Partners in
Thought

Psychoanalysis in a New Key Book Series
Volume 12

PSYCHOANALYSIS IN A NEW KEY BOOK SERIES

Donnel B. Stern
Series Editor

When music is played in a new key, the melody does not change, but the notes that make up the composition do: change in the context of continuity, continuity that perseveres through change. "Psychoanalysis in a New Key" publishes books that share the aims psychoanalysts have always had, but that approach them differently. The books in the series are not expected to advance any particular theoretical agenda, although to this date most have been written by analysts from the interpersonal and relational orientations.

The most important contribution of a psychoanalytic book is the communication of something that nudges the reader's grasp of clinical theory and practice in an unexpected direction. "Psychoanalysis in a New Key" creates a deliberate focus on innovative and unsettling clinical thinking. Because that kind of thinking is encouraged by exploration of the sometimes surprising contributions to psychoanalysis of ideas and findings from other fields, "Psychoanalysis in a New Key" particularly encourages interdisciplinary studies. Books in the series have married psychoanalysis with dissociation, trauma theory, sociology, and criminology. The series is open to the consideration of studies examining the relationship between psychoanalysis and any other field—for instance, biology, literary and art criticism, philosophy, systems theory, anthropology, and political theory.

But innovation also takes place within the boundaries of psychoanalysis, and "Psychoanalysis in a New Key" therefore also presents work that reformulates thought and practice without leaving the precincts of the field. Books in the series focus, for example, on the significance of personal values in psychoanalytic practice, on the complex interrelationship between the analyst's clinical work and personal life, on the consequences for the clinical situation when patient and analyst are from different cultures, and on the need for psychoanalysts to accept the degree to which they knowingly satisfy their own wishes during treatment hours, often to the patient's detriment.

PSYCHOANALYSIS IN A NEW KEY BOOK SERIES

Donnel B. Stern
Series Editor

Partners in Thought

Working with Unformulated Experience, Dissociation, and Enactment

Donnel B. Stern

Routledge
Taylor & Francis Group
New York   London

Chapter 3 originally appeared in *Psychoanalytic Dialogues, 13,* 843–873, 2003.

Chapter 4 originally appeared in *Contemporary Psychoanalysis, 40,* 197–237, 2004.

Chapter 5 originally appeared in *Psychoanalytic Quarterly, 78*(3), 701–731, 2009.

An earlier version of Chapter 6 appeared in *Psychoanalytic Inquiry, 29*(1), 79–90, 2009.

An earlier version of Chapter 7 appeared in *Psychoanalytic Dialogues, 16,* 747–761, 2006.

An earlier version of Chapter 8 appeared in *Mind to Mind: Infant Research, Neuroscience, and Psycho-analysis,* Slade, Berger & Jurist (eds.), © 2008 by Other Press, LLC.

An earlier version of Chapter 9 appeared in *Psychoanalytic Dialogues, 18*(2), 168–196, 2008.

Reprinted with permission.

Routledge
Taylor & Francis Group
270 Madison Avenue
New York, NY 10016

Routledge
Taylor & Francis Group
27 Church Road
Hove, East Sussex BN3 2FA

© 2010 by Taylor and Francis Group, LLC
Routledge is an imprint of Taylor & Francis Group, an Informa business

Printed in the United States of America on acid-free paper
10 9 8 7 6 5 4 3 2

International Standard Book Number: 978-0-415-99969-4 (Hardback) 978-0-415-99970-0 (Paperback)

Library of Congress Cataloging-in-Publication Data

Stern, Donnel B.
　　Partners in thought : working with unformulated experience, dissociation, and enactment / Donnel B. Stern.
　　　　p. cm. -- (Psychoanalysis in a new key ; v. 12)
　　Includes bibliographical references and index.
　　ISBN 978-0-415-99969-4 (hardcover) -- ISBN 978-0-415-99970-0 (pbk.) -- ISBN 978-0-203-88038-8 (e-book)
　　1. Schemas (Psychology) 2. Experiential learning. 3. Experience. 4. Cognitive dissonance I. Title.

BF313.S74 2009
150.19'5--dc22
　　　　　　　　　　　　　　　　　　　　　　　　　　　　2009007473

Visit the Taylor & Francis Web site at
http://www.taylorandfrancis.com

and the Routledge Web site at
http://www.routledgementalhealth.com

To Kathe, Lexi, Babette, and Mikey

Contents

Acknowledgments

For their readings and commentary on various drafts of the chapters of this book, I thank Ghislaine Boulanger, Philip Bromberg, Rich Chefetz, Bill Cornell, Phil Cushman, Muriel Dimen, Stewart Crane, Robert Grossmark, Adrienne Harris, Betsy Hegeman, Irwin Hirsch, Irwin Hoffman, Jill Howard, Ruth Imber, Hazel Ipp, Shelly Itzkowitz, Lawrence Jacobson, Manny Kaftal, Peter Lessem, Howard B. Levine, Sharon Mariner, Russell Meares, Robert Millner, James Ogilvie, Lois Oppenheim, Jean Petrucelli, Barbara Pizer, Stuart Pizer, Bruce Reis, Harry Smith, Steve Stern, Don Troise, Steve Tublin, and Cleonie White. I also thank the International Association for Relational Psychoanalysis and Psychotherapy for proposing an online symposium in November, 2007 devoted to a discussion of Chapter 4, "The Eye Sees Itself." The symposium was organized, administered, and moderated by Peggy Crastnopol and Bruce Reis, and Dan Shaw, Orna Guralnick, Susan Sands, and Estelle Shane participated as panelists.

I am grateful, too, for the opportunities I have had to present chapters of this book to professional audiences around the country, and especially for the discussions after those presentations, which revealed to me points about my own thinking that I would not have considered without the stimulus of those interchanges. Ongoing dialogue with Philip Bromberg, as good an editor as he is a friend, clarified and stimulated my thinking all along the way. Another good friend, Phillip Blumberg, deserves special thanks for his continuous support, interest, and enthusiasm, his ceaseless willingness to read drafts, and his capacity to raise questions that forced me to think through issues that I had not seen clearly prior to his observations. When you are the editor of the series in which your book appears, as I am, you don't have an editor yourself. It is a lot to ask of someone to take on that job. I never asked Phil to do that, but that is, in effect, what he did. Most of all, I thank my wife, Kathe Hift, a psychoanalyst herself, who read and helped me with this book at every step, and whose encouragement over the years made this book a reality.

Introduction

I noticed that this book had been written out of the corner of my eye. After the publication of *Unformulated Experience* in 1997, I found myself drawn to the ideas of enactment and dissociation and the conception of the self as multiple. These interests had been prominent in *Unformulated Experience*. In fact, looking back, I now realize that I also made the link in that book between dissociation and enactment that I am making in this one, although I was then exclusively using the language of transference and countertransference. In the earlier book, however, the link was primarily implicit and therefore less fully theorized (see D. B. Stern, 1997, Chapters 10–12).

In the years that followed the publication of *Unformulated Experience*, the link between dissociation and enactment took center stage for me. During those years I was also writing about other things, though, so that, although I knew that the work on dissociation and enactment was accumulating, it did not occur to me that what I was writing added up to a book. I was brought up short by the realization that a book was already nearly written.

And yet there it was. The papers had thematic unity, each of them coming at the subject matter from a different perspective. For that reason, this book is not a linear account of its subject, developing toward a final conclusion, but a collection of various approaches to the relationship of dissociation and enactment.

In Chapter 1 of this book, I try to formulate the ideas that I believe undergird the chapters that follow. The idea that most meaningfully links them is a particular take on the nature of relationship and its place in unconscious process. I conceptualize unconscious psychic life as unformulated experience, vague psychic material that, under the right circumstances, becomes articulated or realized meaning. Unformulated experience is potential meaning, and in that way quite different from the fully formed meanings that are assumed in theories based on the concept of unconscious fantasy.

Chapter 1 presents the perspective that the meanings that arise from unformulated experience are catalyzed by the states of relatedness in which the meanings emerge. Patient and analyst are, in the most literal sense, *partners in thought* because the interpersonal or relational field they create between them, mostly without their awareness, and the changes that take place within that field, have everything to do with the shape and nature of what they experience together. This point holds, as we shall see throughout this book, not only for the patient's and the analyst's experience of each other and the relationship between them, but for *all* that they feel, think, and perceive in each other's presence—and sometimes what they experience elsewhere as well. The content of the session, in other words, whether or not it expressly concerns the analytic relationship, is the outgrowth of clinical process, conscious and unconscious.

Each time I make this point I feel compelled to add a proviso. Or perhaps I should call what I want to add here my attempt to lend perspective to the problem. It is not the whole story to say that the content of a clinical session is the outcome of its process. Process is also the outcome of the sequences of its content. I will take the position in this book, for instance, that the narratives we create in clinical work are the unplanned expressions of clinical process (Chapter 5). But I am also careful to say in that chapter that the narratives that come about in this unwitting fashion then contribute to the shape and nature of the clinical process that follows them. It may be an expression of nonconscious clinical process, for instance, when the analyst has a new thought about the analytic relatedness; but that new content (i.e., the new thought), in the same spontaneous way, then affects the unfolding of the clinical process that comes after it. It would distort the clinical situation to look at the problem too exclusively from the perspective of either process or content. Each plays a part.

But with that said, I must also say that this book is an attempt to correct what I feel has been too great an emphasis in our field on the construction of clinical reality by the analyst's consciously chosen interpretations, and too little an emphasis on the spontaneous growth of clinical reality from unplanned clinical process. Since clinical process is continuously influenced by unconscious factors contributed by both the analyst and the patient, my emphasis is on the analyst's attempt to understand what we are continuously in the process of unwittingly constructing. As I pursue this point of view, and as a corrective, I lay more emphasis on the creation of content by process than I do on the creation of new process by preexisting content. I do want it to be clear, however, that I recognize that process and content have a mutual influence on each other, sometimes facilitative, sometimes inhibitory.

Rethinking Unformulated Experience

Recently I have reconceptualized the theory of unformulated experience. The change is recent enough to have taken place after most of the work on this book had been finished. I claimed in *Unformulated Experience* that only experience we can reflect on in verbal terms can be formulated at all, and that only experience we have constructed in this way should be described as formulated. In the reconceptualization I have just completed, however, formulated meanings are not limited to the verbal register. I now take the position that both verbal *and* nonverbal meanings can be formulated. I refer to the formulation of verbal meaning as *articulation* and that of nonverbal meaning as *realization*.

These new ideas do not appear explicitly in this book, however; they are instead the core of another book that is now in preparation. But the changes I will propose in the theory of unformulated experience are nevertheless present in implicit ways throughout these pages because the writing of these chapters was what made it inescapable to me that changes in the theory of unformulated experience were necessary. What most gripped me was the nonverbal nature of the clinical events that eventually break up enactments and often make their dynamics possible to experience in conscious, reflective ways.

Let me explain just a bit about what I mean. I observe repeatedly in this book that what eventually interrupts enactments is not verbal insight but a new *perception* of the other and oneself (see Chapters 3–6, but especially Chapter 4). Although in the chapters of this book I do not make an issue of the fact that this new perception is nonverbal, the point has always been unmistakable to me, and once I formulated it for myself I could not stop thinking about it. How could I maintain that the process of formulation must be verbal if I also took the position that the event to which I am pegging therapeutic action—the new perception— is nonverbal?

Even before dissociation and enactment took center stage for me, I had felt for many years that I assigned too exclusive a role to verbal language in the formulation of experience. Furthermore, I had always known, of course, as all of us do, that many significant clinical events take place apart from verbal language. Now, with the "new perception" serving as the straw that broke the camel's back, it was clearly time to redefine the process of formulating meaning in a way that would make it possible to conceptualize the formulation of nonverbal meanings.

But the exploration of that subject, and others related to it, must await the book that is now in preparation. In the book you now hold, I must be satisfied to announce the change in view that is to come and to prepare you to encounter the implicit expression of this change in the chapters that follow.

The Chapters

Chapter 1, in addition to what I have already described about it, contains the first of many clinical examples of dissociation and enactment. In the course of reading that first clinical vignette (which, unlike those that follow, is fictional), most readers will think about projective identification. And so, following the introductory example, I compare projective identification and the modern Kleinian/Bionian view with the Interpersonal/Relational perspective on enactment and dissociation that is the subject of this book.

Chapter 2 presents the hermeneutic ideal of true or authentic conversation, which is the dialogic creation of understanding, also referred to by Hans-Georg Gadamer (2004) as "the fusion of horizons." Authentic conversation is one way to describe the ideal of the psychoanalytic situation; in fact psychoanalysis does work that way much of the time. But true conversation breaks down during enactment. Enactment can be defined as the *interruption* of true conversation. And so Chapter 2 constitutes a hermeneutic portrayal of the dialogic context that enactment destroys and to which, once we are involved in enactments, we try so hard to return.

Following this theme, Chapter 3 examines the link between dissociation and enactment in hermeneutic terms. Starting from the position that all understanding is context dependent, I claim that one of the most significant contexts for clinical purposes is the self-state. How we understand the other, and ourselves, depends on the state(s) we occupy. Dissociations between the analyst's states of self can therefore limit or impede understanding of the analysand by depriving the analyst of a fitting context within which to grasp what the analysand says and does. Such impediments can become what we understand as mutual unconscious enactments. Clinical understanding under these circumstances requires the breach of the dissociations, which ends the enactment. I lay out some of the implications of thinking about transference and countertransference along these lines, with detailed examples illustrating the consequences of both the analyst's dissociations and their eventual resolutions. Among the advantages of this way of thinking is that it amounts to a psychoanalytic account of the hermeneutic circle.

Chapter 4 is probably the heart of my ideas about dissociation and enactment. The chapter addresses the question: If being part of an enactment means being blind to the nature of our involvement with the patient, as I claimed in Chapter 3, how can we *ever* understand the countertransference? How can the eye see itself? I expand the portrayal of enactment offered in Chapter 3, where I introduce the conception that mutual enactment is the outcome of the interlocking dissociations of analyst and patient. Chapter 4 presents the view that, in cases of mutual enactment, neither the analyst nor the patient can experience alternate, or conflicting, views of the other; each is limited to understanding the other through a single lens. These reciprocal dissociations are breached only when either the patient or the analyst can transcend this "single-mindedness" and allow the experience of multiple, conflicting perceptions of the other. Until the conflict can be contained within one mind, it remains split into the pieces rigidly experienced by the patient and the analyst as enactment. I take the position that conflict must be viewed as an achievement. Enactment is not the result of too much conflict in the personality, but of too little.

Chapter 5 focuses on how narrative is created in psychoanalysis, offering an alternative to the views of Schafer (1983, 1992) and Spence (1982), an alternative based in the concept of unformulated experience that shows how enactment derails narrative formation and makes psychotherapy essential. The chapter's title, "Partners in Thought," from which the title of the book is drawn, refers to the kind of productive clinical process, based on what I describe as "witnessing," that becomes impossible in the presence of dissociation and enactment and that takes place once again when dissociation and enactment are resolved. Even in the absence of other people, we learn about ourselves by listening to our own thoughts about ourselves through the ears of the other. We need an emotionally responsive witness, even if that witness is imaginary, in order to know and feel our experience. We need a witness, that is, if experience is to fall into a satisfying narrative order. The origins of the witness lie in earliest infancy, in the roles played by responsive parents in reflecting back to us a version of ourselves that eventually becomes the self. We need a witness to become a self; and later in life, in similar fashion, we need a witness to heal ourselves. Patients listen to themselves as they imagine their analysts hear them and in this way create new narrative freedom. But only what feels like "me" can be witnessed. "Not-me" can only be enacted. The resolution of enactments is crucial in psychoanalytic treatment not only because it expands the boundaries of the self, but also because it reinstitutes and broadens the range within which patient and analyst can witness each other's experience. Narrative is not the outcome of the analyst's objective interpretations, but an emergent, co-constructed, unbidden outcome of clinical process.

Chapter 6 approaches dissociation and enactment through the lens of trauma and memory. Even when trauma can be remembered, the memory often does not infuse the present with vitality or emotionality, as other memories do. To become a vital part of experience, trauma must be linked with other current experiences. Such links are metaphorical, in the sense meant by Lakoff and Johnson (1999). I use their work to suggest that, in metaphor, the meaning of a memory is "carried over" or "transferred" from the past to a present experience. When such transfer takes place, trauma can be reflected on because it can now be seen against the background of other experience. Transfer is made possible by "co-occurrence," or the simultaneous presence in one's mind of a memory and a present experience. I describe such co-occurrences as potential, unformulated metaphors; they can be either actualized or refused. Modell (2003) tells us that when metaphors are unconsciously refused, a common event among trauma sufferers, traumatic experience is prevented from becoming part of "emotional categories." The resulting isolation of the experience is what I mean by dissociation. I therefore refer to the unconscious refusal to tap the potential of co-occurrence, that is, the unconscious, defensively motivated refusal to create metaphor, as *dissociation*. As in any other instance, dissociated states are liable to be enacted. And so the unconscious refusal to create a metaphor is one source of unconscious enactment.

Chapter 7 extends the concepts of dissociation and enactment beyond the bounds of the clinical situation into the kinds of interpersonal patterns seen in long-term romantic relationships. The chapter explores the way that certain kinds of mutual dissociations and enactments can come to define relatedness over long periods of time.

Chapters 8 and 9 compare dissociation/enactment theory to two prominent contemporary approaches to clinical understanding. In Chapter 8 I compare my thinking to the mentalization theory of Fonagy and his collaborators (2002), a body of work that constitutes a profound exploration of the nature and significance of reflective awareness. I ask whether the view of reflective function held by Fonagy and his collaborators is the same as my own. It seems that therapeutic action in mentalization theory requires the analyst to be capable of mentalizing, which is exactly what I believe cannot be done during an enactment; and so it also seems that the therapist must be responsible for avoiding enactments whenever possible. To me, such avoidance is not really possible. Whatever wiggle room we have around enactments exists more often in how we respond to finding ourselves already part of them than in the choice about whether or not to enter them in the first place. And even if it were possible to avoid enactments, it would usually not be desirable, because dissociated material (*not-me*) is not symbolized, but unformulated, and is therefore only available via the experience of enactment. Finally, it is my position that the most clinically significant instances of reflective function take place unbidden. Although the analyst can try to create conditions under which reflection can flourish, I believe she cannot control its appearance in her mind. And so, despite the overlap in our approaches, and despite holding the opinion that mentalization theory is one of the most significant and clinically useful bodies of work in contemporary psychoanalysis, I conclude that the architects of mentalization theory and I probably think at least a bit differently about the place of reflective function in therapeutic work.

Chapter 9 compares dissociation/enactment theory with the work of the Boston Change Process Study Group (BCPSG; 2002, 2005, 2007, 2008; D. N. Stern et al., 1998), another highly influential body of work that has deeply influenced my perception of clinical events, especially in its brilliant conceptualization of the nonverbal and nonsymbolic aspects of what transpires in the consulting room. After presenting these substantial areas of overlap in our work (it is really only the similarities of our thinking that make our differences interesting), I focus on three areas. First, I take the position that the work of BCPSG, to this point, does not address the kinds of emotionally intense enactments that have been presented in the Relational literature, including throughout this book, and I offer a speculative explanation for this difference. I then turn to BCPSG's application of nonlinear dynamic systems theory, observing that that theory is used by BCPSG in a literal sense and suggesting certain problems this leads to for psychoanalysis. I take the position that nonlinear dynamic systems theory should probably be used metaphorically in psychoanalysis, and I offer my explanation why. Finally, I address BCPSG's objectivist, scientific approach to psychoanalysis and psychotherapy and compare it to the constructivist or hermeneutic one I have adopted.

1

The Embodiment of Meaning in Relatedness

One cannot include everything about one's ideas every time one writes so I must refer readers to my earlier book (D.B. Stern, 1997) for a description of the theory of unformulated experience. However, there are points about those views that should be reiterated at the outset of this book, at least briefly, because they are crucial and frequently misunderstood. First, the question of relativism. I conceive unformulated experience as potential experience, and I intend by that point to suggest that the shape of the next moment's formulated meanings is not entirely predetermined, that there is always some ambiguity to be resolved in experience, some formulation of the unformulated that remains to take place, some emergent quality in the creation of whatever is to come next. At times this position about the inevitable ambiguity of the next moment has been mistakenly interpreted to imply that the process of formulation is unconstrained, as if unformulated experience can become any meaning one pleases to give it. That is not what I believe (D.B. Stern, 1997, pp. 28-32, 203-233). I want to avoid altogether the implication of relativism and unconstrained subjectivism. The idea of unformulated experience is a hermeneutic view well described by Sass (1988): "For, though it may be impossible to discover a single meaning, this does not mean that anything goes, that listeners can legitimately ascribe any meaning to any discourse. The hermeneutic view is a sort of 'middle way' between objectivism and relativism" (p. 254).[1]

I have taken pains elsewhere in this volume to describe the formulation of meaning as a dialectical process, but I want to emphasize dialectic

---

[1] Among hermeneutic writers, Hans-Georg Gadamer has had the most influence on my thinking, and therefore on the ideas in this book. For introductions to Gadamer's philosophical hermeneutics, see Palmer (1969), Bernstein (1983), Warnke (1987), Grondin (1997), and Dostal (2002). Gadamer's magnum opus is *Truth and Method*, published in a new translation in 2004. A collection of informative but accessible essays (Gadamer, 1966) is a good point of entry to Gadamer's thought. For the intersection of Gadamer's hermeneutics and psychoanalysis, see Orange (1995), Messer, Sass, and Woolfolk (1988), Sass (1988), and Stern (1997).

here, too, in the beginning, because another implication I want to avoid is that unformulated experience has no structure and that the process of formulation is therefore unidirectional or one-dimensional, i.e., "nothing but" emergent, uninfluenced by the continuity provided by reality and the more structural aspects of personality. That is not the position I take.

The meanings that can be validly created from any unformulated experience are a joint outcome of pre-existing structural meanings and the emergent influence of the present moment. The role of structure, from this perspective, is played by constraints on what unformulated experience can become. From the hermeneutic perspective, reality cannot be directly apprehended; it can be perceived only through the lenses of tradition, history, and culture. But reality is there, and it shows itself in the continuous constraint it exercises on our freedom to create experience. In Gadamer's (2004) hermeneutic view, all experience is interpretation. It is reality that provides the limits within which we are free to create valid experience, and beyond which we recognize experience as lie or distortion.[1]

The degree of constraint on unformulated experience ranges from high to low, and this degree of constraint differs with context, over time, and from one kind of experience to another. In the case of tight constraints, there is little "wiggle room," which is to say that in these cases the range of formulated meanings that can validly be made from unformulated experience is narrow. In other cases, constraints are looser, and the range of meanings that can validly be formulated is therefore correspondingly wider. Consider, for example, a painting consisting of two fields of color, one pink and the other orange, the two fields seeming to float on an off-white background. Let us say that I simply attend to the impact the painting has on me, trying to formulate my reaction, or the kind of affective experience I have while looking at it, or the place of this painting in the tradition of art from which it arises. In the cases of experiences and thoughts such as these, the interpretive quality is undeniable, and the range of formulations that can be made without violating the constraints of reality is very wide, indeed. But if I ask myself instead what are the colors of the painting's two fields, the experiences I can formulate without violating reality are so few

---

[1] This point is too simple in one very important respect that I cannot pursue here, but that needs to be recognized. Uunconscious ideology, the aspect of culture that serves our minds not as the potential for new meaning but as a straitjacket for it, is just as effective as reality itself in setting limits on our freedom to experience. Because reality can only be apprehended via the tools made available by culture, the distinction between limits that are based in reality (and therefore intrinsic to human experience), and those that are ideologically based (and therefore imposed on us for reasons having to do with the invisible workings of power [see Foucault, 1980]) is always at issue and painfully difficult to accomplish.

that the interpretive aspect, while it remains real enough, is constrained enough to seem trivial.

One routine effect of formulating meaning is to provide a constraint on what future meanings can become. The impact of the past, and the presence of continuity in the personality, are thereby assured, because the most significant constraints on what unformulated experience can become in its next incarnation, or in the next moment, are the meanings that have come before. The creation of meaning is once again dialectical: formerly created meanings influence the future to take their shape, while the unique influences of the present and the future encourage the reformulation of past meanings. I made this point in *Unformulated Experience* (D.B. Stern, 1997) in words to which I continue to subscribe:

> The given and the made are a dialectic, neither ever excluding the other and both constituting every meaning and moment. Without the opportunity to change previously structured experience, and without that previous structure to feel and think against, new experience would be impossible. We would be trapped in an evanescent subjectivism. But, on the other hand, without our capacity for an imagination that goes beyond experiential regularities, without the animation of spontaneous expression and the continuous reworking that represents our ceaseless effort to understand, we would never be able to redeem our experience from the stasis of dead convention. It is reflection that saves the unconscious from being nothing more than a set of strictures, and makes it a precious resource instead; and it is the unconscious that offers reflection on the fecund and ever-changing materials with which to carry out its life-giving mission (p. 30).

The Location of Unformulated Experience

Where is unformulated experience? Does the question even make sense? Should we really say that it exists anywhere? Certainly we would not want to say that it is "located" in the kind of hypothetical netherworld that most of us are no longer even willing to call "the" unconscious. The era of psychic geography is dead. Unformulated experience is possibility, the various potential meanings that might expand from the present moment. Only one, or some, of these potentials are ever realized. Unformulated experience is the source of what experience can *become*. And so, because it does not yet exist, it cannot really be said to be located anywhere, not even in the brain.

We can say that the present moment actually exists in our minds (wherever *that is*), but the present is probably the only kind of experience about which we remain confident enough to ascribe to it literal existence. Take the example of memory. We once thought memory had a literal existence. When we think of experience that perseveres over time, we think immediately of memory, and so it was natural for us to think that each memory was represented in stable, physical fashion somewhere in the brain. That natural conclusion is what motivated the futile search for the engram (Lashley, 1950).

But the way we see memory has changed, and in particular, our view of the literalness of what we remember has been qualified. We accept today that we reconstruct memory each time we consult it. We constantly remake the past in the service of present purposes. Citations of this point go back at least to Bartlett (1932), and in fact, cognitive and developmental psychologists have recently come to a broad and striking consensus that remembering is a constructive process (e.g., Tulving & Craik, 2000). In an important sense, then, even the past is unformulated. We continuously reconstitute the events of our lives, even if those reconstitutions often bear a significant similarity to the ones that have come before. And of course, if the past is substantially unformulated, whatever we imagine about the future must be in even greater flux. As soon as we really consider these things, it is apparent that we live as if life were much more stable and predictable than it is. And so, while some psychoanalysts today seem enthusiastic about nailing down the origins of experience in cerebral structure and process, many of the rest of us are skeptical of theories that "source" experience too specifically or concretely, whether the location of that source is said to be the unconscious or the brain.

But there is one "place" in which it may be meaningful to give unformulated experience a home that is at least metaphorical: relatedness. Relatedness is a category of living in which I mean to include not only the relevant conduct that transpires between people, but all the relevant affective, cognitive, and conative experiential processes. In imagining these intrapersonal processes, I am thinking, for example, of interaction between states of self, or for those who prefer a different language, internal object relations.

Relatedness is the nexus from which experience emerges. It is in the crucible of each moment's relatedness that unformulated experience is articulated into knowable, usable, experience-able living: meaning is potentiated and prohibited by what transpires between us. Since the events of relatedness are only partially under our control, we are not the only authors of the meanings that we formulate in what we usually feel is the privacy of our own minds; but at the same time, and paradoxically, because the process of authorship goes on outside awareness, we are unaware, more often than not, of the extent to which we do create the experience that emerges from relatedness.

Mind and Relatedness: Hand and Glove

Contemporary interest in the relationship between dissociation and enactment, each phenomenon significant in its own right, each the inspiration for a literature of its own,[1] is part of the broad interest in psychoanalysis in process theories of treatment. I hardly know whether to call this interest explosive or longstanding, because it is both: process theories have now held the floor in psychoanalytic clinical debate for decades. Across theoretical schools whose adherents otherwise usually claim to differ from one another in significant respects, I believe there has developed an emphasis on the close examination of clinical process, a move toward the study of the events of the treatment for their own sake.

What do I mean by "for their own sake"? I mean to refer to the social aspects of therapeutic relatedness. I mean that today there are analysts of all persuasions who tend to understand the transference and the countertransference as "interlocked" with one another, as Wolstein (1959) so presciently put it, each playing a role in holding the other in place. Now, of course, I hasten to add that I do not mean to equate "social" and "sociological." I am hardly setting aside unconscious influence. In fact, it could reasonably be claimed that I, along with most analysts who identify themselves as Interpersonal or Relational, actually privilege mutual unconscious influence between patient and analyst. At the very least, we emphasize it heavily.

Even those analysts who continue to maintain that the unconscious fantasies of the individual mind lie at the heart of life and of treatment (the majority of analysts may very well hold this view; see Bornstein, 2008) would agree that their interest in process theories of therapeutic action is today extensive. Yet it does seem to me that anyone who accepts the latent/manifest distinction, and who imagines each mind to be housed within

---

[1] Prime examples of the Relational literature on enactment include Aron, 2003a, b; Bass, 2003; Black, 2003; Benjamin, 1998; Bromberg, 1998, 2006; Davies, 1997, 1999, 2003, 2004; Davies & Frawley, 1994; B. Pizer, 2003; S. A. Pizer, 1998; D. B. Stern, 2003, 2004. For the contemporary psychological and psychiatric literature on dissociation, see Dell & O'Neil, 2009. For the contemporary clinical psychoanalytic literature on dissociation, see Bromberg, 1998, 2006; Howell, 2005; D.B. Stern, 1997.

a single skull, has to hold a different view of analytic relatedness than I do. I know that even those analysts who take the most conservative position about transference—i.e., that it is a distortion based on the demands of the inner world—would readily accept that different transference configurations are uppermost at different times. In taking this position, one might say, these analysts are indicating their acceptance that context plays a significant role in analytic relatedness. But most of these same analysts would also take the position that each one of these transference manifestations is attributable to the activation/expression of a particular enduring, underlying unconscious fantasy and the defenses against it. The latent meaning of the transference continues to be, for this group of analysts, the truth of transference. The truth exists in the unconscious and awaits discovery. This book is based in a different view.

The traditional assumption that unconscious meaning is fully formed also has a significant influence on analysts' understanding of their own participation in the treatment. It is acknowledged by adherents of the traditional view, of course, that analysts, like any other human beings, are themselves capable of transference; but many of these analysts also believe that they are supposed to be capable, because of their own analyses, of observing the development of their own transferences in such a way that they avoid being caught up in them. Everyone these days accepts that countertransference can be informative, but it is still common for some analysts to believe that they should be able to stand aside from these aspects of their experience and analyze them before they appear in analytic conduct.

In this orientation toward transference and countertransference, which was dominant until at least the mid-1980s in most of the field, and still exists in some quarters, the analyst's authority is at least partly defined by knowing what is true, and the most important thing the analyst should know, or come to know, is the contents of the patient's mind. It is possible in this frame of reference, in a fairly straightforward way that can be embraced without disrespecting anyone, to believe that the analyst knows the truth about the patient.

But now consider what happens if we think in the frame of reference provided by the concept of unformulated experience. From this vantage point, experience is not uncovered but constructed, and the construction of experience involves the selective formulation of some portion of the available possibilities. Experience ceases to be a given at any level. It is not that we "have" the experience and then interpret it. Rather, we are continuously involved, without our awareness, in crafting the very shape our experience takes. It is very seldom that we know exactly how and why we make experience as we do. Experience, instead, arrives in our minds unbidden; but its unbiddenness makes us no less responsible for its shape than we are in any psychoanalytic frame of reference. Unconscious meaning is not fully formed and waiting to be uncovered; it is instead potential meaning, meaning that might become actualized under the right circumstances—and "the right circumstances" means "the right interpersonal context."

That was the message of *Unformulated Experience* (D.B.Stern, 1997). In these terms, there can be no single reality underlying any transference, no unitary truth to be uncovered. Transference and countertransference can no longer be viewed as distortions, but must be understood instead as unconsciously selected perceptions that are quite real, but that represent only one, or a few, of the possibilities that might be actualized. Transference and countertransference, in other words, are created in just the same way as any other interpersonal perceptions. What sets them off is not the means of their creation, or their sources, but their rigidity. Transference and countertransference are rigid selections from among the possibilities for relatedness. Unlike other interpersonal perceptions, they do not necessarily shift easily and freely with changes in circumstances; the person in the grip of transference turns away from the possibilities for feeling, thinking, and being that might make a new experience of the other available. The experience that would change the transference (that would *be* a change in the transference) is simply not constructed. For the moment, for simplicity's sake, I will not explore the fact that transference cannot be maintained this way without the collaboration of the other. Let me just make the familiar claim that, even (or maybe especially) in the case of unconscious processes, it takes two to tango. Paraphrasing Winnicott: there is no such thing as transference.

As soon as you take this kind of constructivist view, in which meaning is not predetermined but created in dialogue, the idea of a single, objective reality becomes unsupportable. I hasten to add, however, as I always do when I make this point, that the claim that reality is multiple is not at all the same thing as taking the position that reality is relative. The multiple possibilities for meaning *all* have a real existence, even if it is not sensible to refer to those potential existences as objectively verifiable.

I must also make sure to answer another objection I have often heard made to my work and the work of other interpersonal and relational writers. It is claimed by some that in interpersonal and relational views individual subjectivity has been eclipsed—that is, that the individual mind has disappeared, leaving only the dyad. That simply is not the case. To recognize the role of the other in the selection of the conscious contents of one's own mind is hardly synonymous with suggesting that one's mind does not have its own, separate existence. Even the idea that the mind is distributed, a claim I make later in this chapter, is perfectly consistent with individual subjectivity. Let me be as clear as possible about this point: the recognition of the influence of the other, even the recognition of the influence of the other on the contents of one's own mind, does not imply for one moment the rejection of the individual mind.

Of course, as soon as we reject a single objective reality, the analyst's old status as the arbiter of such a reality also becomes impossible to sustain (e.g., Benjamin, 1988, 1995, 1998; Cushman, 1995; Aron, 1996; Elliott & Spezzano, 1996; Hoffman, 1996; McLaughlin, 1996; Mitchell, 1997, Chapter 7; Greenberg, 1999; Zeddies & Richardson, 1999). A training analysis can no longer be considered an inoculation against countertransference enactment, because countertransference and its enactment are not different in kind from everyday interpersonal life. We can no longer define countertransference as irrational and then contrast it with a rational non-countertransference. All experience is subjective, the analyst's as thoroughly as the patient's. (This point has now been made so often that I would not know how to limit citations of it.) We must now understand that we all continuously, necessarily, and without awareness apply ourselves to the task of selecting one, or several, particular views of another person from among a much larger set of possibilities. That is the way we all deal with one another, all the time. We can no longer specify psychopathology as a certain *kind* of mental content, or even, as some writers have redefined unconscious fantasy (e.g., Sugarman, 2008), as a mental *process*. All we can really specify is the degree of freedom or rigidity that characterizes a person's approach to experience, and even that specification must be understood as a judgment, vulnerable to unconscious influence. The only clinical question about transference and countertransference that really matters becomes how thoroughly *willing* and *able* each person is, under some specified set of circumstances, to consider alternative meanings.

Before I go any further, I think I should reinforce a point I made in beginning this chapter: my perspective does not require the dismissal of the concept of character, or any of our other ways of grasping the continuity of the personality. Those ideas are far too useful to be dismissed. But our notions about continuity, or what are commonly referred to as structural aspects of personality, do have to become multiple. We can no longer do with a single character structure, for instance. That idea needs to be replaced with a more flexible conception in which different *aspects* of character appear under different circumstances, circumstances that we then need to specify. Even those of our ideas that refer to the mind's continuity, in other words, must become more responsive to context.

Now, when I say that the only clinical question about transference and countertransference that really matters is how thoroughly willing and able each person is to consider alternative meanings, I mean by "willing" and "able" to refer to phenomena that transcend consciousness. This kind of will and ability should probably be called intentionality, a commitment thorough enough to extend into unconscious life. In Chapter 3, for instance, in the case of Hannah, the patient's commitment to her treatment, and her willingness to become vulnerable to me at a frightening, risky moment that one might have expected to provoke an unconscious defensive maneuver, were powerful enough to create a collaborative dream instead—a dream that proved to be what she and I needed to end a lengthy and rather dire enactment.

To hold out for meanings alternative to the ones that pop up with least effort in our minds is an admirable kind of choice. At the same time, though, because freedom of this kind is rooted in intentions that reach so deep in us, these are "choices" that, in an important sense, can hardly be made otherwise. They define us; they are what make us ourselves. And they are the motives that create the possibility of psychoanalytic treatment. Hannah, the patient in Chapter 3 to whom I just referred, did not "choose" her dream, of course, not in the sense in which we usually use that word; but in another sense she did, because the dream was her invention, however unconscious the creative process may have been.

It has been several decades since the revelation of the mind's contents, or their manipulation in the service of creating a different kind of content, has been the core of anyone's theories of therapeutic action. We have come to believe that the way the mind works is far more important than what it holds. For many of us, the way the mind works is inseparable from the mind's context; and the mind's context is relatedness. Mind and its context are a ceaselessly changing unity. It has been many years since most of us thought of the analyst as a decoder of the patient's unconscious secrets, those congealed nuggets of meaning that were supposed to exist in a hidden, timeless realm in which context was only relevant to the extent that it provided the canvas on which disguised expressions of those secrets were projected. Those of us who have made the shift from models of content to models of context and process think and write about psychoanalytic work only infrequently as the interpretation of a greater truth that lies behind or underneath appearances. Instead, we believe that whatever we can have of emotional truth is most often embodied in the nature of our relatedness with one another and what we do with it.

Ongoing Interaction and the Formulation of Meaning

In any particular moment, with any particular person, some of what one "is" with the other stays unformulated, while other parts of one's being-with-the-other are available to us as perceptions. What we either perceive or leave unformulated runs the gamut: we feel our own emotions and infer the emotions of the other; we attribute intentions to ourselves and the other; we perceive conduct, to which we ascribe meaning, and so on. All of these phenomena may be either perceived or left unperceived, their potential untapped. When they are left undeveloped, we are making the "choice" to leave them—in a word—unformulated. But if they are formulated, perceptions of oneself or the other may take either a verbally symbolized form that allows reflective consciousness, or a nonverbal form that then becomes part of the intuitively organized relating to come.

Our perception of interaction is always several steps behind our participation in it. Perceptions of self and other, including our perception of our own and the other's affects and ways of being, arrive in our minds *after* the relatedness that embodies them, not before it. And that observation then leads us to the conclusion, perhaps counter-intuitive, that our perceptions of self and other are at least as deeply shaped by interactions as interactions are shaped by pre-existing perceptions (cf. Renik, 1993a).

For the most part, we take it for granted in everyday life that things are the other way around—i.e., that it is perceptions that shape interactions, not interactions that shape perceptions. We generally take it for granted, in other words, that it is our views of others that determine how we treat them. There is truth in that view, of course, because once we absorb the self/other perceptions embodied in one moment of interaction, that new awareness participates in shaping the interaction that comes next. And so, to attain a balanced view we must recognize that the relationship between perception and action is, like the relationship between content and process that I discussed in the Introduction of this book, reciprocal: each plays a role in creating the other.

I mean "perception" to include what it seems to us that we and the other person are *like*, and what it *is like* to be involved with each other. It is affect, the "feel" of the situation, that gives an interpersonal perception its boundaries or wholeness, that gives us a meaningful way of demarcating one perception from another; it is affect, in other words, that makes it meaningful to refer to what something is like. When we say that perception is what it *is like* to be with the other, *that is*, and what the other *is like*, what matters most to us is what it *feels like* to be with the other and how it *feels like* the other is being with us.

If we are to perceive what something or someone is like, we must experience the possibility of alternative (D.B. Stern, 1990). To take advantage of the potential meanings embodied in interactive experience is to be open to multiple interpretations of oneself and the other. This is the mature form of the capacity to reflect on one's own experience and that of others, or mentalization (e.g., Fonagy et al, 2002), in which we are not necessarily attached to any particular interpretation of our own and/or the other's feelings and motives, but remain open to whatever we come across. To absorb the potential meaning of interpersonal events is to be curious, to allow oneself, with a willingness that derives not from moral force but from desire, to imagine as freely as possible the ways of grasping and feeling one's own and the other's conduct and experience. Unfettered curiosity is an ideal, never actually created but worthy of our aspirations toward it.

And that is to say that, even after the lag between the event and its perception, we never absorb all the potential meanings embodied in the interactions in which we participate. We develop only some of the potential meanings of relatedness, leaving the others unformulated. This selective process goes on continuously. We could hardly develop every potential relational experience; if we did, we would be so preoccupied that we could do nothing else. For this reason, much of relatedness is on "automatic pilot," and it is this automaticity that is responsible for a large portion of what we never perceive. The necessity for automatic relating also allows us to maintain in our daily lives highly selective, problematic, and meaningful patterns of perception, patterns of perception that make up a substantial portion of what we call transference and countertransference, without ever facing the challenge to notice them.

We are able to symbolize in words some of our perceptions of the meanings embodied in relatedness—that is, we can name and think about some ways of being. Other ways of being, while not available in words, nevertheless are perceived either nonverbally (e.g., in the form of imagery) or subsymbolically (i.e., in experience that is not represented in conventional verbal or nonverbal symbols, but in affect-laden procedural forms closely related to the original experience).[1] Especially significant is the subsymbolic, which, Bucci (1997) tells us, is the primary means by which affect can be represented. The Boston Change Process Study Group (BCPSG; 2002, 2005, 2006, 2008; Stern, D.N. et al., 1998) has brought a key aspect of the subsymbolic to our attention under the rubric of implicit relational knowing (IRK). IRK can be sensed or felt, but usually it cannot be symbolized in verbal language. Conceptions like Bucci's subsymbolic mode and BCPSG's IRK show us why it is so often crucial to ask patients, "What was (is) it like?" The question invites a kind of groping toward explicit meaning without insisting on a precise verbal formulation. Verbal language cannot specify or articulate IRK or the subsymbolic; but there are moments in which it can be used in a loose, relaxed way that draws our attention further into places that are hard to illuminate, perhaps making possible our nonverbal or subsymbolic appreciation of phenomena that might otherwise remain wholly in the dark.

We are seldom explicitly aware of this part of what we perceive, but when we do notice it, it is comfortable enough; it does not feel alien or disturbing. Most of the time, IRK, the nonverbal, and the subsymbolic simply unfold in a "natural" way that we never explicitly notice at all. Perception in these modes is the primary language, as BCPSG suggests, in which the moment-to-moment, unnoticed negotiation of relatedness, or what we might call nonreflective living, takes place. If we can comfortably "be that way" with the other person, or can comfortably perceive and tolerate the other "being that way" with us, then, we can say that that way of being is available to us for use in nonreflective living.

Conceptualizing Enactment

To this point I have been discussing parts of our experience of relatedness that, while sometimes inconsistent with explicit symbolization, are unquestionably tolerable. But some of the potential meaning embodied in relatedness is not tolerable at all. These unformulated parts of relatedness seldom, if ever, become meanings we use in living. That is, even if we otherwise *could* formulate them in reflective consciousness—even if their modes of representation were consistent with registration in reflective awareness—they remain unformulated for unconscious dynamic

---

[1] See Bucci (1997) for a description of what she calls the verbal, nonverbal, and subsymbolic modes of information processing.

reasons. They are, that is, *dissociated*. In the Interpersonal/Relational model I introduced in *Unformulated Experience* and expand in the present book, dissociation is the primary unconscious defensive process, replacing repression. Dissociation and unformulated experience are the building blocks of a psychoanalytic model of mind (D.B. Stern, 1997, 2009).

I mean dissociation to refer to the process by which, for unconscious defensive reasons, either the patient or the analyst, or both, fails to potentiate some portion of the verbal, nonverbal, or subsymbolic meaning available in the interaction of which they are part. Some of this selective perception takes place as a result of dynamically-controlled inattention to certain possibilities for social meaning, which I (D.B. Stern, 1997) have described as "passive dissociation," or "narrative rigidity" (an attachment to certain narratives so strong that other alternative narratives are never imagined, and the relevant observations are never formulated). In other instances, selective perception is the outcome of more typical unconscious defensive processes: the specific rejection of certain meanings, the unconsciously motivated turn away from the possibilities for formulation. This is what I have referred to as "dissociation in the strong sense" (D.B. Stern, 1997).

The unconscious motive for dissociation is conceptualized differently from the unconscious motive for repression. That is, the motive for dissociation is not the unconscious intention to avoid certain kinds of experience, i.e., certain aversive or anxiety-provoking affects, meanings, or memories. Instead, what moves us to unconscious defense in the theory of dissociation is the need to avoid assuming a certain kind of *identity*. The unconscious purpose is to avoid the creation of a certain *state of being*, or *self-state*. The unconscious necessity is that we *must not be* a certain person; and we suddenly *would be* that person if we were to formulate certain key parts of an interaction in which we are involved. I give illustrations of what I mean in most of this book's chapters. For the time being, let me just say that the person one must not be—the self-state one must not find oneself inhabiting—is someone who felt disappointed, bereft, frightened, humiliated, shamed, or otherwise badly hurt or threatened. One must not be the person to whom that thing happened, the person who has the feelings, memories, and experiences that come with being that person. What we defend against is not any single feeling, fantasy, thought, or memory, but a state of identity, a way of being. I refer to this dreaded state of being, after Harry Stack Sullivan (1954) and, more recently, Philip Bromberg (1998, 2006), as *not-me*. Quite literally, this is the part of subjectivity that must not be me.

But of course life does not necessarily cooperate with our intentions, this intention included. Circumstances—interactions with others—sometimes conspire in such a way that the dissociated way of being threatens to erupt into awareness. Interaction, for example, might seem to be moving in a way that we unconsciously perceive as a threat to wrest us into a position in which a certain kind of humiliation cannot be avoided. That must not happen. The only course of action left to the dissociator who needs to protect himself from such imminent danger is the externalization of the way of being that one must not take on oneself—*the interpersonalization of the dissociation.* Enactment is the last-ditch unconscious defensive effort to avoid being the person one must not be, accomplished by trying to force onto the other what defines the intolerable identity (see especially Chapters 3–8).

A Fictional Illustration

One manages relatedness most of the time in such a way that the possibilities for the eruption of not-me are minimized. Let us imagine a simplified illustration, a man who, on the basis of his relationship with a parent whom he feels experienced his needs as selfish and burdensome, is in danger of being overwhelmed by shame when he feels a certain degree of self-interest. Awareness of self-interest, especially self-interest that might conflict with someone else's interests, is, for him, not-me. These aspects of his character are observed by certain others in the man's life; but he himself has never formulated them. Nevertheless, he manages to construct characteristic states of relatedness with others in which his self-interest almost always takes a back seat to theirs. He does this on the basis of the process I have described as passive dissociation, dissociation in the weak sense, or narrative rigidity. That is, he is so attached to living out a narrative of self-sacrifice that he is never faced with circumstances that would make him feel greedy. And generally, this way of living works for him: he is known as generous by some people, masochistic by others. In any case, he is generally able to avoid having to be keenly aware of his self-interest, and this is especially true when his self-interest would conflict with the interests of the person with whom he is interacting.

I restrict the use of the phrase *mutual enactment* to interactions in which *both* the patient and the analyst are, individually, sufficiently threatened by awareness of their own dissociated material to unconsciously interpersonalize it. This happens when the patient, enacting his own dissociated material, accuses the analyst of something that the analyst cannot tolerate being, or treats the analyst in a way that threatens to arouse the same intolerable identity—that is, the patient awakens a dissociation in the analyst. The analyst, who is no more able than the patient to use his mind effectively in a situation of this kind of imminent threat, in some fashion—perhaps subtly, perhaps openly—turns around the patient's accusation or the way the patient is treating him, thereby interpersonalizing his own (the analyst's) dissociation. In mutual enactment, in other words, both the analyst *and* the patient externalize dissociated material; both analyst *and* patient are caught in an unconsciously motivated way.

Let us say that the fictional person I have just introduced becomes a psychoanalytic or psychotherapy patient. And let us say that paying his analyst's fee has been a bit of a strain, and might even mean that he will have to forego something he wants, such as a vacation to a place he has been thinking about visiting for years. At this point the analyst brings up raising the fee. The patient is taken by surprise. He was not prepared for this, and he is attached enough to his vacation plans that he cannot adopt his usual, automatic attitude of self-sacrifice. He is threatened with feeling a powerful surge of self-interest, one that will conflict with the interests of his analyst. If this happens, the patient will be not-me: he will feel intolerably greedy, ashamed, and self-hateful. Instead of trying to negotiate the issue, which is just too risky a course, the patient conveys, in words or in conduct, something like this to the analyst, thereby interpersonalizing the dissociation: "You're some kind of greedy bastard, aren't you, charging such a high fee? Aren't you already getting plenty out of me?"

If the analyst is *also* someone who cannot tolerate a certain degree of self-interest (and many such people do become psychoanalysts, after all), he responds in a way that interpersonalizes his *own* dissociation, his *own* version of not-me, conveying in one way or another that (for example) the patient is wildly unreasonable, that he (the analyst) has perfectly justifiable expenses that require that he collect thus-and-such a fee, and so on.

This is not the only thing that could happen, of course, and not even the most common. Let us say that the analyst *can* tolerate his own self-interest without feeling too greedy and ashamed. In that case, the clinical interaction still qualifies as enactment, but not as *mutual* enactment. This kind of enactment is what takes place when, in the face of one person's enactment, the other person in the interaction manages to respond in a way that recognizes the dissociation without responding from within a dissociation of his own. The analyst who is not caught in a reciprocal enactment is instead able to mentalize (Fonagy, et al, 2002) his own experience, saying to himself something like, "OK, I'm bent out of shape here. This person is getting under my skin. I hate feeling this way. I'm angry at the patient over the accusation, and maybe a little guilty about my fee. But exactly what is happening to me? *Why* am I angry? *Why* guilty? What exactly is the patient setting off in me? What can I learn about the patient from my reaction?"

Let us go back for a moment to the observation that our perception of events lags behind the events themselves. The perceptions that would allow you to know or sense what is happening with the other are not immediately available, under even under optimal conditions. And so we must conclude that there is *always* a brief period after every interpersonal event during which we literally don't know what we are doing. If we think of enactment as unconscious participation in relatedness, the time lag might lead us to take the position that *all* interactions are enactments, or have enactive qualities, even those interactions in which both participants' perceptions of ongoing interaction are relatively unobstructed. I have not adopted that way of defining enactment, however, because the phenomenon would then have to be understood as omnipresent. We would never cease enactment; and in this way the term would lose any specific meaning. And so, despite my acceptance that all interaction does indeed have unconscious aspects, I prefer to restrict the use of the term "enactment" to the interpersonalization of dissociation. I offer a fuller exploration of these issues in the chapters that follow, especially in Chapter 4.[1]

---

[1] It goes without saying that *all* conduct, both the patient's and the analyst's, is partially the outcome of unconscious motivation. I want to be clear that I am restricting only the use I am making of the term "enactment," not the range of unconscious motivation that is involved in ongoing interaction between analyst and patient. A great deal of nonconscious motivation and other kinds of influence do not qualify as dissociated, i.e., are not unconscious for defensive reasons. Think of all the mutual regulatory influences we pass back and forth in the clinical situation without ever being aware of doing so (e.g., Beebe & Lachmann, 1998, 2002), or consider the procedurally represented experience that the Boston Change Process Study Group (1998, 2002, 2005, 2007, 2008) refers to as "implicit relational knowing." In Bucci's (1997) multiple code theory, much of the experience encoded nonverbally, and especially subsymbolically, is nonconscious (at least in verbal-reflective terms), although not necessarily for any kind of defensive reason. Bucci suggests that affect, in particular, is encoded subsymbolically.

This point is hardly unique to the dissociation model, of course. The same point can be made in classical models, in which much nonconscious influence on conduct and experience comes from sources that are descriptively but not dynamically unconscious—i.e., not repressed.

Dissociative Enactment and Projective Identification

No doubt my fictional example provokes some readers to think about pro-jective identification. It does seem that the two conceptions are similar in certain respects. Most meaningfully, both are ways of thinking about how unconscious influence is conveyed from one person to another, and a suc-cessful outcome in both cases has to do with transformation of experience from a "raw" form that cannot be used in making meaning (not-me in the terms of dissociation theory; *beta* elements in Bion's [1962, 1963] frame of reference) to a more benign and useful form (me; *alpha* elements).

The similarities, but particularly the differences, between these two views deserve much more careful study and exclusive focus than I can give them here. The issues are complex, both because of the concepts themselves and because different authors employ them differently. Neither enactment nor projective identification means the same thing to all those who use the terms.

And yet, because I imagine that the clinical examples that appear in most of the chapters of this book will continue to make readers think about projective identification, I will hazard the beginning of an analy-sis of the difference between the concepts. I do so, though, as an aid to the reader rather than as an attempt to stake out a position. That larger goal requires more scholarly study and documentation than I give the hypothesis here.

The differences between the ideas of enactment and projective iden-tification that are most relevant to the clinical problems I am discuss-ing in this chapter revolve around the ways the analytic relationship is conceived. Among those analysts for whom projective identification is central, analyst and patient occupy complementary roles, container and contained, and the most affectively charged exchanges between the two participants are understood to take place mostly *within* psychic life, less frequently in the actual conduct of analyst and patient. If the exchange spills over into conduct in a notable way, especially if the conduct is the analyst's, and especially if it is the kind of distressing conduct that is often the heart of the matter in what are considered enactments by Interpersonal and Relational analysts, the containing function is under-stood to have failed.

For Interpersonal and Relational analysts, on the other hand, for whom the roles of patient and analyst are more mutual and reciprocal than complementary, the stage on which enactments are played out has a more complex geography. It encompasses psychic life, of course; but the unconscious parts of both the analyst's and the patient's psychic lives are also expected to play out on the field of actual conduct. There is a greater emphasis than in the work of those for whom projective identification is central on the way analyst and patient treat one another. The examination of what is happening in the room between the two people—the details of what is taking place, and the meanings each participant (i.e., not only the patient, but the analyst as well) ascribes to those things—is a routine part of Interpersonal and Relational practice. This way of working derives from the emphasis on relatedness that is the subject of this chapter.

Of course, psychic life is hardly the exclusive precinct of those who think in the terms of projective identification, nor are Interpersonal and Relational clinicians the only analysts who investigate clinical relatedness. Analysts from both orientations see unconscious material reflected in both the minds and the conduct of the participants. It is a matter of emphasis: Interpersonal and Relational analysts, I believe, simply look more routinely than their colleagues for reflections of enactment in their own conduct and that of the patient. It is an important aspect of what is distinctive about Interpersonal or Relational practice. The kind of enactment that is often felt to be a failure of containment by those who use the concept of projective identification is often the very event, for Interpersonal and Relational analysts, that sets in motion the most important work of the treatment. For these analysts, it is frequently only via affectively charged enactments that not-me, because it cannot be symbolized, can appear in the treatment at all.[1]

---

[1] Mitchell (1997, Chapter 4) argues that interaction in the Kleinian frame of reference is not fully mutual, that there remains in that body of work the (unstated) assumption that there are important limits on the vulnerability of the analyst to the patient's unconscious influence. On that view, because the Interpersonal/Relational perspective is fully social, one might argue that projective identification and dissociative enactment differ on the basis of the degree of their acknowledgment of the analyst's unconscious involvement with the patient. That may be the case. But the problem is complicated by the fact that it is primarily Bion's revision of the concept of projective identification that is used today; and those who use Bion's revision do not necessarily describe either Bion or themselves as Kleinians (e.g., Ferro, 2005a), and in fact feel that Kleinians did not know what to do with Bion's revisions of Klein's ideas. Ferro (2005a) writes that Bion, "while he derives from a definitely Kleinian matrix," developed his thinking to the point where "it was no longer a linear expansion of the previous [model], but one which brings about a quantitative leap" (p. 1535). And so analyses like Mitchell's of Kleinian writers do not necessarily apply to the understanding of writers such as Ferro, who is one of the contemporary writers best known for his use of projective identification. All of this complication is the reason that the comparison of dissociative enactment theory and contemporary models of projective identification requires careful study and documentation.

Not-Me Does Not Require Trauma

Sometimes, perhaps because of my use of dissociation, readers have been left with the impression that not-me is routinely the outcome of trauma. I want to be careful to avoid that implication. Trauma is indeed often central in the creation of not-me; but not-me can also be the outcome of much less easily observed psychic processes.

The fictional patient I just discussed, for instance, might have grown up worrying that, if he were demanding about the satisfaction of his wishes, he would have hurt or overwhelmed a parent whom he believed to be weak and emotionally inept. To demand too much from a loved person who is nevertheless perceived in this way could provoke the sense that one's own demands are hurtful enough to others to be intolerable to oneself. Such a person might come to feel, too, that his angry reaction toward the parent's perceived weakness was also not-me, since it might very well seem to the patient that the parent would be helpless in the face of the patient's anger, resulting in guilt and shame on the patient's part. Under the right circumstances, such guilt and shame might come to seem intolerable. The patient might also worry that he would enjoy causing the parent pain, for example, and might be unable to bear the guilt provoked by the formulation of this recognition.

The point I want to emphasize about this elaboration of my example is this: it would be possible for the fictional patient I have described to develop and hold his perceptions of the parent for any number of reasons, and some of these would be unformulated reasons with dynamic significance. That is, the relational origins of not-me are not limited to observable, traumatic events. To put it another way, the origins of not-me are not limited to events that have actually taken place in the external world.[1] No trauma would necessarily have had to take place in order for the fictional patient I have described to grow up feeling that to be demanding or angry is not-me.

Note that in this example, the patient's "worries" about the parent's emotional capability would never have been formulated. These "worries" can be conceived as something other than unconscious fantasies, as that concept is usually used; they can be understood, that is, as possibilities for meaning that are dealt with by never being fully known, felt, or sensed.

---

[1] Any psychoanalytic understanding of trauma, of course, includes more than external events. The case has also been made, though, that psychoanalytic views of trauma have given short shrift to the actual traumatic events, especially in the case of adult onset trauma (Boulanger, 2007).

These possibilities for experience are dissociated for unconscious reasons without ever having been formulated, and are then maintained in an unformulated state; that is, they remain potential experience that has never been actualized, not fully formed experience that has been repressed. Unless or until the interpersonal field allows enough safety to formulate the experience (and that outcome requires the successful resolution of enactment), not-me remains unformulated indefinitely, and enactment of not-me comes and goes as the interpersonal context shifts. The way the concept of dissociation is used in this book, then, is not specific to trauma. Instead, as I have already claimed, dissociation and unformulated experience comprise a model of mind (D.B. Stern, 1997, 2009).

Unformulated Experience/Unmentalized Experience

Links have frequently been drawn between the idea of unformulated experience and certain other conceptions of unconscious experience, particularly Bollas's (1987) "unthought known," Stolorow's (Atwood & Stolorow, 1984; Stolorow, Brandchaft & Atwood, 1987; Stolorow, 1988) "prereflective unconscious," the "prelogical experience" of Tauber and Green (1959), and Wolstein's (1982) "transconscious experience." But there is another link that is at least as relevant to emphasize, the one between unformulated experience and the various ways of understanding unmentalized experience. There is by now a substantial literature having to do with what Lecours and Bouchard (1997), in a review of that body of thought, describe as "the necessity of the mental transformation of raw, concrete, 'unmentalised' experiences" (p. 855). Unmentalized experience is "raw" in the sense that it has not been symbolized. Mentalization is symbolization of one kind or another, and it makes thought, feeling, and the life of the mind possible.

I have already cited Fonagy et al. (2002) in the context of unmentalized experience. I add to that the work of Mitrani (1995) and, most recently, Botella and Botella (2005). Earlier influential contributors to this literature are Bion (1962, 1963), Segal (1957), and the Psychosomatic School of Paris (Fain & David, 1963; Fain, David & Marty, 1964; Green, 1975; McDougall, 1985; Chasseguet-Smirgel, 1990; Marty, 1990, 1991). The task of mentalization, broadly defined, is one of the greatest challenges of infancy and, in intrapsychic views, pre-exists the development of repression, which can only come about once experience of a certain degree of structure has been created. The wish, too (again, from within the classical perspective) is possible only after it becomes possible to think (e.g., Green, 1975). In models in which repression is central, experience can only be expelled from consciousness—repressed—once it attains the kind of symbolic form that awareness requires. Experience that is not symbolized cannot be thought, nor can it be repressed, because such experience can never have been conscious in the first place.

That is the position I have always taken about unformulated experience, although I reached it from a very different direction, one in which, among other differences, the primary defense is dissociation, not repression (D. B. Stern, 1997, 2009). Here is an early presentation of the point (D.B. Stern, 1983):

> Unformulated material is experience which has never been articulated clearly enough to allow application of the traditional defensive operations. One can forget or distort only those experiences which are formed with a certain degree of clarity in the first place. The unformulated has not yet reached the level of differentiation at which terms like memory and distortion are meaningful (p. 73).

Not-me, and all experience that has remained unformulated for unconscious defensive reasons, therefore conveys something important in common with unmentalized experience: it has not been formulated and then expelled from consciousness; rather, it has never been symbolized at all. And therefore, as in theories of mentalization, the task of treatment as conceived in this book is to make formulation possible where it was impossible before, and in that way to expand the limits and the capacities of the self or mind. Furthermore, accounts of mentalization and the theory of unformulated experience share the position that the rendering of symbolically mediated experience is a continuous and vulnerable process that can be interrupted, temporarily or for longer periods, by the ongoing conscious and unconscious events of psychic and relational life. Both kinds of theory conceive the creation of experience that can be used in making meaning as a continuous process.

Relatedness and the Future of Meaning

Those who theorize the roots of transference to lie in unconscious fantasy—even if, like many Freudian analysts today, they think about unconscious fantasies not as configurations of drive and defense, but as repressed narratives—are at the very least taking the perspective that clinical relatedness does not itself constitute the object of clinical interest. Relatedness is instead conceived as a means of access to that object—an expression of the mind or something outside the mind, not part of the mind itself. For those who depend on the concept of unconscious fantasy, clinical relatedness is like the image projected on a movie screen: it contains what you want to know, but if you want to affect the image in any permanent way you had better ignore the screen and go find the film.

I believe, on the other hand, that the possibilities that, if actualized, open experience in just the ways intended in psychoanalytic treatment, are quite literally the possibilities of clinical relatedness. We do not need to try to see "through" clinical events to the real substance, the fantasies lying behind or beyond them. The future of any treatment instead exists in the unseen, unformulated possibilities embodied in the conscious, and especially in the unconscious, parts of clinical process, right there in how the patient and analyst grasp one another's personalities and intentions, what they do with one another and how they feel about it. As the possibilities for this jointly created interpersonal field unfold—some of them disappearing without ever having been realized, others becoming actualized as they emerge into a moment of relational relevance—they continuously set the changing parameters for what patient and analyst can experience in one another's presence. In the simplest terms, what I want to say is this: The experience that it is possible for the analyst and the patient to have in one another's presence is shaped by the nature of what takes place between them. The possibilities between them are not contributed by a separate source of meaning—i.e., fantasy—that shapes and influences relatedness to conform to its image. The possibilities between analyst and patient are instead the unformulated possibilities of relatedness itself.

This is what I mean by when I claim that meaning, at least the most psychoanalytically relevant meaning, is embodied in relatedness. Relatedness is mind in action, and so what you see is, in an important sense, what you get. It is often reasonable to take the position, and especially often reasonable in clinical work, that what mind does is what it is. Relatedness is simultaneously the site of the mind's potential and a very significant part of what it does. Relatedness does not, therefore, bear the relation to mind that the image on the screen bears to the film. That is, relatedness is not merely an *expression* of mind—relatedness is *part* of mind. This is one of the most important areas in which it makes sense not to conceive mind as unitary, not to conceive it as contained in the brain or the head, or even as located somewhere inside the person, but as *distributed. The future of meaning is embodied in relatedness.* That is, to repeat the point of this chapter, the nature of the interactions in which we participate, and that we are partially responsible for creating, has a great deal to do with which versions of our unformulated experience we articulate or realize.

Psychoanalysts do not know in advance which new emotional/relational contexts will transform old meanings into new ones, and it is unlikely that they could set out to create those contexts even if they knew before-hand which ones they were. Spontaneity is required. We must feel our way toward the fulfillment of our intentions, allowing those intentions to create and recreate themselves along the way. That is one of the lessons of Alexander and French's (1946) now long-ago experiment with correc-tive emotional experience: we are all aware now that, for any number of reasons, it just does not work to try to suss out the transference and then calculate the correct way to avoid confirming it. The problem is not only that we cannot predict the meaning to the patient of our interventions. We certainly can't predict such things—that is true as far as it goes. But our inability to predict is not the primary problem. We must be both more authentic and less calculated than the Alexander and French technique allows, however well intentioned it was at the time. It is not enough to know how to do our work, although knowing how to do it is essential. We have to mean what we do.

We do not necessarily have any idea when we and our patients will find ourselves in a transformative context. It just happens. I (D.B. Stern, 1983, 1997) have referred to this event, after Bruner (1979), as "effective surprise," and have described the process by which we try to encourage these events (we cannot simply cause them or will them into being) as "courting surprise" (D.B. Stern, 1990, 1997). Under favorable conditions, that is, under conditions that allow therapeutic action, we notice, after the fact, that the emotional/relational context has changed, and we see its impact on us. In the chapters that follow this one, those moments come about over and over again. The heart of our work takes place beyond our capacity to grasp the events that make it up. That does not mean that it is unlearnable; it means, rather, that it is a form of praxis. Like art and like craft (e.g., Sennett, 2008), and like the mind itself, psychoanalysis is what it does.

Enactment is a kind of extreme selective attention, a set of perceptions of the other, and of oneself in relation to that other, that are so rigid that no other possibility can be imagined, at least temporarily. Because any perception that grows from need inevitably has a constricting effect on the range of interpretive understandings we can allow ourselves to have, any perception of the other person that represents greater freedom or curiosity is inevitably broader than the transference and countertransference that preceded it (D.B. Stern, 1997, Chapter 7). Need stifles curiosity by shining light only into certain corners; it requires continuous effort, and the kind of intentionality that I have claimed goes beyond consciousness, not to succumb to this selectivity, to stay open to our capacity to allow alternative perceptions to form in our minds. Over and over in this book, it will happen in clinical illustrations that enactments end in the appearance of a new perception of the other.

And so, here at the beginning of this book I reaffirm and extend the theme of *Unformulated Experience*: we best serve those with whom we work not by attempting the revelation of pre-existing psychic content, but by working toward a greater freedom to experience, an unlocking of the affective/relational problems, large and small, that arise between our patients and ourselves. As we unlock those problems, the possibilities for the analytic relatedness expand; and as they expand, the possibilities for the experience analyst and patient can have in one another's presence also expand.

Because both the analyst and the patient are involved in the relatedness that grows up between them, offering help of this kind requires that not only the patient, but the analyst, find a way to accept a greater freedom to experience. Patient and analyst must become partners: partners in thought, yes, but also partners in feeling and every other aspect of experience. We work toward a wider range of affects, thoughts, and perceptions that allows us to feel and sometimes formulate meanings that have remained outside our capacity to live. We work toward a resumption of the therapeutic conversation that has been interrupted by enactment, a resumption made possible by our acceptance of some small part of what has been *not-me*. The interruptions are as important as what they interrupt. The aim is less to know something different than to *be* something different. I hope that the chapters of this book contribute to the articulation of such a vision of our field.

2

Conversation and Its Interruptions

We say that we "conduct" a conversation, but the more genuine a conversation is, the less its conduct lies within the will of either partner. Thus a genuine conversation is never the one that we wanted to conduct. Rather, it is generally more correct to say that we fall into conversation, or even that we become involved in it. The way one word follows another, with the conversation taking its own twists and reaching its own conclusion, may well be conducted in some way, but the partners conversing are far less the leaders of it than the led. No one knows in advance what will "come out" of a conversation. Understanding or its failure is like an event that happens to us. Thus we can say that something was a good conversation or that it was ill fated. All this shows that conversation has a spirit of its own, and that the language in which it is conducted bears its own truth within it—i.e., that it allows something to "emerge" which henceforth exists.

—Hans-Georg Gadamer (1965/2004, p. 385)

What Is Conversation?

In the chapter following this one, I discuss dissociation and enactment from within a hermeneutic frame of reference. In this chapter, I contextualize that chapter, and the ones that follow it on dissociation and enactment, by revisiting the way that the hermeneutic philosopher Hans-Georg Gadamer (1965/2004), who has influenced me for many years, thinks about the matter of true conversation, or collaborative, authentic dialogue.[1] I have been drawn to think of dissociation and enactment as the uncontrollable, unconsciously motivated interruption of that kind of dialogue (e.g., D. B. Stern, 1990, 1991, 1997; see also Chapter 3). And so understanding

---

[1] Gadamer's magnum opus, *Truth and Method*, was published in German in 1960, but it was not published in English translation until 1975. In 1965 a second edition of the book had appeared, and it is this edition that was translated into English. Then, in 2004, a revised translation of the second edition was published. I have used the revised translation throughout this book. To represent this complex bibliographic history, I cite the book thusly: Gadamer, 1965/2004.

the nature of true conversation in its uninterrupted form should set us on the path for the chapters to come.

Hermeneutics is rooted in historicity, the perspective that what we consider good and bad in life—in fact, what it is possible for us to find meaningful at all—is the outcome of our embeddedness in history. Our time and place simultaneously define the range within which we can create our possibilities for meaning and limit our access to possibilities outside that range. By participating in what Gadamer calls true or genuine conversation, we can understand the limitations imposed by history to some degree, thus making it at least somewhat more feasible for us to take them into account and sometimes even to transcend them. Gains of this kind come, first and foremost, from the conversation itself, of course; but they also arise from the assumption of historicism we start with, which encourages us to assume that we are blind to possibilities that, if given the opportunity, we might rather know about.

For Gadamer (1965/2004), understanding emerges in dialogue; and dialogue has a very particular meaning to him, a meaning that lies at the heart of what most psychoanalysts believe is the ideal of clinical process.

> Conversation is a process of coming to an understanding. Thus it belongs to every true conversation that each person opens himself to the other, truly accepts his point of view as valid and transposes himself to such an extent that he understands not the particular individual but what he says. What is to be grasped is the substantive rightness of his opinion, so that we can be at one with each other on the subject. Thus we do not relate the other's opinion to him, but to our own opinions and views. (p. 387)

The idea that we should try to understand "not the particular individual but what he says" may seem to contradict the aims we pursue in clinical practice. But I do not believe it does; Gadamer is merely trying to say that any conversation that matters must be *about* something, and that the dialogue is successful to the extent that the conversants find their way to common ground about whatever that is. Furthermore, in consonance with contemporary thinking about the analyst's use of her own experience, Gadamer believes that we understand the other's position by understanding ourselves. It would be better, actually, to make this point reciprocally: we reveal ourselves in our own eyes by understanding the other, and we understand the other via what we learn about ourselves. In any case, the route to an understanding of what the other is trying to say lies through our own experience. We must change our own experience of the other to understand her.

Gadamer's reference in this passage to "substantive rightness" may be jarring to those of us who think of psychoanalytic work as a matter of subjectivity and intersubjectivity. But Gadamer is not speaking epistemologically; that is, he is not embracing objectivism. Rather, he is emphasizing that the partners in a conversation are not acting directly on each other, as they would be, for instance, if they were yelling at each other or kissing each other. That is what would constitute subjectivity in his frame of reference: some kind of statement or action that conveys, "This is what I want *from* you; or this is what I am going to do *to* you." The substantive rightness Gadamer is describing is defined by an attempt by each conversant to address what he understands the other to be thinking and feeling. The focus, in other words, is on developing a sense of the other's meanings, not in getting something from the other or making something happen.[1]

The process of conversation is therefore inevitably and continuously interpretive; and the interpretations are motivated, to whatever extent each participant can manage, by the attempt to see the object of the dialogue the way the other is seeing it. Along the way, of course, this extended interpretive process also features other kinds of interpersonal processes, such as disagreement, paradox, prescription, cajoling, and exaggeration. And sometimes, of course, the therapist will think she is simply attempting to understand the patient, but unconsciously she is attempting to make something happen.

Each partner in the conversation begins the process of understanding from within his own horizon of understanding. When the conversation is successful, the interpretations of each by the other come closer and closer to each other, each participant repeatedly modifying her interpretation to conform to what she now understands the other to mean. There occurs what Gadamer repeatedly refers to as "agreement," a word that is not meant to imply that the conversants believe the same thing, but that they *understand* the same thing. Belief is an entirely separate matter, in the same way that it is in clinical process, where the question of whether we believe the patient is right or wrong is virtually never a primary consideration, or even a relevant one, in guiding our listening. Gadamer's

---

[1] Of course, if we are to be true to clinical reality here, we also have to add that, in the very act of understanding the other, we participate in creating the meanings to be understood. We must acknowledge that our attempt to understand is hardly "pure," in the sense that we are doing nothing else with the other than pursuing understanding. We must acknowledge, in other words, that we are always also *acting* on the other in ways that we may or may not be aware of. We are, in other words, always mixing our attempt to understand with other intentions that actually *do* say "This is what I want from you" or "this is what I am going to do to you." More about this later in the chapter.

famous expression of this idea of agreement is "the fusion of horizons" (see Chapter 3).

And so, for Gadamer, the conversation that works its way toward truth focuses on what emerges *between* two people, not on what one of them finds within the other. Perhaps most immediately, this part of Gadamer's thinking reminds psychoanalytic readers of the ideas contributed by Benjamin (e.g., 1999, 2002, 2004) and Ogden (e.g., 1994, 2004) that two subjectivities working together in the analytic space co-create an "analytic third," an intersubjective relationship between them that has an independent existence. In a more general sense, Gadamer's description of a true conversation is what all clinicians understand as a smoothly progressing analytic inquiry.

Gadamer himself had little to say about psychotherapeutic conversations, except (oddly enough) to indicate his belief that his work was probably not applicable in that setting. For example, just after the passage I quoted above, Gadamer goes on to say this, contrasting a focus on what he calls "individuality" with the more hermeneutic emphasis on what is said: "Where a person is concerned with the other as individuality—e.g., in a therapeutic conversation or the interrogation of a man accused of a crime— this is not really a situation in which two people are trying to come to an understanding" (p. 387). It is clear from Gadamer's (1965/2004) equation of "therapeutic conversation" with "the interrogation of a man accused of a crime" that he does not view psychotherapy as we do. Apparently, Gadamer thought that psychotherapy was limited to some kind of attempt to influence, examine, blame, or change the other—and that, of course, would not be what he meant by a true conversation. He does not seem to grasp that individuality could itself become the object of true conversation. What those of us who practice it understand as psychotherapy, of course, is consistent with both individuality *and* true conversation. The ideal of psychotherapy and psychoanalysis, like the ideal of true conversation, is the relatedness of I and Thou.

Gadamer's work is, in part, a response to the early 19th-century Romantic hermeneutics of Schleiermacher, one of the great hermeneutic innovators. A review of Gadamer's divergence from Schleiermacher illuminates the source of Gadamer's antipathy to the view that understanding is a grasp of the other's mind. For Schleiermacher, says Gadamer (1965/2004), "the author can really only be understood by going back to the origin of the thought" (p. 186). What does that require? It requires that one reconstruct the very process of creation—from within the mind of the creator. It requires that one "identify" with the creator. In the end, because the reconstruction of the creation reveals many aspects of the process that were unconscious to the original creator, the one who understands what an author has written, according to Schleiermacher, aims *"to understand a writer better than he understood himself"* (p. 191; emphasis in the original). Keep in mind that this reconstructive understanding does not require the contribution of the other; the other has nothing to do with it, apart from, of course, being himself the object of the understanding. That is, Schleiermacher developed the Romantic belief that understanding requires neither mutual understanding nor conversation or dialogue, but rather an empathic understanding of the individuality of the creator of the thought, an understanding that is created in the monadic or isolated mind of the one who understands. Gadamer believes that Schleiermacher's hermeneutics has been handed down in an uninterrupted way from then to now; the understanding of the other through identification is "a formula that has been repeated ever since" (p. 191). "It is ultimately a divinatory process," writes Gadamer (1965/2004):

> a placing of oneself within the whole framework of the author, an apprehension of the "inner origin" of the composition of the work, a re-creation of the creative act. Thus understanding is [for Schleiermacher] a reproduction of an original production, a knowing of what has been known ..., a reconstruction that starts from the vital moment of conception, the "germinal decision" as the composition's organizing center. (p. 186)

Contrast this view with Gadamer's claim that understanding cannot be monadic, but must be mutual and must concern not the source of what must be understood, but its actual nature. We understand not by reconstructing the mind of the other, but by doing more and more to remove the differences between his view and our own. From the other side of the dialogue, the partner in conversation is doing the same thing. There is a process of mutual accommodation. Each of us begins by identifying the other's meaning with what it most reminds us of. Gadamer calls the initial meaning we bring to bear a "prejudice" or a "preconception," words that are used without opprobrium in this context. In true conversation, we deal with the other via preconception only at the outset, because as soon as possible we allow the other's contribution to the dialogue to query us about what we mean. Sometimes the query from the other is literal. Imagine that my preconception of the other's meaning is that he is angry with his spouse. Perhaps I say, "So you must have been very angry." But the other was not angry, or at least he did not think he was, and he responds by saying, "Well, no, I wasn't really angry. I was more baffled than angry."

My impression of what he intends to say now changes, and whatever I say next reflects that change. The situation continues to develop.

A similar sequence of questions and answers might occur on a more implicit or nonverbal level. Let us say that, in response to my own impression that the patient is angry with his spouse, I make a sympathetic noise; or maybe I convey something by the very absence of a response. The patient understands, in any case, that I have the wrong impression and says, "No, no, I was actually more baffled than angry." And in addition, of course, we could construct a scenario in which *both* sides of the conversation went on without explicit symbolization.

The kind of mutual questioning that furthers a true conversation can take many forms. We often hold psychotherapeutic conversations, for instance, in which, despite one's acceptance that the other person believes what he says, one still thinks it is possible that a different meaning is submerged, or potentially present, in that content. In other words, true conversation can include the attempt to discuss meanings that one member of the conversation believes are either unconscious or implicit in what the other says. In my example, perhaps I think that the other patient *really is* angry with his spouse, but does not want to know it; that is, I think that his bafflement, while sincere, is defensive. Gadamer's model can be expanded to include this kind of psychoanalytic example because the fusion of horizons is not necessarily defined by an agreement between partners in dialogue that an unconscious meaning is present between them; the fusion requires only that the partners both grasp either that the unconscious meaning is a reasonable implication or that it is not. Of course, in the end, the implication of an unconscious meaning by the analyst helps, when it does, because it organizes experience of the patient that had not been organized before (Loewald, 1960), and so the fusion of horizons usually is comprised by an actual agreement about the nature of the meaning. What I mean to emphasize is that Gadamer, like psychoanalysts, rejects the authoritarian imposition of meaning; and like an increasingly large group of analysts, he insists that meaning is jointly created.

Offering an understanding, provoking a question, modifying one's understanding—this is the stuff of conversation for Gadamer. We do not reconstruct the literal history of the meaning that we find in the other, as Schleiermacher believed. We do not directly construct the other's mental process. Each conversational partner *interprets the meaning* of the other, absorbs the answering reaction, and then interprets again, until a fusion of horizons comes about.

In this way, Gadamer's portrayal of understanding is intersubjective. It requires two people; it is inevitably and continuously dialogic. Schleiermacher's is not; the object of understanding is more passive. He need only make his meaning known. He need not simultaneously participate in the more active way necessary for the one who understands in Gadamer's frame of reference.

Gadamer's hermeneutics holds an implication for our theories of empathy. As long as we mean by empathy that two people come into mutual understanding, we do not contradict the hermeneutic perspective. But a true conversation cannot take place between two people if only one of them is trying to understand the other; nor can it take place if the understanding that is sought is felt to be grasped directly from the experience of the other, as Schleiermacher portrayed it, as if, that is, the one who understands somehow looks into the mind of the other and absorbs it through identification. Empathy is an interpretive process, not a direct apprehension of meaning (e.g., D. B. Stern, 1994), and it must be reciprocal. Of course, the psychotherapist or analyst is usually more focused on the patient's experience than the patient is on the therapist's; but the ongoing process needs to be reciprocal in at least the sense that therapist and patient intend to understand what the other means by what she says and by her conduct. Each needs to understand his or her task as the ceaseless contribution of meaning, the querying of the meaning offered by the other, and acceptance of the other's queries of one's own meaning. When empathy is reciprocal, it issues in mutuality, not in the grasp of one person by the other. Racker (1968) puts this point beautifully: "To understand is to overcome the division into two. ... To understand, to unite with another, and hence also to love, prove to be basically one and the same" (p. 174).

One of the points in Gadamer's thought that has always fascinated me and that I think links it most closely to clinical process is the fact that conversation, if it is going on between two people who are doing their best to understand each other, takes its own course, and that that course is unpredictable. (See the epigraph at the beginning of this chapter.) The course of an analysis can never be planned, even from one day to the next, from one moment to the next. We do not know what will happen, and we cannot sense where we will end up.

Why is this the case? In Gadamer's (1965/2004) terms, it is because of "*the priority of the question* in all knowledge and discourse that really reveals something of an object. Discourse that is intended to reveal something requires that that thing be broken open by the question" (p. 357, emphasis in the original). Gadamer goes on:

> To ask a question means to bring into the open. The openness of what is in question consists in the fact that the answer is not settled. It must still be undetermined, awaiting a decisive answer. The significance of questioning consists in revealing the questionability of what is questioned. It has to be brought into this state of indeterminacy, so that there is an equilibrium between *pro* and *contra*. The sense of every question is realized in passing through this state of indeterminacy, in which it becomes an open question. Every true question requires this openness. (p. 357)

And so true conversation moves in mysterious ways. Seeing what is questionable is its heart. I return to my simple illustration, which I will now embellish a bit for my present purpose. Let us say that I think my patient may actually be angrier with his spouse than he seems to think he is. How do I bring up this possibility? I could just ask him about it, of course. But I will be much more effective in bringing something new into the open if I can say something that conveys what suggests to me the questionability of his conclusion. I need to make his denial of anger toward his spouse seem possible within the terms of his own experience. And to do that, I must try to grasp enough about what he means by what he says to make his own prior, denying interpretation seem questionable in even his own eyes. So after I say that he must have been angry, and he responds by saying that no, he was really just baffled, maybe I say something like: "Well, a person certainly *could* be baffled by what she said to you. But it seems to me that a person could also be annoyed. Especially you. After all, your wife was questioning your judgment about something that you pride yourself in knowing about. It wouldn't be surprising if you had felt annoyed, and as a matter of fact, there was something in the way you said you were baffled that made me wonder if you were. Do you know the tone of voice I'm referring to? Do you think that's possible?"

Now, whether the patient responds in an accepting way to this remark of mine has to do with many things. But if he feels reasonably safe with me, and we have managed to develop at least the beginnings of a collaboration about this aspect of his relationship with his wife, he may very well be able to see, on the basis of my questioning, new possibilities in his own previous utterances. Something new has been brought into the open. He may respond by filling out what I said, adding detail and emotional resonance to it, until it once again begins to become something more than it was; and at that point, perhaps I have another comment or question that opens it even further. The outcome is unexpected and unpredicted because it depends on the autonomous, emergent development of the subject matter that exists in the *between*, not on the separate, individual experiences of the participants. Something is, as Gadamer says, broken open.

And of course the same process could take place in reverse: The patient might see possibilities to query something I said or did, and it might then be me who, seeing the patient's take on what is questionable in what *I* have said or done, expands the material in an unexpected direction. No doubt I also do not need to add that this kind of inquiry, in psychoanalysis, often concerns the nature of the ongoing relatedness between the two conversational partners. In such instances it is the analytic relationship itself that is brought into the open.

It is no accident, of course, that good psychoanalytic sessions often go by quickly and effortlessly, and that bad sessions usually require backbreaking work and can seem nearly interminable. Gadamer says that the forgetting of ourselves is what happens when conversation is authentic. The subject matter, or the play (a term that Gadamer shares with Winnicott, and uses in a way that Winnicott would recognize), is all that exists; the players disappear, at least in their own minds (see Gadamer, 1965/2004, pp. 110–118). We are familiar with this phenomenon in psychoanalysis, where we write things such as this about it: "There is the remarkable experience of being carried along by something larger than both the therapist and patient: A true sense of an interpersonal field results. *The therapist learns to ride the process rather than to carry the patient*" (Levenson, 1984, p. 122, emphasis is in the original).

At these times, analyst and patient are not living as much within their individual consciousnesses of themselves as they are within the boundaries of a joint event that is happening between them. Of course, this is a complicated thing to say, because this joint event has everything to do with the individuals who are part of it, and it requires from each participant a continuous and nuanced appreciation of his or her own experience. I think I will have to leave it at this: Anyone who has been a psychoanalytic clinician or a psychoanalytic patient knows what I am referring to.

But perhaps that is not all there is to say about it, after all, because, actually, even those who have been neither patient nor analyst probably know what I am referring to. As Gadamer tells us, the immersion of one's self to the point of feeling its loss is something that happens to everyone in true conversation.

The phrase of Gadamer's that is translated as "true conversation" can just as well be translated as "authentic conversation." This authenticity is key both to hermeneutics and psychoanalysis. But there is a seeming paradox here. Authenticity, Guignon (1965/2004) points out, is defined in two ways that can appear to contradict each other. In one sense, the ideal of authenticity is to own oneself, to achieve self-possession. We long to be all that we can be, to self-actualize, to become what we are. In another picture of the good life, though, the ideal is what Guignon calls "self-loss" or "releasement," the giving over of one's life to something greater than one's own feelings or needs. Do these two ideals not conflict? How can we own ourselves if we give ourselves away?

The ideals actually do not conflict, for either Gadamer or psychoanalysis. We have already seen that good sessions fulfill both ideals: In good sessions we become more ourselves through a process in which we are, in certain important respects, released from awareness of ourselves. Here is what Guignon (2004) says about the matter. It applies as well to psychoanalysis as it does to Gadamer's thought, which is what Guignon is addressing.

> Gadamer shows how the participants in the [authentic] conversation can leave behind their self-preoccupations as they give themselves over to the to-and-fro of the discussion. What becomes central in a dialogical situation of this sort is not the opinion of this person or that person, but rather the subject matter under discussion. We all have experienced conversations in which we get so involved in the topic being discussed that we seem to become totally absorbed in the discussion. The center and focus of an intense conversation is defined by the ongoing play of ideas as they carry the matter at hand forward. The locus of the activity as we experience it is not my mind and yours, but rather the "between" made concrete in the issue of the *truth* of the matter we are discussing. In vital, intense discussions, egos fall away and are replaced by something much more important: the matter that matters. (pp. 164–165)[1]

There are differences over the question of what implications this view of hermeneutics holds for psychoanalysis. I am going to develop what I want to say on this point against the foil of a paper by Zeddies (2002), a paper that I admire in every other respect than the one I am about to comment on here (see D. B. Stern, 2002a, in which I make use of the points from which I have learned). Like Guignon, Zeddies emphasizes that Gadamer's true conversation is not focused on the individual participants but on the subject matter of the conversation: "In order to be carried along and transformed by the subject matter, no participant can regard his or her

---

[1] Philip Cushman (personal communication, 2009) comments on this quotation: "Perhaps we could say that we are most ourselves when we are in the process of dialogue, of giving and receiving, immersed in what Gadamer meant by the great circle of life. One way of thinking about this is to draw from both Gadamer's and Heidegger's ideas about historicity. Through an encounter with difference, we come face to face with the enormous influence of history on us, and its limitations on us as well. Through our social world, history constitutes us, and yet by encountering other social worlds we come to realize our world is only one of many worlds, the truths of our world are not the only truths. This is what prevents hermeneutics from being a historical determinism."

own opinion or perspective as inherently superior, nor attempt to move or coerce the conversation in any predetermined direction or toward any particular goal" (p. 19).

So far, so good. But Zeddies develops this point in a direction it is hard for me to follow, and that will be equally difficult, I think, for most psychoanalysts. Zeddies starts out in a familiar enough vein. He writes that, in transference/countertransference work, it may be necessary "to understand what each individual contributes to the dialogue." But then he writes that this point applies mostly to "those who are in therapy to have better relationships in life," suggesting that this is a subgroup. For me, having better relationships in life is no doubt the most important or frequent reason for psychoanalytic treatment. It is over what Zeddies says next, however, that I most disagree with him:

> However, in contrast to much recent psychoanalytic writing, an overfocus of [sic] subjectivity or intersubjectivity may actually prevent or obscure Gadamerian true conversation. There must, Gadamer would say, be a third element in the dialogue about which or through which the individual and collective subjectivities are concerned. Conversation and relationship cannot simply be about us, lest we risk becoming disconnected from vitalizing traditions and customs and consumed by narrow individual purposes and incentives. From a hermeneutic perspective, it is through mutual concern with the subject or topic of conversation that the individual subjectivities are enhanced and transformed, and not through an open-ended, exhaustive exploration of individual subjectivity itself. (p. 20)

Zeddies (2002) goes on to say that unless psychoanalysis looks "beyond itself for moral and dialogical inspiration and grounding, its promises will ring a bit hollow and its identity will be lacking in purpose and meaning" (p. 20).

If I understand properly, psychoanalysis, with which Zeddies is generally quite sympathetic, is here being accused of navel gazing—or, in more serious language, of being unwittingly hospitable to the expression of ideology in the guise of therapeutics. I *think* that Zeddies is saying that an ongoing focus on transference/countertransference can be excessive and self-indulgent and can thereby lead to self-preoccupation and a turning away from the things that most matter in life, probably social issues and the ideal of community. If that is what he means, he seems to be suggesting that to make the study of subjectivity the central preoccupation of psychotherapy and psychoanalysis is to court self-centeredness, a perspective with which I wholeheartedly disagree.

The point of psychoanalysis, it seems to me, is the *mutual* exploration of subjectivity and intersubjectivity. In mutual study, these phenomena become, in Gadamerian fashion, the matters that matter; they become the objects of true conversation; they are precisely the "third element in the dialogue" to which Zeddies refers. As a matter of fact, as far as I am concerned, the ideal of "better relationships in life," which Zeddies seems to find wanting, is not only *not* self-indulgent; it is actually one way to represent the ideal of community. To have better relationships in life is to accept one's own narcissism fully enough to choose to live otherwise, is it not? To have better relationships is not only to find in relationships more of what one wants out of life, but also to be of more use to those one cares about— more loving, authentic, courageous, generous. I do think that most psychoanalytic clinicians share this body of ideals.[1]

Zeddies has been among those who have made the point that psychotherapists must examine their practices with an eye toward revealing the incursion of ideology.[2] All these writers urge us to use the historicity of hermeneutics to see how psychoanalysis is embedded in the larger cultures to which it belongs. In particular, they have warned that psychotherapy can have the effect of valorizing self-contained individualism and self-interest while drawing attention away from the ideal of community, and that such an effect upholds the worst aspects of capitalism and the rampant commercialism of our time.

The question is how best to address this concern. For me, there is a danger in any recommendation about psychoanalytic treatment that represents the straightforward imposition of a moral program. To follow such a recommendation would be to fashion psychoanalytic conduct along lines that do not grow out of whatever we can sense of ongoing clinical relatedness. That does not mean that psychoanalysis is not closely related to morality, of course. I have elsewhere taken the position that our field is actually *rooted* in morality (D. B. Stern, 1996). We do need to find a way to apply hermeneutic principles to psychoanalysis and psychoanalytic psychotherapy, but we need to do

---

[1] I want to make sure not to be misunderstood about the question of ideals. What I am *not* proposing is that this list of characteristics ("loving, authentic, courageous, generous") comprises some kind of humanistic catalog of the characteristics of human nature, or some essentialist vision of morality. I am *not* suggesting that humans are "naturally good" or anything else in such a vein. This is not the place for me to lay out in any detail what I do believe about the origin of human values. Suffice it to say, for the present purpose, that I take a hermeneutic view: We derive our values from the traditions that comprise our possibilities for meaning.

[2] See also Cushman (1990, 1995, 2005a, 2005b, 2007); Layton (1998, 2002, 2004a, 2004b, 2005); Richardson and Zeddies (2001, 2004); Zeddies & Richardson (1999).

so by asking how we can use the insights of hermeneutics within our existing convictions about the centrality of conscious and unconscious clinical process.

If I read Zeddies correctly (now between the lines), he encourages us to make a point of discussing moral and political issues with patients, or, if not moral and political issues, then at least matters with moral and political heft that fall outside the exploration of subjectivity and intersubjectivity. Now, it is true that we discuss with patients matters outside the analytic relationship, and we do it all the time; but we do it from within the context of what we sense is happening in the room.[1] In other words, we do not limit our clinical interest to an understanding of subject matter the patient brings up; we also ceaselessly try to imagine that other subject matter, often unexpressed, that always contextualizes the subject under discussion: the place of the patient's concern in the unfolding of the analytic relatedness. Because we are always doing both these things, we never disregard clinical process, and we always seek to embed our interventions in what we can grasp and feel of that process. If we were to replace our focus on clinical process with a different kind of focus, no matter how well intentioned— some kind of concern with raising consciousness, for example—the treatment could very easily become clumsy, inauthentic, argumentative, and intellectualized. To structure psychotherapy according to any rule or technical prescription, without embedding the technique within what can be sensed of the emotional environment being created in the here-and-now with the patient, is to leave a psychoanalytic orientation behind.

What is it that is so significant about the value of clinical process as a guide? Here I think we return to the matter of authenticity. Focusing ourselves on what we can sense about the ongoing emotional situation in the room, and then listening and participating from within the context of that situation, is perhaps the most we can do to ensure the authenticity of our work. Isn't it the absence of a sense of authenticity, and especially of any sense of releasement or self-loss (Guignon, 2004), that makes bad sessions so hard and unproductive? And isn't our most significant and challenging analytic task to find ways of participating that are both analytically meaningful and personally authentic? Very often we feel that we are most effectively satisfying our clinical demands of ourselves when we are least aware of having to think about how to do the work; and we are least aware

---

[1] Philip Cushman (personal communication, 2009) writes that this view amounts to "the encouragement to notice moral and political issues, but to do so when they emerge in the conversation, not to force them, impose them, or invent them." In this connection, Cushman cites Gerber (1990).

of thinking about what to do next when we are so thoroughly immersed in the emotional sense of the session that we do not need to ask ourselves what to do. We just know.

And yet, of course, we also have to admit that clinical process, and our habits in understanding it, are just as thoroughly the products of history, and thus just as completely moral and political, as any other social phenomenon. Relying on clinical process as a guide hardly gives us a pass on the necessity for developing a moral/political awareness of our work. So what are we to do? It seems that we must do something (talk about social issues, for instance), on the one hand, that we must *not* do, on the other.

Cushman (1995, 2005b) says that the task of writing about how to recognize and discuss the political in psychotherapy is difficult, but not impossible, and seldom attempted. He follows this proviso, though, by plunging in, offering clinical vignettes that illustrate his contention that discussing the political in the clinical situation requires fashioning some kind of compromise between Heidegger and Foucault. That is, it is not enough to recognize the traditions that comprise our very being (Heidegger), nor is it enough to deconstruct those traditions (Foucault). We must do both (see also D. B. Stern, 2002b). Cushman intends his vignettes to illustrate how he has managed this compromise, and the vignettes do convey what he intends. But I find them more notable for something Cushman does not comment on and probably did not set out consciously to convey: their rootedness in the emotional atmosphere of the sessions in which they take place. (Cushman 2005b) manages to consider the political and the clinical simultaneously. Take as an example the following vignette:

> Toward the end of a long therapy, [the patient] was struggling with a problem at work that had profound implications for his life: when to accept jobs from customers and when to turn them down. He came to realize that the moral understandings about the good in his family of origin fit well with those of the unscrupulous work world with which he was involved. He often felt placed in the same moral predicament from which he suffered in childhood. He is in the position of being both victim and perpetrator: He is a victim because he is forced to live in a framework he never agreed to and that he hates, and a perpetrator because in order to emotionally survive he must not care even though he has promised to care, and because he has promised to do, properly, a job that ultimately cannot be done properly, given his standards. "In other words," I responded, "you are in the middle of a moral conflict. According to the moral code of your family and the society, you should accept the double bind: detach and yet pretend to care, work conscientiously and yet know that the work is impossible to accomplish, and all the while pretend not to notice that you are feeling enraged, unsatisfied, and deadened."

We came to realize that he is in the process of … [shaping] a new understanding of what is moral. He has a sense that if he takes the job, he will be cheating the client, living a life of detachment, denial, and falseness. And now he thinks that is the wrong thing to do. But to refuse is to break the old family rules [and the rules dominant in today's society], to act in ways that they would think immoral. He is caught in a dilemma

… Hoping to find others to encourage him to refuse the job, my patient began asking his colleagues what they thought he should do. Contrary to his hopes, each of them, without hesitation, advised him to take the job. The money, they thought, was too good to turn down, no matter how damaging it might be to him emotionally. …"It was like they stood up and spoke with one voice! The voice was my mother's voice, and it said, 'Hey, your feelings don't count.'"

"Well," I said, "it sounds like your mother isn't the only one who thinks that money is more important than emotional well-being."

My patient smirked. … "Maybe it's everyone—hell, it's the system. That's the voice."

"I think the voice you heard speaks through all these people, because it's sedimented in each of us. …"

My patient was silent for a moment. … "It's speaking through everyone, he said angrily, "my buddies, my competitors, everyone. It's not just my mother, as much as I'd like to blame it on her. It's the whole system." He thought for a while, and then he looked up and smiled. "This is going to be more difficult than I thought. How are we going to get the whole damn system into the room?" We laughed together and I said, "You know, if it's all the same to you, I'd rather you take your ideas out there, instead of bringing … [everyone] in here." (pp. 440–441)

There is nothing arbitrary about what Cushman (2005b) is doing here; if he does have an agenda to raise the patient's consciousness, you have the sense that Cushman is subordinating it to his grasp of clinical process. The words he contributes grow from his emotional sense of the session and are responsive to the patient. Nothing is directly spoken about the transference/countertransference, and yet everything that is said seems to grow from it. One senses that Cushman is important to the patient, and that the patient feels a kind of safety in his presence. I especially like the laugh they share at the end, which conveys the comfort between them. In my imagination, this comfort could accommodate an exploration of feelings about Cushman that are less comfortable than those we see in this example. It does not matter whether the patient actually has that degree of freedom with Cushman—the example does its work by demonstrating the viability of that possibility. This session does not sound intellectualized or defensive; it strikes us as an authentic conversation, one in which something new emerges.

Gadamer's description of authentic conversation is a good fit for the parts of psychotherapy and psychoanalysis that proceed with relative smoothness, such as the basically friendly and collaborative interchange between Cushman and his patient. A great deal of the time, actually, our work does proceed that way. But that kind of work is not the most difficult part, and in the end, it may not be the most important. Much of the remainder of this book concerns *interruptions* of true conversation, how we understand such interruptions, and what we do about them. I want to situate the following chapters in the general characterization of conversation I have just offered; but I also want to make sure to convey that true conversation is precisely what dissociation and enactment make impossible. Gadamer's subject was the ideal of conversation; this book, by contrast, concerns the problematics of conversation. On the other hand, we can also say that true conversation, as will become clear in the clinical examples I offer in the following chapters, is what is restored once dissociation is breached and enactment dissolves.

But exactly how *does* enactment interrupt authentic dialogue? The answer to that question is actually fairly simple. True conversation requires that the partners to the conversation not work at cross-purposes. I have already emphasized, for instance, that true conversation cannot be about who is right or whose views are superior. There can be no attempt to prove the other wrong.[1] As soon as the partners try to *act on* each other, rather than understand each other, true conversation breaks down. But of course enactment is precisely the attempt to act on the other, not to understand him or her. Usually there is a sadomasochistic element in enactments, an attempt to deal by domination and submission with what is unconsciously felt to be an irresolvable difference.

Gadamer does not consider the nuances of this issue, but we can. He was a philosopher, not a clinician, and so he had the luxury of taking the position that collaboration was simply present or absent. Psychoanalysts are used to working with a much messier situation than that, because we take for granted that all people are acting on one another all the time, even during episodes of collaboration. That is the meaning of unconscious process. Without our own awareness, we are all continuously attempting to influence the other, and we are just as continuously absorbing the other's unconscious influence on us. And so, for a psychoanalyst, collaboration is

---

[1] "There is, of course, a time and a place for those conversations, but dialogue isn't one of them. In fact, dialogue might make those other kinds of conversations go more smoothly and/or effectively. Perhaps, indeed, those other kinds of conversations might be impossible without dialogue" (Cushman, personal communication, 2009).

always a relative matter. It is impossible to believe that any conversation is *nothing but* collaborative.

But with that proviso, we can still define true conversation, in psychoanalysis, as relatedness that is *relatively* collaborative, relatedness in which the partners' primary intention is to understand the other, even if there are other ways in which they are undercutting the fullness of that collaboration by their unconscious attempts to act on each other.

Sadomasochism obviously interrupts the open, nondefensive, often implicit, questioning of one another that makes up true conversation. We have no choice, though, in our attempts to deal with enactments, but to continue to *try* to understand, to restore true conversation. Often enough we may as well try to put out an inferno with a garden hose; and when the enactment is mutual, as it often is, we do not even have the hose. The following chapters are an attempt to comprehend our difficulty in understanding at these times, the failure of our capacity to see what is questionable in the other's experience and in our own.

I do not take up the political aspects of enactments in the chapters to come, but that does not mean that such a study would not be productive. It is certainly true that the kind of conversation Cushman had with his patient becomes quite impossible in the heat of an enactment. But the fact that such a dialogue is impossible at such times does not mean that the events in question do not have a political or moral side. As a matter of fact, it seems to me that the very intensity of the happenings and the fact that they so often end up being expressed through the operations of power mean that enactments probably carry even more expressly political and moral meanings than other clinical events. It sometimes behooves us to think about these possibilities during the course of an enactment and to bring them up with our patients once they end. Who is attempting to dominate whom? Is a man angry with a woman? A woman angry with a man? What might the *reason* for the anger have to do with the genders of the participants? Whenever the race, class, gender, sexual preference, or ethnicity of patient and analyst differ—meaning that there exists some kind of power differential, in addition to the differential built into the distribution of the roles of patient and analyst—the same questions can and should be asked once the atmosphere cools enough to allow it. And the question of power hardly ceases to be meaningful just because two people have the same identity position. I can testify, having been there, that power relations between two middle-aged, upper-middle-class, straight white men are hardly absent!

3

The Fusion of Horizons
Dissociation, Enactment, and Understanding

Context and the Fusion of Horizons

We understand our patients when we locate their speech and conduct within suitable or fitting contexts. We understand ourselves the same way, by feeling our way into the contexts within which we feel that our own experience and behavior are most convincingly situated. Contexts, for this purpose, are enveloping atmospheres, at least as much matters of mood or affect as of content, within which some kinds of experience and interaction can take shape and others cannot. A fitting context is one that allows the meaning of the other's speech and conduct, or our own experience, to unfurl: it enables the expansion of meaning, and it unlocks some significant portion of the capacity of experience to signify. A poorly suited context does not enable or potentiate in this way, but instead prevents, stunts, or inhibits the meanings that might emerge. A poorly fitting context ensures that new meaning remains locked away; it forces understanding down paths that lead only to familiar destinations.

Once one is able to supply a suitable context, a meaning emerges; one has understood. But the advent of new meaning not only marks the union of conduct with a fitting context; new meaning actually constitutes this union. In recognition of this view, the hermeneutic philosopher Hans-Georg Gadamer (1965/2004) describes the birth of new understanding as the "fusion of horizons." The explicit new meaning that arises in the fusion is only one of the possibilities that might have come into being; it did not exist previously in the mind, at least not in finished form, but was given its shape in the moment of the fusion. The potential meanings that preexist the fusion of horizons, only some of which will come to explicit fruition, therefore are less aptly described as unconscious in the usual sense (that is, as hidden but fully formed) than as unformulated (D. B. Stern, 1983, 1997). Thus the task of making the unconscious conscious is not best described as allowing oneself to accept what is already there, but rather as freeing oneself to articulate or construct what one has refused to think about. Unformulated experience is not "there" to be revealed.[1]

Situating conduct in a fitting context, then, is not like finding the right spot for a piece of a jigsaw puzzle. More often than not, our grasp of both conduct and context is at least partially constructed in the act of understanding, a mutual accommodation that the phrase "fusion of horizons" is meant to convey. Conduct and context modify each other until, in the fusion, one finds that one can sense the goodness of fit from the inside of what one is trying to understand. Uncertainty vanishes, at least for the time being; one knows that *this* is *right*. And yet, as right as the new understanding may feel, what the next moment demands us to understand is liable to be no less ambiguous than what we needed to understand the moment before.

Once the fusion of horizons has taken place, one can speak to the other person from within that other's frame of reference. But the process by which the analyst arrives at such a clinical interpretation, especially when that interpretation concerns matters of some emotional significance in the analytic relationship, often requires that a step take place prior to the fusion between the horizons of analyst and analysand. Frequently a fusion must first occur *inside* the analyst's experience, a fusion between the horizon of what-feels-like-me and the horizon of part-of-me-that-feels-alien, the other in myself.

This fusion of the horizons of two or more parts of the mind allows the analyst fuller conscious and preconscious access to his own subjectivity (a term I use to signify the entire range of a person's psychic life, including its unconscious aspects), a freedom that then informs the clinical process, sometimes allowing understanding where none was possible before. In everyday psychoanalytic guise, just as the fusion of horizons (in the analyst's

---

[1] The claim that all experience is continuously constructed does not contradict our everyday recognition that some meanings are remarkably enduring. It is entirely consistent with the idea that we continuously create our experience anew and suggests that in some cases we construct the same meaning, or the same pattern in experience, over and over again. To put the point in conventional psychoanalytic language: Unformulated experience can be highly structured, though never so structured that multiple interpretations are excluded. Even those structured meanings remain processes. Even the most highly organized unformulated meanings are therefore not static objects or ruts worn in the brain, and never absolute, but predispositions toward certain kinds of meaning-making and away from others.

mind) between analyst and analysand is the most significant aspect of what we refer to as clinical interpretation or the attainment of empathy, the fusion of horizons *within* the analyst's subjectivity is familiar to us as the successful analysis of countertransference. (It would take me too far afield at the moment to explore the point in detail, but the same two kinds of fusion take place in the *analysand's* experience, that is, in the analysand's understanding of the analyst's experience, a process corresponding to the growth in the analyst's capacity to interpret and provide empathy and containment; and in the analysand's understanding of himself, corresponding to the analyst's understanding of the countertransference.)

One of my intentions in this chapter is to show how productively the hermeneutic portrayal of understanding dovetails with the psychoanalytic conception of the multiple self. As I have already hinted in referring to the fusion of horizons within one's own subjectivity, it seems to me that it is productive to think of self-states as some of the most significant of the contexts we employ every day in the clinical situation. One understands conduct when one is able to imagine the self-state from which it arose and then grasp it from within that context. I argue later that notable episodes of misunderstanding in the analytic situation—that is, circumstances in which the possibility of a fusion of horizons between analyst and analysand seems remote—often can be attributed to a dynamically enforced separation, or dissociation, of the analyst's relevant self-states. The analyst unconsciously denies himself access to the context, to the state of his own self—to the other within himself—from within which it would be possible to construct the experience of the analysand. In more familiar terms, the analyst does not understand himself well enough to understand the patient.

In hermeneutic philosophy, the process by which conduct and context are fitted to each other—the creation of understanding, the fusion of horizons—is called the hermeneutic circle. The scope of application of this idea is very wide: It includes our grasp not only of thoughts but of feelings, and our understanding not only of other people and ourselves, but also of art, literature, drama, and even science.

Not surprisingly, and as has already become clear in Chapter 2, the hermeneutic literature focuses much less on unconscious motivation than psychoanalysis does. Gadamer, in particular, whose work centers on the phenomenology of understanding—the moment-to-moment episodes of interpretation and understanding that constitute human experience—has little to say on the subject. Other hermeneutic philosophers, especially Habermas (1971) and Ricoeur (1970, 1977, 1981), have had closer relations with psychoanalysis, but their accounts do not really address the moment-to-moment construction of experience Gadamer (1965/2004) deals with so well. And so, while preserving Gadamer's picture of understanding, I set out here to present what Gadamer has not: a psychoanalytic account of the hermeneutic circle.

How does the hermeneutic circle work? Whenever we are trying to understand, we are working with part–whole relations. We try to comprehend something new by grasping it partially, just enough to identify it as an instance of something familiar, a meaning we already know. Then we project this "whole" meaning onto the "partial" one we have constructed, completing the partial meaning—and the circle. (I am not adapting psychoanalytic vocabulary by using "projection" here; the word is employed in hermeneutics in a more general sense than in psychoanalysis and implies nothing about defense. It signifies, rather, our imposition of meaning on what faces us, based on what we are already capable of understanding.) The "whole" meaning is what I have been calling "context" and what Gadamer refers to as "prejudice." Gadamer does not use the word prejudice in its most common, negatively valenced sense; he employs it instead to signify that the contexts we project are expectations or biases based on past experience, both our own personal history and the cultural traditions sedimented in us. And, therefore, although prejudices, if they remain unexamined, may obstruct understanding, they are also what make understanding possible: Novelty can be grasped only from within what is already familiar to us.

The key problem for any kind of understanding, clinical work included, arises when the prejudice or context we project is not a good fit for what we are trying to understand. In fortunate instances, the working psychoanalyst sees that the context within which he is trying to understand the analysand is inadequate; he sees that the meaning he has projected is inappropriate. Of course, this understanding requires that the analyst be able to treat the context or prejudice as a hypothesis, that is, that he be able to question the validity, for this purpose, of the familiar understanding he is projecting. He must be sensitive to those moments when the detail that faces him challenges the familiar thesis he intends to project: He must maintain enough uncertainty to be in a position to reject what he may otherwise be tempted to believe.

When everything is working well, the process of understanding, this hermeneutic circle, is what anthropologist Clifford Geertz (1974) calls "a continuous dialectical tacking between the most local of local detail and the most global of global structure in such a way as to bring them into simultaneous view" (p. 69). We use the parts to grasp the whole, and the whole to grasp the parts. The reciprocal aspect of the process is the source of its description as a circle. As Geertz puts it: "Hopping back and forth between the whole conceived through the parts that actualize it and the parts conceived through the whole that motivates them, we seek to turn them, by a sort of intellectual perpetual motion, into explications of one another" (p. 69).

This is an engaged, interactive, dialogic view of understanding. We need the collaboration of the other. We cannot understand him by ourselves; we cannot somehow choose, on our own, to experience exactly what the other experiences. The value of empathy is not at issue; it is just that in a hermeneutic view empathy is not some kind of monadic immersion in the experience of the other. It is a process that requires the involvement of the one who is to be understood. This point holds both for our understanding of other people and for our understanding of the otherness within us: Understanding is dialogue, even if it is a dialogue we have within our own skins.

But of course it is usually more comfortable to think along familiar paths than to strike out in a new direction. It is easier to gloss over what is different about the other than to keep ourselves open to possibility. How do we maintain our curiosity and open ourselves to the other? What do we do? The analyst begins by trying to keep in mind the strong likelihood that he *does not* experience what the analysand experiences (and that he does not fully comprehend what he himself experiences).

In other words, the analyst ceaselessly imagines and reimagines the limits of his own grasp. When the analysand speaks, or the analyst notices something about what the analysand has done, the analyst notes the interpretation that occurs to him and then asks himself what else the analysand might mean. What else could this speech or conduct signify? This is one of those paradoxical, recursive, look-at-your-own-eye-seeing operations: The analyst tries to query himself about what he might not be thinking. What could he see differently? What might he be missing? He must find a way to allow the other's experience to have its voice, to "speak," perhaps even to speak in ways the analysand did not know he intended. The analyst must allow the other's experience to disconfirm assumptions the analyst did not even know he was making.

But now consider what happens when the analyst has no idea that he is selecting an inadequate context for what he is trying to understand: That is, the analyst does not understand, but believes he does. There is no dialogue here, no reciprocity, no fusion of horizons. What may appear to the analyst to be an interchange is no more than the unwitting and unilateral imposition of an interpretive frame on the patient's experience, monologue disguised as dialogue. Under these circumstances, the analyst is liable to feel critical of the patient or baffled by him. The analyst does not see that he is looking for evidence of what he already knows and, as a consequence, is liable to feel (however guiltily) that the patient is recalcitrant.

Here we have what we might call the "vicious" circle, not the hermeneutic one: It does not open into anything new, but leads only to the conclusion that set it in motion in the first place. We are inside the vicious circle when we know the answer before we ask the question, when, in fact, we are not really asking a question at all. But when we are in its grip, the vicious circle may not feel vicious: Until some later time, we may remain utterly convinced of our openness to the other. The vicious circle sustains our continuing projection of poorly suited contexts. It is what happens when we cannot (or do not, or will not) see enough to sacrifice our preconceptions: We stifle or stunt the other person's meaning and, as a result, inevitably find ourselves in some kind of relational bind. We shall see that the vicious circle, in psychoanalysis, is the outcome of the dissociation of the analyst's self-states from one another.

The Multiple Self as Context in Flux

As a result of the work of a number of writers,[1] it is today a familiar idea in interpersonal and relational psychoanalysis that the self is not simple and unitary but a more or less cohesive collection of self-states. These different self-states may be simultaneously knowable; there is no implication that a person need be uncomfortable about knowing one self-state while he is "in" another. The multiple self as the expectable, everyday condition of identity is, among other things, a very helpful addition to our conceptualization of the role of context in understanding because our frequent shifts from one self-state to another emphasize the continuous change in the context of all understanding.

The idea of the multiple self in psychoanalysis owes much to Sullivan (1950), who suggested that the interpersonal field determines the contents of consciousness. The kind of relationship we establish with another person has everything to do with what we can be aware of in that person's presence

---

[1] Most notably, Bromberg (1998, 2006); Chefetz (2003); Chefetz and Bromberg (2004); Davies (1996, 1997, 1998, 1999, 2003, 2004); Davies and Frawley (1991, 1994); Howell (2005); Pizer (1998); Slavin (1996); and Slavin and Kriegman (1992, 1998). See also Flax (1996); Harris (1996); Mitchell (1991, 1993).

and what the other can be aware of in ours. (I use "presence" now both in its physical sense and in the more metaphorical, intrapsychic sense as the symbolic presences of the inner world.) It was Sullivan (1950), after all, who said over half a century ago, "For all I know we have as many personalities as we have interpersonal relations" (p. 221).

Admittedly, Sullivan was not proposing a multiple-self theory at the time. He was criticizing the reification in the traditional idea that each of us has something that we are justified in referring to as a unique, unitary self. But add to this critique Sullivan's emphases on trauma and on disso-ciation as a defensive process, and you have the seeds of what has become the multiple self in the hands of interpersonal and relational writers. Sullivan's great insight that what we can experience is defined by the field becomes, in multiple self theory, the idea that each self-state is defined by the experience that we are capable of creating, feeling, and formulating from within it. When, for defensive reasons, we cordon off certain self-states from contact with the others, and then restrict ourselves only to some of these and not others, we also restrict our access to the fullness and depth of the experience it is possible for us to have. We thus reduce the imagination, precision, and affective nuance of the formulations of the experience we are capable of articulating.

In each life, the multiple self arises in the first place because each of us is different in the presence of different others. Our selves are originally called out by others, although soon enough our own states of being begin to exert their influence on the lives of those same others, so that each of us is, in some sense, called out over generations. The various selves of the multiple self are the patterns of experience and conduct, especially emotionally salient experience and conduct, that coalesce around the differences in our conscious and unconscious interactions with different people. Such coalescences form around the patterns of others' direct impact on us and our reactions to them; but just as significant in the genesis of our states of being is the process of identification. (Identification and the "direct impact" of others are not necessarily easy to tease apart, though. I make separate reference to them to emphasize that self-states have their sources in both the intrapsychic and the interpersonal. But the dividing lines are hazy, since we have no reason to identify with someone with whom we have not been deeply involved in the interpersonal world.)

One good vocabulary here is Racker's (1968): We might say that our self-states are sometimes shaped around our identifications with the way those with whom we interact experience themselves, what Racker calls concor-dant identifications, or identifications with the other's ego; and sometimes our identifications arise from the way other people have experienced those with whom we interact, what Racker terms complementary identification, or identification with the other's internal objects.

In any case, the upshot is that very early in life we begin to be different with different people, and often enough different with the same person under different circumstances, each significant change in our world calling out particular patterns of feeling, thinking, behaving, and being. We are familiar with the process by which, over time, patterns of being such as these are internalized, so that even those self-states that originated in direct interpersonal experience may come to be intrapsychic, thereafter to be elaborated and reconstructed according to the purposes of the inner world as well as the outer one.

The existence of multiple self-states, to the extent that they overlap more or less freely (that is, to the extent that we can tolerate remaining aware of one self-state while also existing at that moment within another, what Bromberg [1998] calls "standing in the spaces") is the definition of "normal" or "expectable" dissociation, a relatively permeable kind of separation between parts of the self that occurs simply as a consequence of human relatedness. Under these circumstances, the boundaries between self-states present little or no obstacle to the mind, traffic across the lines proceeding with no more notice or effort than it takes to cross the demarcation of one municipality from another.

But often enough traffic across the boundaries is choked and obstructed, and our theories reflect this. Dynamics and defense are also part of everyday life, and in the conception of the multiple self, defense is the other meaning of dissociation. In this second sense, dissociation is the unconsciously enforced separation or disconnection of the kinds of experience associated with different selves, a separation motivated by an unconscious discomfort, or even a sense of doom or dread, about certain kinds of experience being simultaneously known, sensed, or felt. The more separate the experience of two self-states must remain, the more dissociated, in this second, defensive sense, we describe them to be.

We define defensively motivated dissociation, then, as the unconsciously enforced disconnection between experience and its most fitting context(s), a disconnection that prevents some of the understandings and new meanings that would otherwise be possible. Under these conditions, boundaries between states of self that, in less troubled circumstances, can be crossed simply by focusing attention on experience and making a minimal effort (like crossing that border from one town to the next) become less like boundaries and more like fractures or chasms in a glacier: The effort required to cross them is considerable, and there may be danger.

In the clinical setting, dissociation, because it deprives the analytic participants of the emotional and intellectual contexts they would need to be able to apply in order to understand the ongoing clinical interaction, is, in a sense, really just another way to describe the origin and maintenance of transference and countertransference. Transference/countertransference enactments, in other words, are instances of mutual dissociation; and they may represent the breakdown of the dialogue critical to the hermeneutic circle. Enactments resolve only when one or the other member of the analytic couple reestablishes dialogue by gaining explicit awareness of how, at that particular moment, the context he is supplying is inappropriate to the other (or the "other" within himself); but at those times, by definition, it is precisely that crucial, explicit awareness that is unavailable to either one.

What I am saying may make it seem that I am implying that mutual dissociation occurs only in the most dramatic kinds of enactments—impasses, breakdowns, or deadlocks; but that is not at all what I want to say. Many instances of understanding ourselves or one another must overcome a mutual dissociation; the dramatic enactments are only the most obvious of these. All instances of successful understanding begin with the absence of understanding; if they did not, there would be nothing to be understood. The absence of understanding between two people often means that they are occupying self-states that do not allow a fusion of their horizons, at least for the time being. In any particular instance, new understanding may arise with virtually no resistance to the participants' grasp of one another's meaning; but that ease of understanding merely masks the fact that the process is roughly the same (though less intense) in those facile moments as it is when understanding is much more difficult to accomplish. In both kinds of moments—the unremarkable episode of comprehension and the breaking of an impasse or deadlock—the two participants must find their way to understanding and accepting that the context they have been applying to the meaning of the other is inadequate to the meaning the other wants to convey, or, for that matter, to the meaning the other conveys unwittingly. In the unremarkable moment, the event of grasping and sacrificing the old context and adopting the new one occurs so instantaneously that it hardly seems worthy of note; in the deadlock, it may be so difficult that it never happens at all.

We are grateful for the times when the analysand is able to see the rigidity in his own selection of self-state and is able to amend it in such a way that the deadlock is broken. And that probably happens much more often than we write about. But we do feel, after all, and rightly so, that it is our responsibility not to depend on the patient, but to find our own way to an explicit awareness of what is wrong with the context within which we understand the analysand. Often, at these times, we manage to learn something important about the analysand by observing our own experience. Sometimes, for instance, as I describe in Chapter 4, we sense the effects of the analysand's self-states in the way the clinical interaction provokes a kind of affective "chafing" in our experience. It is especially changes in the analysand's self-state that we sense this way. Something feels inconsistent to us; something counters an affective expectation we did not even know we had until that moment, something feels subtly "wrong" or contradictory or just uncomfortable.

Therapeutic work is often the psychic equivalent of what we do when an otherwise unremarkable walk in the woods is suddenly interrupted by finding that our sweater has snagged on a twig or branch: We stop to investigate the source of the difficulty. Now bring this snag into the consulting room and make it metaphorical. Perhaps that snagged feeling makes us attend to a subtle change in our mood or even makes us note the presence of a different feeling. We ask ourselves about that change, and we find that we are responding to something about the analysand that we have not yet explicitly noticed.

Such hints, which amount to our recognition of our own, previously unformulated state of self, are often the first things that alert us to a shift in the analysand's self-state. A change in the analysand's self-state, in other words, is likely to provoke a change in our own state of self. The reverse is also true, of course. Neither the analyst's nor the analysand's state shifts are useful to the task of explicit understanding unless the change in state that is provoked is noted and accepted by the one who wishes to understand.

We recognize the analysand's self-state from within a part of our own being that is responsive to the analysand's; and, in its turn, our adoption of a responsive state of being has occurred because we have found a way to accept the impact of what the analysand is saying and doing. We cannot observe the other's self-state directly, but only through its effect on us; the other's self-states are visible only as a consequence of their impact. Similarly, we understand our own self-states, and shifts in them, from what we can sense about changes in our ongoing, conscious experience.

The analyst's direct awareness of his state of self, of course, is the exception and not the rule. It is crucial, but only for the task of explicit understanding. Unnoticed changes in self-state ceaselessly oscillate between analyst and analysand and constitute over time the spontaneous, unanalyzed relationship that is the background against which the more purposeful analytic work becomes meaningful and without which it could not proceed.

Reaching an Understanding

Consider the following incident: Daniel, a very bright and articulate middle-aged professional man, was in the early stages of his analysis. We had already established a warm, collaborative relationship and were both well aware, even at this early time in the work, that my reaction to him carried particular importance. If he felt I was warm and affirmative in a session, the time between sessions tended to go well for him; but if he left with the nagging feeling that I was critical, disapproving, or cool, he could become rather depressed ("deflated" was the word that seemed to him to fit best), often about matters that, on their face, had nothing to do with the analysis. In neither instance (that is, when he felt good or when he felt deflated) was he necessarily aware, between the sessions, that these feelings had to do with our relationship; but he was very open to understanding them in this way when he returned for his next session, and he felt that we were on to something significant. We both felt that way.

On the day in question, Daniel heard me rustling around behind him (he was on the couch). He turned around to face me and snapped, "What are you doing?" He has very good peripheral vision (this had already been established), and so, because my chair is not positioned directly behind the couch but slightly to the side, he had been able to see that I was leaning forward to look at my appointment book. I asked him what he imagined I was doing. In the same reproachful tone, he said that I must be thinking about some other patient's appointment.

In fact, I had been thinking about him. It was significant, of course, that he chose his particular interpretation of my behavior; and, with many or most patients, I would have made the conventional move here and suggested that we explore the sources of that interpretation. But I had a different feeling with Daniel. From what had taken place in the treatment to that point, I knew perfectly well that he was capable of conventional analytic exploration and that he even thrived on it. But I also had the sense that this particular episode, because it concerned his belief that, emotionally, I had disappeared from the room, was painful to him in a way that exploration would exacerbate.

Unpacking Daniel's reaction to the feeling that I had deserted him, of course, might have been useful, but he and I had done this before: We both already knew that he worried about whether I had a sustained interest in him. And so I had some doubts that the pain the exploration would cause would be worth whatever we would learn from it. Those doubts were especially acute given the fact that I actually had been thinking about him and so, in that sense, had not disappeared at all. I imagined that we might get further by exploring his sensitivity to the possibility of my disappearance at a moment when he knew I had not left him. All this led me to feel that carrying out a conventional inquiry at that moment would have amounted to following the rules for the wrong reasons; I would not have been choosing my course on the basis of the experience growing out of this particular analytic engagement.

And so I pointed out to Daniel that, just before I looked at my schedule book, he had been telling me about having made plans on a particular afternoon to go out with a woman he was excited about. I reminded him that we had rescheduled an appointment for an afternoon in the near future, and I told him that I had thought the appointment and his date with the woman might be on the same day. (They were a day apart, in fact.) I had been checking the date and had no idea that he would hear me doing so, and certainly no idea that he could see what I was doing.

I imagine that my curiosity about the date of the make-up appointment would be as objectionable to some patients as it would be if I were thinking about another analysand. In both cases, after all, I would not have been paying attention only to what the patient was talking about. I have no doubt that my concern with scheduling would be interpreted as self-serving by some patients, while others would be sure I was looking to see if I would get an hour to myself or away from them, or (in fewer cases) to see if I would have to be disappointed by their absence. For myself, once Daniel drew my attention to the direction of my own thoughts, I wondered if I was checking to see if I was to be replaced by his woman friend.

Was this an instance of unconscious communication? Was I experiencing my own version of what Daniel was feeling—he being replaced by another patient, I being replaced by his woman friend? To him, however, as you might expect from what I have already said, my explanation was unalloyedly good. I was thinking about him, after all. He wove his associations to this event into the rest of what he said that day. He was not as interested in exploring his sensitivity to feeling that I was emotionally absent as he was in the good feeling he had that I had cared enough about his presence to wonder if his date conflicted with a session. He fretted, though, about how I felt about his having snapped at me, since my revelation indicated that I did not "deserve" it.

When I saw Daniel next, after the weekend, I learned that during the intervening couple of days he had found it difficult to maintain hope that his career plans would come to fruition. He had been mildly depressed. He began to talk about circumstances that might have led to these feelings. After a few minutes I asked him about how he had felt about the previous session and whether his feelings over the weekend might be an instance of the "deflation" with which we had become familiar. I made reference to the interactions around "What are you doing?" He recognized immediately that there was something to this and plunged in. He talked about the "snap" for a few minutes, and I eventually somehow got the drift (it was implicit, unformulated in his mind, though somehow available to me in what he said) that, in fact, there had been a kind of sly twinkle about his delivery that I had missed. When he asked "What are you doing?" it had been with the tone of an annoyed but just slightly amused parent catching his four-year-old snitching from the cookie jar.

Make no mistake, he did mean to snap at me. But he also meant to do it in a way that had a certain intimacy about it, with a kind of wink accompanying it, and I had missed that completely. He had not been able to articulate that I had misunderstood this subtlety (he never did have the words for it until it somehow surfaced in what I could glean from what he said on this second day), so he had just suffered with it. He had felt, between sessions, that I must hate somebody like him who caused so much trouble.

I had the sense, as a matter of fact, that although he had not explicitly formulated the affection in his rebuke, his "deflation" would have been less painful to him, and perhaps would not have occurred at all, if I had been able to respond to the intimacy he was offering and not just to the hostility. It seemed even clearer to me now that it had not been so much my reaction to the irritation in Daniel's snap that had worried him, but the fear that I would emotionally disconnect. He was less worried about the damage I would do if I retaliated than he was about my turning away from him. If I had better understood the warmth in his rebuke, perhaps I would have accepted the hostility in a way that would have reassured him about the connection.

Enactments, which are always a variety of misunderstandings, are not necessarily deadlocks. Plenty of them, this one being an example, are situations in which, although the analyst participates unconsciously (my mistaking the afternoon of the rescheduled appointment for the afternoon of the date; my missing the irony in his complaint about what I was doing), the problematic aspects of this unconscious participation can be brought to the analyst's attention by relatively minor events. (The qualification "problematic" is necessary because much of what facilitates the analysis is equally unconscious, but never formulated.) In the terms I am using, this is an example in which the boundaries between my relevant states of self were obstructed but could be cleared easily enough that the treatment was not badly snagged or detoured.

Take one detail: In one of my states of self or mind—let's say, a state that may have originated in my response to my mother's characteristically veiled criticism—I respond to criticism, in a prickly and defensive way, and laughter doesn't come as easily to me as it does otherwise. If I had heard Daniel's "snap" at me in that vein and did not have available to me, simultaneously, countervailing states in which criticism is a little less freighted, it is not surprising that I would have missed the irony in his complaint, an irony so subtle, after all, that Daniel himself had not explicitly formulated it prior to my query about it in the next session.

And yet, in that next session, after the intervention of a period of living, I was different; somehow that subtle irony was available to me, although it was now only an echo. In workable enactments, the relevant dissociations are unstable; an intervening period of living is usually enough to destabilize the relevant dissociations between the analyst's states of self, and that destabilization, in turn, by freeing the analyst to use his mind, allows the reframing of the situation and suggests a line of inquiry or interpretation. Or it just allows the analyst a different state of being-with-the-other.

The vignette of Daniel illustrates our everyday experience that the contours of our own self-states are seldom explicitly visible except by contrast to those that come just afterward. Shifts in our states of mind reveal the presence of prior contexts we usually had little choice but to live through unwittingly. In this case, I could see neither my (apparently) defensive portrayal of Daniel's hostility nor the state from within which I had that picture until I noticed my new portrayal of him on the following day. I did not and probably could not know the "me" who reacted defensively until I had also become the "me" who constructed the fuller portrait.

I might add here, to complete the picture, that despite my conviction that I selected the best course in telling Daniel that I was actually thinking about him and not about another patient, I might think differently in the future. I can imagine my decision eventually appearing to me as an unwitting installment in a deadlock, a much more problematic (and potentially even more informative) kind of analytic interaction than the easily destabilized one that took place between Daniel and me. Perhaps my paternal countertransference to Daniel will seem stifling to him one day, or even patronizing. Perhaps even now it feels that way to some parts of him in ways neither he nor I yet appreciate.

Or perhaps (as I am inclined to think), if his feeling about my countertransference changes, my feelings will change as well, or perhaps, in resonance with him, my feelings already will have changed by the time the old ones become objectionable to him. Much of what is most mutative about the analytic relationship, after all, happens in unnoticed reciprocity, evolving without words, sometimes visible in retrospect, but probably most often never noticed at all. At this point I believe that the loving parts of my relationship with Daniel are good and useful and will remain so; but I remain open to the possibility that they will also turn out to be more complicated than that. In any case, to whatever degree it becomes possible for us to attend to them, they will be analyzed as time passes.

Breaking the Grip of the Field

If the vignette of Daniel illustrates a hermeneutic circle that could be completed with only minor difficulty, the vignette I am about to discuss is an example of a vicious circle, a deadlock, a closed system of stubborn and stable dissociations on the part of both the analyst and the analysand that prevents understanding for long periods, or even indefinitely.[1]

The crucial difference between these two enactments is the kind of dissociation that underlies them in both the patient's mind and the analyst's. My enactment with Daniel grew, on my part, from "weak dissociation" or "narrative rigidity" (D. B. Stern, 1997), defined as an involvement with a particular storyline exclusive enough that alternative possibilities

---

[1] The literature on enactment has become so immense that to cite it is impractical. There also exists, though, a recent and smaller body of writing offering conceptions of impasse or deadlock. A representative sample: Russell (2006a) on the "crunch," an aspect of the repetition compulsion; Elkind (1992) on the problematic interaction that takes place when the patient's transference hits the analyst squarely in his "primary vulnerability"; Ogden (1994) on the "intersubjective third" turning into "the subjugating third"; S. Pizer (1998) on the "nonnegotiable"; Ringstrom (1998) on a variation on Bateson's "double bind"; Benjamin (1990, 2000) on "breakdowns" of intersubjectivity due to especially recalcitrant "doer–done to" complementarities; B. Pizer (2003) on the "relational knot," a form of Russell's "crunch"; S. Pizer (2004) on impasse as "weak dissociation." I thought that the word *deadlock* had arisen spontaneously in my mind during the writing of this book until I read Irwin Hirsch's (2000) interview with Benjamin Wolstein and was reminded that Wolstein coined the phrase "transference–countertransference interlock" in 1959 (!) to refer to enactments. Perhaps my word is an unconscious appropriation of his.

are not noticed or articulated. Weak dissociation does not specifically exclude certain possibilities; those possibilities just happen to be unnoticed alternatives to the story we are so focused on telling or experiencing. Because of my own background, I was so "taken" with the storyline in which Daniel's snap was an expression of criticism that I missed its other half. (S. Pizer [2004] also offers a moving and detailed illustration of the use of the concept of weak dissociation to understand an enactment.) "Strong dissociation," on the other hand, is specifically defensive: whatever is being defended against *must not* be experienced (D. B. Stern, 1997). Strong dissociation is deployed in the service of avoiding specific, consciously accessible experience; it is simply not allowed to coexist with the rest of the personality. Manageable enactments are those in which the reciprocal dissociations are weak ones; in deadlocks, on the other hand, the dissociations binding the experience that analyst and analysand can have of each other are more likely to be the strong or defensive kind.

I had been working with Hannah, a middle-aged professional woman, also very bright and articulate, for about six months when her sometime complaints that I was understanding her inaccurately or narcissistically began to become more frequent. When I asked her to explain what I was missing, what she told me convinced me that I was missing nothing at all, that we were, in fact, saying exactly the same thing. I could not grasp how she could think I was *mis*understanding her. When I would point that out and express bafflement about any differences between what we had said, she only felt that I was understanding her less and less.

I tried over and over again to get it just right. Yet she still said that I was hurting her more with each one of my mistakes. She was angry at me about what she felt was my refusal to see things from her point of view; but what I responded to more directly was her hurt. Despite my very clear awareness that she and I had to be participating in some kind of enactment, I began to feel guilty that I could not grasp what she was talking about, guilty that I was hurting her and annoyed at what seemed to me to be her influence on my taking these emotional paths.

I knew there had to be another way to see this situation, and I continued to ask her about our differences in the greatest detail. I hoped to be able to claw my way to a more empathic attitude; but more often than not I did not find my way there. I came to feel that her complaints were more significant as a kind of blaming operation than as attempts to convey meaningful content. Increasingly, I found that my attitude toward her was irritable. I would not have objected to making this problem between us the focus of joint inquiry if I could have found my way to an open-minded enough perspective, but I was not able to do that.

I felt that, if I were to try this kind of analysis from within my current state, all I would accomplish was to blame her. I did not have to blame her openly and explicitly to continue to hurt her, though, because I could see plainly enough that my annoyance leaked through, and so she felt increasingly blamed, anyway, and thus more hurt and angry than ever. I felt quite alone, without a collaborator. I knew that there must be some way to understand what was transpiring between us so that would release us without requiring either of us to give in, but I just could not seem to formulate that understanding. I could see that she felt the same way I did, and I conveyed my understanding of this deadlock in an empathic way, which helped, of course; at least she knew that I understood that she was hurt, and I think she did believe, at least at times, that it mattered to me. She knew that I imagined that there could be an understanding that would help, but that I could not construct it. As useful as this empathic appreciation may have been, though, it did not help nearly enough, because it did not change our basic positions vis-à-vis one another.

This was not a good situation. I found it increasingly painful. I felt more and more guilty about my feelings and my seeming inability to stifle their expression (which I hardly thought was a good solution, but I had no other for the time being). And, of course, I also felt guilty about what seemed to me to be my failure to be of use. I knew better than simply to blame myself, but there is no inoculation for certain emotional impacts, even if you do know better. I felt locked in.

This very painful period was more complicated than any single telling can capture, as any treatment is, which is to say that it should probably come as no great surprise that we also did good work during this time. The relatedness never ceased being analytic: We continued to make the deadlock the focus of our curiosity and analytic concern. And so, during this period, it seemed in keeping with the work we were doing that Hannah continued to bring in dreams. She is an imaginative person who works well with dreams. One day she brought in a dream that turned out to have special import for both of us.

In the dream, Hannah was in my waiting room, except that, unlike the waiting room in my real office, this one was in an apartment that she knew was also my home. She was alone in the waiting room, but she could hear people in the adjoining kitchen. She somehow could tell that they were my family, laughing and enjoying one another's company. On the table in front of her was an open safety pin, the kind that used to be used to fasten diapers. It was her impression in the dream that I had a baby and that this pin was used for his diapers. She remembered (in the dream) that during her own chaotic and disorganized childhood (her mother had been deeply depressed, and Hannah had been lonely, frightened, and poorly cared for), open safety pins had sometimes been lying about. During those years Hannah had heard awful stories of babies and toddlers swallowing pins that had been left open. The open pin on the table suggested to her my carelessness about my baby and, worse, my murderous hostility. Yet it was entirely clear to her in the dream that she was not about to close that pin. She fully intended to leave it right where it was, wide open. She woke up with the thought that we were both full of hostility. And that was what she said to me in the session.

After everything I have said, it may be surprising that this was a revelation to me. I had been focused on her hostility as a problem to be addressed and on my own hostility primarily as a reaction to hers, which it may very well have been to begin with. But even if that were true, we were far beyond that now. I had not seen clearly that each of us was separately hostile, that it was accurate to say that we were playing on a level field, and that each of us was individually responsible. I had surely been aware of my hostility, but my guilt about it and frustration over it had prevented me from thinking clearly about what part it played in my own subjectivity. I had not been able to think about it effectively and so had been able only to suffer over it and wish to expunge it, once again, despite knowing better. Now suddenly I could ask, why exactly *was* I angry?

Suddenly I had hypotheses about that. Suddenly I could use my mind again. I was finally able to ask myself exactly who Hannah would have to be, and how she would have to feel, to treat me as she did. In short order, Hannah and I laid out a series of thoughts about the nature of our problematic interactions. We were able to stand back from them and think about them effectively for the first time in months. My projections (I use the word in its hermeneutic sense), which I had not been able to stop from becoming certainties about her impossible treatment of me, shrank once again to the manageable level of hypotheses.

Hannah and I have become involved again in this kind of exchange. Understanding is not a magic bullet aimed at the future. As of this writing, as a matter of fact, Hannah and I just faced another deadlock of this kind; but, given that first experience, and our capacity to make individual and mutual reference to it, I felt confident this time that we would find a way to loosen the noose, and we did. It took much less time and effort than before to reduce the vicious circle to the hermeneutic one. Perhaps we will have to do this several times, or even many times, until it is worked through. One of the simple and recurring lessons of psychoanalytic work is that principles never substitute for experience. Each episode in the transference/countertransference must be addressed and either resolved or not, on its own terms.

There are any number of points that could be made about Hannah's dream, of course, and she and I explored many of them. For the present purpose, what is important to me is that her interpretation of the dream broke the grip the interpersonal field had on us both and allowed me to occupy simultaneously the various states of self that I needed to occupy in order once again to be free to think.

One might say that it was not so much the interpretation itself, but Hannah's sudden offer of collaboration that made the difference. That hypothesis may be right. Whether we focus on her collaboration or on the insight she offered me, I take for granted that the episode could not have taken place without the previous occurrence of other, perhaps silent processes that must have been occurring over a significant period of time between us. I feel sure that my dogged attempts to understand what was going on, for instance, although they were unsuccessful, made a considerable impression on the nature of Hannah's willingness to work with me. Even in the worst of moments, I retained certain important aspects of my capacity to be an analyst, as Hannah retained hers to be an analysand. We continued to work successfully, however suffused the hours often were with the effects of the deadlock.

What happened in response to Hannah's interpretation of her dream was not as simple, then, as the resumption of my analytic capacity or Hannah's to be a collaborative analysand. Hannah's offer of collaboration, as surprising as it was to me, grew from both a conscious and an unconscious context. Although I could not sense these contexts, no doubt I was as central as she was in their development. That is the nature of many of the surprises that occur in psychoanalysis: in fact, surprise is the feeling we have when an event in the relationship takes place in a way that feels out of the blue, devoid of context.

Hannah and I did not simply resume our analytic capacity. What we resumed was our ability to think about this particular problem. It is partly that specificity that draws me to the idea of the multiple self, with dissociations between various of its aspects, as an especially suitable way to think about what happened. With any patient, we adopt many states of mind in the course of the work. In my example, however, it was just one of those states that was problematic—a key one, of course, and apparently isolated, but just one nevertheless. It is equally important, though, that our eventual ability to deal with that one state was embedded, in ways that she and I created but will probably never know, in all the others.

Where was my affective "chafing" in this illustration? That is not difficult to pick out. I knew that Hannah must be saying something that I did not understand, because she was hurt and I was unable to offer an effective analytic response. In a deadlock, it is often only the analyst's awareness of the inadequacy of his own response that prevents the situation from degenerating into a common argument and keeps hope alive that the analyst (and the analysand, too) will find some solid ground on which to stand and think.

In a deadlock, the analyst may be able to do no more than try to be open to influences from outside the state of mind within which he is mired. A deadlock means, after all, that the participants' freedom is curtailed, which suggests that neither can choose to pull the treatment up by its bootstraps. In the case I have just described, it was the analysand's generosity, courage (she took the risk that I would not accept her observation), and powerful motive to further the treatment (powerful enough that it infused a dream) that made change possible. Both of us very much wanted something like what she did to happen. As angry and hurt as she was, I think she was aware that, in my way, I regretted the deadlock as much as she did, and I think she must have had a pretty good idea that I would welcome her offer of collaboration. So I cannot say that I had no freedom; better to say that what little freedom I had took the form of my regret and sincere desire for therapeutic movement. I may not have been able to shift my state of mind, but I certainly wanted to, even if, outside my awareness, I must also have wanted not to. Without the analysand's belief in my desire to work and to help, I suspect that it would have been just too dangerous, under the circumstances, for her to make herself as vulnerable as the dream, and her interpretation of it, made her.

In such a case, then, the analyst must wait, recognizing that he is in the grip of a dissociation that he cannot control. He has no choice but to accept that he cannot will a change. He can only remain open to the foreign element that may reveal a path to freedom. Sometimes that foreign element is an intervention by the analysand, as it was in this case; sometimes it is a consultation sought by the analyst; sometimes it is a movie, a conversation with a colleague, a play, a novel, or a psychoanalytic article. Sometimes the analyst, in retrospect, can identify in the clinical interaction a variety of that affective chafing, that unprovoked signal of the unexpected, that alerted him to something about the patient, or about himself, that he had not noticed before.

Perhaps most often, though, the foreign element is impossible to identify. In these less easily describable cases, at some point the interaction between the analyst and the analysand seems to become infused with some new quality that neither participant consciously set out to create. Then, in response to these new meanings, the inner world (which may actually have contributed the new shades of meaning in the first place) shifts as well, making it possible for at least one of the participants to have a deeply felt new experience of how the other feels. In the meantime, while analyst and analysand both try to protect what they can of their collaboration and curiosity through the storm, the analyst can do no more to melt the deadlock than to register whatever he can of alternative ways of experiencing and focus on the details of his experience of the interaction.

For the sake of perspective, leaving the case of Hannah, I return to the case of Daniel. He and I both felt that I understood him rather well most of the time. But remember my oversight: It turned out, you will recall, that Daniel's "snap" at me had an intimate, humorous edge that I completely missed at the moment it happened. Daniel had spoken to me in this way frequently enough over the previous months of the treatment that I might have been expected to be familiar with a certain wryness he has. My oversight was clearly a kind of temporary blindness, a notable but relatively unproblematic dissociation of the state(s) of self within which I could have sensed and articulated the emotional nuance I missed. It is not my own motivation that interests me so much here. The case of Daniel is a reminder that dissociations and the enactments they inspire are seldom as noisy, dramatic, and painful as the deadlock with Hannah was. The more subtle dissociations and enactments, and our clinical responses to them, are part of every analyst's more or less unremarkable daily work.

A Note on Imagination

In this chapter I have described dissociation as an unconscious unwillingness to experience certain states of being simultaneously. Elsewhere I have placed much more emphasis on dissociation as the inability or unconscious unwillingness to articulate certain aspects of one's experience in verbal language (D. B. Stern, 1997). These two meanings are really different ways of making the same point. To refuse unconsciously to enter a certain state of being is (among other things) to refuse unconsciously to create the particular explicit meanings that would be available from within that state.

Dissociation is a constraint on the freedom of thought. It is sometimes total, as in the absence of any shred of memory of early childhood abuse; but more often the inability to articulate is not total at all. I may be able to remember, for instance, or to formulate in the present moment, that Daddy is angry at me; but depending on the history of the relationship and the residue of that history in my mind, I may or may not have access to the additional interpretation that Daddy is angry because he loves me and does not want me to wander into the street. If I do not formulate the latter experience, I come away feeling that he is unfair. Or perhaps, in a different and more abusive situation, the field I put together with my angry father allows only the interpretation that his anger is due to my badness, so that I cannot articulate the perception that he is sadistic. Or I can articulate it in some states of self and not in others. Or, like Hannah, I may be able to see that my analyst is irritable, but I cannot formulate an interpretation of my own behavior as provocative, so I feel only victimized. Dissociation makes it difficult to reflect on certain aspects of experience; these things just happen.

It is not only the freedom of thought that dissociation prevents. It is just as significantly the freedom to feel. To stay with memory as an example: We sometimes have a hazy recollection of traumatic events, or even a fairly explicit one, but it is flat, dead, merely factual, lacking the affective nuance we might expect to accompany it. Or perhaps a storm of affect is present, but the emotional subtlety that would be needed to give the experience a fuller meaning is absent.

In the largest sense, though, dissociation is not fully described as a failure of either thought, memory, or feeling. Dissociation is a failure to allow one's imagination free play. In many instances one can think of the failure of imagination as the collapse of transitional space (Winnicott, 1971) into deadness or literalness. Merleau-Ponty (1964a, 1973), who captured the sense of what I mean by imagination as well as anyone, writes that "speech takes flight from where it rolls in the wave of speechless communication" (1964a, p. 17). He tells us that creative speech, which is the domain of imagination, "tears out or tears apart meanings in the undivided whole of the nameable, as our gestures do in that of the perceptible" (p. 17). Imagination is our capacity to allow language to work within us as it will; dissociation is our inhibition of that capacity. If we wish to do so, we can use Lacan's terms here: Imagination takes place in the realm of the Symbolic, dissociation in the Imaginary. Merleau-Ponty (1964a) put it this way:

> To make of language a code for thought is to break it. When we do so we pro-
> hibit ourselves from understanding the depth to which words sound within
> us—from understanding that we have a need, a passion, for speaking and must
> (as soon as we think) speak to ourselves; that words have the power to arouse
> thoughts and implant henceforth inalienable dimensions of thought; that they
> put responses on our lips we did not know we were capable of, teaching us,
> Sartre says, our own thought. (p. 17)

The absence of dissociation is not defined by the presence of some particular experience that has been prevented from existing. That way of thinking would be a simple-minded dualism, as if experience could be only present or absent, formulated or unformulated. The absence of disso-ciation is defined, instead, as (relatively) unfettered curiosity, a point that immediately allows us to say that experience ranges from highly imagined to highly dissociated, with all the implied variations in between. In the case of Hannah, for instance, it certainly is not my intention to say that I did not formulate my experience. Rather, I did not formulate it in certain ways; I was not able to allow myself an open kind of curiosity, a freedom of thought and feeling, an unconstrained imagination. I did formulate my experience of the interaction with Hannah; it is just that the experiences I formulated were too incompletely imagined to be useful. My experience was constricted, highly and rigidly selective. I could not ask myself the questions that would have opened up my own experience. I could not use the possibilities my experience afforded me. I needed to be able to expand my context—that is, my state of mind—to imagine more fully, to be able to wrap my mind around a more inclusive and nuanced picture of what Hannah and I were doing with each other.

Just as dissociation is a failure of imagination, enactment, too, is a sign that imagination has failed. The failure is usually understandable, informative, temporary, and relative; but it is a failure nevertheless, because it is a kind of estrangement from within which we are locked out of curiosity. Simultaneously, of course, enactment is also a kind of unconscious communication, the only way that some experience can be brought into the analytic situation. In that sense, enactment is a boon, not a failure at all. Without it, in fact, imagination would have that much less to transform. That these two interpretations of enactment seem to contradict each other is merely one more evidence, if we needed one, of how rich and manifold reality is: The world allows us interpretations that logic might tell us cannot coexist; and yet they do. To complicate matters further, many of us now think of the analyst's unconscious involvement as continuous.[1]

But, of course, imagination in some ways goes on continuously as well. Experience is formulated and unformulated, free in some ways and constricted in others. Each moment can be conceived in both ways, and probably should be.

When the Patient Reveals the Path to Freedom

We can describe the crucial element in a deadlock as each participant's loss of the capacity to see or value the other's perspective; and so it follows that perhaps the chief means of relaxing a deadlock is the reawakening of that capacity. Such a reawakening is easier to refer to than to accomplish, of course, because people in deadlock with one another are, by definition, trying to force one another into a certain set of perceptions. Seeing the other person's perspective is precisely what neither wants nor is able to do. Consequently, most direct expressions of one participant's feelings or perceptions about the other, or about the situation between the two, contain some variety of blaming; and blaming, obviously, resolves nothing.

But there are certain kinds of direct expressions that, even from within a deadlock, can and do change the nature of the analytic field. If the analyst makes a nonblaming observation of the analysand that is precisely descriptive and heartfelt (but that may nevertheless convey anger or other aspects of the deadlock's affective charge), there is the chance that the analysand's capacity for empathy about the circumstance in question may be awakened, or reawakened (and I might add here that the analysand's empathy for the analyst is something we depend on more often than we acknowledge). Once the analysand's empathy for the analyst's position is aroused, the analyst finds it much easier to occupy the states of mind in which the analysand's self-state can be formulated. Of course, this may also happen the other way around, which is actually more direct; that is, a direct, heartfelt, precise expression from the analysand may loosen up the

---

[1] For the reasons I described in Chapter 1, I prefer not to define this continuous unconscious influence as enactment, but prefer instead to preserve the word "enactment" for episodes in which dissociation is interpersonalized.

analyst in such a way that the necessary states of mind become available.[1] In these instances, the analysand's emotional expression is the foreign element that reveals to the analyst a path to freedom.

One of my favorite examples of this sort of intervention comes from Bollas's (1983) report of his treatment of a maddeningly controlling patient: "It is impossible to convey, I fear, just how maddening this woman can be as the reality of her self presentations is truly so unbelievable as almost to defy communication altogether" (p. 28). After a lengthy and thoroughly unsuccessful period of trying to interpret in traditional fashion what he faced, Bollas began to fantasize, when he was with his patient, that she would move away, become disillusioned with him and go to someone else, or have a breakdown and be taken off his hands by the hospital: "More than a few times I thought I would have to tell her that unfortunately I would not be able to continue with her and I would tell her about how private practice has its limits and so forth" (p. 27). However, one day she made a complaint that made Bollas sit up and listen: She told him that he had become cold and removed from her. He knew immediately that she was right, although he had not formulated the observation before: "I had withdrawn from her and was always on the alert for her next use of herself as a kind of afflicting event" (p. 28). Bollas then said to his patient:

> I am very glad that you have said this, because in a way, I think you are absolutely correct. I have become somewhat cold as you put it and am aware of being distanced in these sessions, something that I think you are well aware of. But let's wonder, shall we, about how this happened. You see, it's my view that if you could convince yourself to stop being so God damned traumatic then I could be quite a bit more at ease with you and we could actually get down to the task of understanding you. (p. 28)

Later Bollas added that he thought she had brought up his distance from her because she knew this was something in her life that needed work. The patient responded to all this with a level of maturity Bollas had not seen before.

---

[1] I certainly do not mean to imply, though, that empathy for each other's emotional positions is always the most therapeutic kind of situation that can occur between analyst and analysand, or even that such a state of relatedness is always a goal. To take such a position would be to deny the significance of the analyst's complementary identifications (Racker, 1968) and the authentic responsiveness they inspire in the countertransference. It would also ignore the crucial importance of holding, in which empathy cannot and must not be reciprocal; the analyst must simply accept the analysand's feelings, positive or negative, sometimes a rather heavy dose of them over a rather prolonged period. All of us believe that the analyst's freedom to experience in the countertransference and the patient's freedom to experience in the transference (in the patient's case, a freedom almost always unencumbered either by the realistic danger of frank retaliation or by any demand to understand the analyst's experience) are important aspects of therapeutic action.

At first glance it might appear that it was Bollas's intervention that allowed the patient to treat him differently, with the consequence that he could adopt a state of mind that allowed him to formulate her perspective. But why did Bollas come up with this very influential intervention? It was the outcome of his response to the patient's direct expression of *her* observation about *him*, however much the message may have been clouded by her status as "afflicting event." Note that Bollas had not been able to see his coldness and emotional distance from the patient until the patient observed them. That means, in the terms I am using, that he was trapped in an isolated (dissociated), unproductive, and unresponsive state of self, one in which he had not even thought to formulate either his coldness or the pain his patient must have felt about it. Bollas's angry state of mind, that is, was dissociated from the state of self in which a more productive perception of the patient would have been possible. It seems that his recovery of the use of his mind to help this woman with her hysteria was at least partially the result of her intervention, very much as Hannah destabilized my dissociation with her interpretation of her dream.[1]

Perhaps we should even wonder if, in cases in which deadlocks are resolved, patients come to the aid of their analysts very frequently. Take those cases in which, like Bollas, the analyst breaks the grip of the field by offering a direct emotional response. How does a beleaguered analyst, caught in and struggling with his own desire to control the patient, suddenly find it possible to offer a direct, nonblaming, recognizing but noncontrolling observation? Doesn't the very capacity to make such a response suggest that the important shift has already taken place? Sometimes the analyst may find his own way to such a resolution; but very often it must be the patient who, however maddeningly, sets this kind of mutative event into motion. Unexpected aid from the patient, it seems, is one of the most significant of those foreign elements, often announced by that persistent affective chafing, that the analyst must try to allow himself to perceive if he is to resolve his own dissociation and find his way to understanding.

But no matter whether it is the analyst or the analysand who resolves the dissociation first, the story does not end here. Understanding is more mysterious than the mere absence of dissociation; it does not necessarily fall into place as soon as our unconscious reasons to avoid it vanish. The view that comes to us from Heidegger, Gadamer, Merleau-Ponty, and

---

[1] We shall see in Chapter 4, thaat enactments end when one participant becomes capable of a "new perception" of the other. The new perception is what Hannah contributed to me, and what Bollas's patient contributed to him. Once such a new perception comes into being, neither the patient nor the analyst can treat the other as they did during the enactment.

others is that there is no way to codify the process by which understanding is reached. No one can say exactly why understanding comes about when it does, why horizons fuse now and not five minutes ago or yesterday, why language becomes able in one moment to contain experience that the moment before it could not. Even after dissociation has been resolved, the most we can do is allow history, or tradition, or the speech and conduct of the other to act freely within us. We cannot decide to understand, even under the best of circumstances; we can only strive to put ourselves in the best position for understanding to occur. And so, while the resolution of the analyst's dissociation is crucial, it guarantees nothing: It merely means that the circular movement that may result in the expansion and flowering of meaning can occur with less obstruction by unconsciously held motivation. New understanding may follow immediately or it may not. Resolving dissociations gives language its head, but what language will do then is beyond our capacity to know.

4

The Eye Sees Itself
Dissociation, Enactment, and the Achievement of Conflict

Part I: Must the Eye See Itself?

The analyst's unconscious participation in the therapeutic relationship interests us today for a very different reason than it used to. The significance of countertransference no longer lies in its status as primary obstacle to the analyst's perception of the truth. As the goals of psychoanalysis have shifted from the acquisition of insight to authenticity, the freedom to experience, and the expansion of relatedness (e.g., Mitchell, 1993), we have recognized that countertransference is as much what the analyst does as what she feels, thinks, and fantasizes, and these enactments, as we have come to call them, have become opportunities as much as obstacles. Insight remains crucial because it increases our range of choice. But no longer is the appearance of new understanding always viewed as the heart of the matter, as it was almost uniformly just a few short decades ago. Now, at least in some analytic circles, insight is just as likely to be viewed as a sign that the important change—the shift in analytic relatedness that allowed the new understanding to arise in the first place—has already occurred. Ghent (1995), for example, writes:

> In the early years of psychoanalysis, the prevailing view was that therapeusis was essentially informational—insight and awareness would bring about changes in the ways one would experience events and respond to them. Over time, there has been a subtle shift from the informational perspective to the transformational, where insight is often retrospective rather than the active agent. (p. 479)

Among many others, the members of the Boston Change Process Study Group (BCPSG, 2002, 2005, 2007, 2008; D. N. Stern et al. 1998) are working this vein. Their transformational view of therapeutic action grows from the application of complexity theory to psychoanalysis, an area bursting with theoretical and clinical potential.[1]

And yet, while loosening the constrictions in analytic relatedness has become the main event in therapeutic action, and despite the fact that many enactments relax for reasons that seem to have little to do with the effects of our consciously intended interventions, we know no other means of focusing our effort on dealing with enactments than to try to feel our way to a speakable understanding of where in our experience and interactions with patients enactments exist and what they are about. Even in the era of transformation, the analyst must know the countertransference but does not; and what she is deprived of is precisely the practical grasp she is able to construct in the case of many other aspects of her experience with the patient. What we need is what it seems we cannot have. In this ironic sense, insight as an agent of change is alive and well.

And right there we come across the rub that challenged me to write this chapter: How is it that we *ever* come to know what we are doing in the unconscious parts of our relatedness with the patient? How can the eye possibly see itself? How can we conceptualize countertransference awareness?

Although virtually every contemporary psychoanalyst would agree that it is crucial for the analyst to find a way to reflect upon as much of her unconscious relatedness to the patient as possible, we have nothing even approaching a similar agreement about how that capacity for self-reflection comes to light. As a matter of fact (and oddly enough, if you ask me), the question of how it is that analysts put themselves in a position to know the countertransference is seldom even broached.

By using the word "how," though (as in "how we know the countertransference"), I do not mean to pose a question about technique. I do not mean to ask what the analyst should *do* in order to become aware of the countertransference. Though I shall offer clinical remarks and an illustration, the quandary I want to address is not technical at all, but theoretical:

---

[1] The term "complexity theory" often refers collectively to complexity theory, nonlinear dynamic systems theory, and deterministic chaos theory. Recent psychoanalytic work in this area (in addition to what I have cited in the text) includes Galatzer-Levy (1978, 1996, 2004); Ghent (2002); Grossmark (2007); Harris (2005); Kieffer (2007); Levenson (1994); Mandel and Selz (1996); Miller (1999); Moran (1991); Quinodoz (1997); Palombo (1999); Piers (2000, 2005); S. Pizer (1998); Shane and Coburn (2002); and Spruiell (1993).

how is it *conceivable* that we observe our own unconscious participation in ongoing relatedness? If our unconscious involvement with our patients is inevitable and continuous, how in the world do we ever develop a conviction we can trust about which interpretations or relational interventions might be most useful in any particular moment? Why isn't every clinical intention simply swallowed up in an enactment? This seemingly endless circularity is what Edgar Levenson was describing in the title of his first book, *The Fallacy of Understanding* (1972): The analyst's insights are not only what the analyst thinks they are; they are also, and more importantly, participations in what most needs to be understood.

When the issue is put this way, does it not seem that the analyst ought *never* to be able to know the countertransference? Where is the "perch" (Modell, 1991) from which the unconsciously involved analyst somehow gains a clear-eyed view of the very involvement that is standing in the way of the view in the first place? From a purely logical perspective, the task of observing one's own unconscious involvement with one's patients seems to be a contradiction, a "bootstrapping" operation (Mitchell, 1993) of impossible proportions. "I have met the enemy," said the immortal Pogo, now many years ago, "and they is us." For years after the appearance of Levenson's book, many of us did not know whether we were more excited by its ideas or despairing about what it meant about our control over our clinical work. But we got used to it, we began to live with it. Perhaps we got too used to it. It is time to return to the unanswerable question that Levenson's work, and much else that came after it in Relational and Interpersonal psychoanalysis, seems to pose: how can the eye see itself?

The Nature of the Problem

Each participant's conduct plays a very important role in "locking" the other participant into the unseen or rigidly perceived patterns of the transference and the countertransference. I have referred elsewhere to this phenomenon as "the grip of the field" (D. B. Stern, 1989, 1997), and Wolstein (1959) refers to it as "the transference/countertransference interlock." It is partly because of the way the analyst's experience is affected by the transference that the countertransference is unconscious; and it is also partly because of the way the analysand's experience is affected by the *counter*transference that the *transference* is unconscious. Because they are mutually embedded, transference and countertransference are reciprocal and inseparable parts of a whole.

This interlocking often enough leads to a situation in which alternative patterns of relatedness are invisible to both participants, and negotiation is therefore difficult, if not impossible. The relatedness has a certain mutual intransigence that no good intention is enough to relax. Each person's attitude toward the other is frozen. When this unyielding quality is conscious and obvious to both participants—that is, when it is reflected in both participants' explicit views of one another, a therapeutic impasse neither can deny—the demand for interpretation (or rather, reinterpretation) is clear enough. Under such circumstances, both analyst and analysand are painfully aware of the need for a different kind of understanding and relatedness between them. Every clinician knows, though, that even then—even in the presence of a mutual, ardent, conscious wish for it—a different and useful way of seeing the situation may still be maddeningly elusive.

The more common and even more difficult situation, however, is for analyst and analysand to be locked into an unconscious enactment that neither of them even knows is under way. The rigidity in the interaction, that is, is not apparent to either the patient or the analyst. Quite often, when we look backward in time from a wider understanding, the patterns we conclude were crucial for us to identify—because they were the sources of difficulty or puzzlement in the analytic work—were not visible at all during the sessions within which they were most influential. Because the analyst had no reason to attend to and formulate such patterns during those sessions, the relevant relatedness was no more conceptually distinct than the air the analyst breathed. But our ignorance of the intransigence does not mean that it was not there; it merely means that neither analyst nor patient saw the appropriateness of characterizing the relatedness as intransigent until later on.

And so we face what seems to be a contradiction: On the one hand, the field must change if it is to become possible for analyst and analysand to learn something new; but on the other hand, it is quite often precisely because the field needs to change that neither the analyst nor the analysand can identify what to address in order to provoke these changes. It seems that the needed alterations in the analytic relatedness are themselves the conditions for their own accomplishment. We therefore appear to be left with no way to account for the fact that psychoanalysis is not endlessly circular.

Wolstein and the "Private Regions" Solution

This conceptual problem does not arise in such a pointed way for those analysts who believe that a significant part of the self exists in a nonsocial realm, in a part of the psychic geography that exists completely apart from interaction with others, untouched and unmediated by social interchange. Obviously, these analysts, most of whom think in the terms of modern Freudian or Kleinian theory, have the same clinical difficulty we all do in understanding the enactments in which they are involved.[1] But at least in theoretical terms, from their vantage point the problem is less thorny than it seems from interpersonal and relational perspectives. Theorists who conceive the self to be partially disconnected from social interchange can at least hypothetically conceive how the analyst is able to construct an understanding of the enactments in which she is involved, even if finding a way to that understanding is painful, difficult, and slow. If there is some part of self-experience that exists in a nonsocial realm, that is, there exists a metaphorical high ground, or as Mitchell (1993) puts it, a "platform," onto which the analyst can climb to observe the fray between herself and the analysand; there is a "place" in the self where one can stand, a private place uninfluenced by any aspect of the other. The analyst can retreat to these private regions, and from there, even if she meets internal resistance to grasping her own unconscious involvement, there is at least the theoretical possibility of a view of the involvement from an uninvolved perspective.

A "private region" that would be useful in this way would need to have two characteristics. First, it would be asocial, existing outside the influence of the countertransference, because only a "platform" unaffected by the countertransference could allow the analyst to step away far enough from her unconscious involvement with the patient to be able look back at that involvement and make it the object of understanding. Second, such a private psychic "place" would have to be a portion of subjectivity experienced as the analyst's own, not as alien or other. In other words, if the analyst is going to be informed about her unconscious involvement by a part of her own mind, that part has to feel like it belongs to her. If it does not feel that way—if it is not "self"—she has no reason to "listen" to it, and perhaps (as in the case of the unconscious) she cannot.

---

[1] For an examination of these issues in the work of contemporary Freudians, including those of a liberal bent, see Hirsch (1996); for a view of the same problems in modern Kleinian thinking, see D. B. Stern (2001) and Mitchell (1997, Chapter 4), who also describes a similarly problematic position held by some contemporary interpersonal analysts (1997, Chapter 3).

If we put these ingredients together, we conclude that a clinically usable private region of self would be, as Winnicott (1960) describes "true self," an "incommunicado" aspect of experience that nevertheless feels like one's own. But even Winnicott (1949), despite his early interest in the use of countertransference, did not use the "private region" argument to grapple with the problem of how the eye could see itself. That line of thinking could only be developed by someone who appreciated both the embeddedness of the analyst in the field *and* the private region argument for dealing with it. The single writer to have done this, as far as I know, is Benjamin Wolstein (1954, 1959), one of the first to take the position that transference and countertransference are inevitably reciprocal, though he is seldom credited as he should be in this respect. Beginning in the 1970s, Wolstein (1971a, 1971b, 1972, 1974a, 1974b, 1975), at about the same time that Levenson was formulating the idea of the analyst's inevitable unconscious involvement with the patient, took a drastically different course, 180 degrees in the other direction. He began to add to his earlier views a conception of what he called "the psychic center of the self," a core of personhood that, whether it founders or is actualized in the course of living, cannot be altered in any essential respect. The psychic center of the self is not necessarily unreachable from the outside (i.e., by contact with others), but when it does enter social interaction, it can only be denied or recognized, never changed or influenced. Wolstein came to believe that the most meaningful aspect of therapeutic relatedness only occurred once the transference/countertransference interlock had been dissolved. Only then did it sometimes become possible to communicate directly from the center of one self to another. Wolstein felt that the most meaningful of these communications concerned matters that the other might not even be aware of. He looked forward, in particular, to the capacity of his patients to observe unconscious aspects of the analyst—himself. The success of these observations, however, was not necessarily to be judged, as Sullivan would have had it, by whether they were clearly understood by the other. What mattered more to Wolstein than consensual validation was whether what you observed and communicated about the other was true to your own experience.

For the present purpose, the significance of the psychic center of the self is that it allowed Wolstein to pose and solve the riddle of the eye seeing itself. Wolstein explicitly noted that, as far as he could see, unless we conceive a kind of experience that remains uninfluenced by the other under any and all circumstances, there was no way for the analyst *or* the analysand to understand their unconscious involvement with each other.

There must be a place in psychic life from which, as we become familiar with it, we can observe our unconscious involvements. Resolving transference/countertransference interlocks, therefore, is not so much the point of psychoanalytic treatment as it is a prerequisite to love, which is for Wolstein the capacity and willingness to know and accept one's deepest view or sense of the other. In an interview with Hirsch (2000), Wolstein said that "a uniqueness of self is the most direct way to get over and out of that interlocking; it makes it possible, it opens up, the love, as distinct from the intimacy, to let it go" (p. 198). And then a moment later, sounding the same note Bollas (1989) strikes when he describes the notion of personal idiom, Wolstein adds, "We all have a unique sense of self that is inborn: Clinical psychoanalytic inquiry doesn't create it; we find it there" (p. 199).

If one can accept such an argument—that there is some inviolate, non-social core in the self—one can work out the problem of countertransference awareness fairly simply: One simply observes from within the nonsocial core.

But however appealing Wolstein's position is, and however wistfully I regard it, I cannot accept it. It certainly makes sense to posit temperamental differences in the self, as well as important inborn constraints on, and potentials for, what the self can become.[1] But it is only within a later social world that these inborn constraints and potentials take on their meanings and exert their effects. The self is a social construction. That is not to say that social construction has no limits; it does have limits, significant ones (D. B. Stern, 2000). Nor does this position require us to deny the uniqueness of each self.

Even if I cannot agree with Wolstein about the nonsocial core of self, though, I admire his early recognition that we must think out the problem of countertransference awareness. That recognition is still very much the exception. Of those clinicians who continue to work and think as if they have access to an objectivity that allows them an impersonal view (whatever that is) of their own unconscious involvement with their patients, most have not really reflected on how they conceive that objectivity.[2]

---

[1] Recent influential conceptions of inborn dispositions of this kind include, besides Winnicott's (1960) true self and Bollas's (1989) personal idiom, Kohut's (1984) idea of the self's destiny or nuclear program and the description by Fonagy et al. (2002) of implicit procedural primary emotion states.

[2] See Friedman (2000), though, for a thoughtful recent defense of objectivity in psychoanalysis, though in my view Friedman, too, underemphasizes unconscious social embeddedness and overemphasizes the degree to which people are capable of observing their own motives.

"Where" in subjectivity is it? Wolstein sidesteps that problem altogether, as we all should, by dealing with it without recourse to a mythical objectivity. All one can do, he believes, is know and remain true to one's deepest feelings and perceptions, the psychic center of the self.

The rest of us, though, to the extent that we can accept neither Wolstein's solution nor a belief in objectivity and impersonal understanding, must look elsewhere. We know we manage to succeed in what we cannot explain how we do. In the search for an understanding that Interpersonal and Relational analysts, too, can accept (the irony here, of course, is that Wolstein was one of the most prominent of interpersonalists), I turn to a clinical illustration. I offer it with certain misgivings, though, because if I am not careful to say exactly what I think I am up to, this kind of presentation (the discussion of a particular enactment) might convey the impression that the analyst's unconscious participation in the process is a sometime thing. For that reason I state my perspective at the outset. Along with the many other analysts who share my orientation, I take the position that the analyst's and the analysand's unconscious involvement with each other is inevitable and continuous.

Now, as soon as I say that, of course, I have stepped yet again right into the middle of the dilemma. How can we maintain that unconscious involvement is continuous without destroying the significance of the analyst's (and the patient's!) thoughtfulness and capacity for observation? That is the paradox with which I begin. Unconscious involvement is ceaseless, and yet we do not doubt that the analyst makes valid and useful observations and interventions.

But enactment is only one variety of the analyst's unconscious involvement. There is a great deal of mutual interactive regulation going on between any two people, and most of it occurs outside awareness (see, for example, Beebe & Lachmann, 1998, 2002). In the way I want to define the word, though, mutual regulation is not enactment. Mutual regulation, especially of affect states, is frequently carried out without conscious design, it is true. Mutual regulation is descriptively unconscious. But it is not dynamically unconscious. Neither is the kind of responsive participation that is a key part of most treatments, the kind of reparative and facilitative unconscious involvement—accepting, loving, humorous, or playful—that self psychologists might refer to as self-object functioning. One has to "mean it" in order for this kind of relatedness to be useful to the other, and so it has to be more deeply felt than mere conscious decision could make it. It has to be part of the analyst's nonconscious involvement. The same is true of holding and containment and the host of other noninterpretive participations that have become so important in our understanding of our work. But none of these participations is a dynamic necessity. Although the analyst may not consciously think about doing such things (though of course sometimes he may), neither does he feel compelled to carry them out. The analyst's agency is not compromised; he could stop participating this way if he wished, but generally he judges it best to continue. In the most important sense, then, all these kinds of relatedness are freely chosen. Enactment, by contrast, is rigid and unyielding for both analyst and patient; it either feels irresistible to both or is recognized, after the fact, to have been a (unfelt) necessity.

It is usually not painful for the analyst to feel and think about his participation in mutual regulation, affirmation, empathic understanding, reparative and facilitative involvements, holding, containment, and so on. It may not always be possible to say what unconscious sources are being tapped at these times, and there may be an emotional cost to be paid for participating in one of these ways in the face of a strong countertransferential pull to behave otherwise; but there is little or no internal resistance to formulating whatever there is to know about such clinical attitudes and interventions. One is not deprived of the freedom to think. And so the problem of the eye seeing itself does not come up in these circumstances. In enactments, on the other hand, the analyst is more or less blind to what he is doing and feeling, and he is likely to suffer. He cannot find his way for some time to a kind of being with the patient that would relieve both of them. And therefore, while the analyst's continuous unconscious relatedness is the rule, the problem I am setting out to explore arises only in that portion of the analyst's unconscious functioning that, because it is dynamically unconscious, deserves to be called enactment.

An Enactment: Guilt and Narcissism

In deceptively smooth treatments, we find in retrospect that, all along, each participant was influencing the other to maintain the *status quo*. In one case of mine, the patient, a talented but immature man in his 30s who had managed to deep-six virtually every one of the many academic and professional opportunities he had had, worked very hard in treatment and expressed deep appreciation to me, though he also expressed his fear that I would somehow indoctrinate him and make it impossible for him to continue the somewhat self-destructive "fringe" life he had been leading.

During one of his high school years, he had been in a once-per-week psychotherapy for his academic problems, but that treatment had seemed to him to be nothing more than tutoring, and useless tutoring at that. According to him, his therapist, like his teachers (and himself, for that matter) had been completely baffled about why this very bright and apparently well-meaning young man, who seemed quite sincere about wanting to do well, just could not seem to get his work done.

After a year and a half or so, during which time the treatment seemed immensely productive to both of us, I began to feel a vague sense of unease. Something bothered me. Over a period of a couple of weeks, I began to formulate what was the matter. The treatment had begun to feel to me very subtly less alive, less continuously intriguing and animated. Certain moments that I knew would have been interesting in the recent past were now perhaps a little flat or stale, maybe just a bit forced. Simultaneously, the analysand, while insisting he was trying as hard as he could, was failing quite spectacularly in certain academic activities that he had felt, with my tacit agreement, would represent progress for him.

We found out somewhat later that the analysand was doing with me precisely what he had done with his parents, though as is so often the case, he was doing it with such utter naturalness that it shaped our interaction unobtrusively. On the face of it, he was the dutiful, cheerful, and loving son; but he was simultaneously failing in an unconsciously purposeful way that he was able to believe consciously had nothing at all to do with his own intentions. We eventually learned that he had always been angry and depressed at the expectations he faced from his parents, which had never seemed to him to have much to do with what he wanted from life or how he felt; but because of his parents' narcissistic vulnerability and his loving feelings toward them, he had felt too guilty to protest directly. Instead, he acted out in a way that was invisible to him but that hit them where it hurt: He failed dramatically to accomplish anything that would have pleased them, a mission that had ruined every one of the opportunities they had found a way to offer him. With me, the patient had begun the relationship in a genuinely collaborative mode in which we had accomplished a great deal. I have not felt the need to revise that initial impression. But we also discovered that, as I had begun to enjoy his collaboration, he had begun to resent my pleasure, and had revised our history together, beginning to suspect (without quite realizing that he felt that way) that we had instituted our collaboration more for my reasons than for his own. He then began to treat me as if I needed this narcissistic pleasure, as he had felt (again, in an unformulated kind of way) his parents had. For a while, I had not noticed this change, or had registered it only as a subtle affective shift, most of the time continuing to enjoy what was fast becoming a pseudo-alliance and ingratiation, just as his parents, by what I could gather from his reports, had always taken pleasure in what seemed to be his adoration and good cheer. It came to my attention in these weeks that I had also been enjoying his appreciative responses to my interpretations, and I now realized that I had been making more of them recently than I usually do. The analysand, in other words, was playing to what he unconsciously fell into assuming was my narcissism, and I was enjoying it enough that he had reason to believe that he needed to keep me well supplied if we were to continue to get along together.

For my present purpose, the point of the illustration is that I responded to the analysand's way of relating to me by developing a countertransference that, in turn, reinforced his transference; and as a result, as is usually the case, he and I locked each other so securely into an unconscious set of interpersonal patterns that it soon became irrelevant, actually, which of us was responsible for having provoked the interaction in the first place. The very idea of determining such a thing, as a matter of fact, would have been (and often or even usually is) nothing more than a blaming operation.

Once the nature of our relatedness came to light, there was the possibility for change; and so my example illustrates not only the interlocking of transference and countertransference, but also the breaking of this mutual grip. How and why that happens is my primary question. Why did I not simply continue to play out this scenario of narcissism? Where did the vague discomfort that helped me to see things differently come from? Eventually, once I had made some sense of my feelings, I drew the patient's attention to what I had noticed about the change in the atmosphere between us and invited him to investigate it with me. The results I have already described. I turn now to what made this turn of events possible.

Snags and Chafing

If we accept that the analyst and the patient comprise an immensely complex, changing, self-organizing system, it seems virtually inevitable that some impasses will relax for reasons we understand only in retrospect, if we ever understand them at all. But that is only one of the possibilities. In another scenario, the analyst is alerted to examine her experience for clues to her unconscious involvement with the patient—for hints at the nature of the system, if you will. More often than not, the alerting signal is something small and subtle. It often has a mildly bothersome quality. One feels an emotional "chafing" or tension, an unbidden "hint" or "sense" that something more than one has suspected is going on in the clinical interaction. Something feels inconsistent, countering an affective expectation we did not even know we had until that moment; it feels subtly "wrong" or contradictory or just uncomfortable. For the curious analyst, therapeutic work is often the psychic equivalent of walking along a forest path in a wool sweater that snags now and then on a branch or twig. When it does, we stop, investigate, and disentangle ourselves. We note some kind of change in our feelings, ask ourselves about it, and find that we are responding to something about the analysand that we have not yet explicitly noticed. A new perception comes about. This quiet and self-reflective process is just as important during impasses, deadlocks, or stalemates, of course, in which the noise and drama of the interaction is endlessly uninformative, as it is during the more silent kind of enactments that only become visible in retrospect.

All well and good, says my personal version of what Sullivan (1950) described as "an illusion, an illusory person, in the sense of a critic, more or less like what we think the hearer is" (p. 214). This illusory critic is an essential but less than entirely inspiring amanuensis who insists that I think through problems in a publicly verifiable fashion. And in this case, he has an objection: Even if we can all agree that we often find our way to an awareness of enactments via affective signposts, such as the subtle diminution of aliveness in the treatment I described, why does this contribute to solving the conceptual problem I have set out to address? Do we not simply face the same dilemma in another guise—the problem of the eye seeing itself? How can we account for our capacity to notice the signs of our unconscious involvement? Shouldn't our capacity to notice what points to the enactment be swallowed up in the enactment itself? Why should enactments be black holes in some respects but not others? If they suck into themselves our capacity to observe them and to know what to do about them, why in the world would the same fate not befall subtle affective hints at their existence?

Well, we know better than to accept the black hole argument; but we still have to admit that the objection makes sense in a purely logical way. Although we know perfectly well that we experience emotional snags and chafing and that they eventually help us grope toward some kind of grasp of the most significant of the enactments that emerge in a treatment, so far we do not have a way to say why any of this is possible.

Part II: A Theory of Enactment

Dissociation and the Multiple Self

The very existence of my internal critic offers a hint, though. Why does it take him (her) to notice that what I have written does not really answer the question I have asked? Why does *he* notice that it seems to be contradictory to say that we can experience hints, but that we cannot just leap directly to new perceptions of the enactment? *He* notices because he has a different agenda than the part of myself that tries to solve the problem. *I* am trying to contribute a creative solution; *he*, on the other hand, is trying to make sure that what I say meets the standards of public discourse. "His" is a different task than "mine"; I (now in the larger sense of the whole person) am divided. These two purposes of mine are identified with what we call "parts" of ourselves or, in the current parlance of Relational thinking, "self-states" or even "selves."[1]

I am able to see the inadequacies in my own argument because the "me" who tries to think creatively acknowledges the "me" who audits my thoughts—or more properly, because the "me" who tries to think creatively *experiences conflict* with the "me" who audits my thoughts.

Is it conceivable that I might *not* experience the conflict with the other "me"? Of course. In that case, we could say that these two aspects of me, these two self-states or personifications, were *dissociated* from each other. If I identified with an imagination dissociated from its critic, I would be grandiose: My ideas would encompass too much significance, apply too broadly; and by implication I would assume an unjustified self-importance. If I felt more closely identified with an internal critic who was, in his turn, dissociated from (did not experience conflict with) my imaginative side, my writing would be flat, uninteresting, overly cautious. In fact, I might very well never write at all because, in my illusory critic's estimation, there would always be something that someone could find wrong with what I would say (and of course he would be right). Just this sort of dissociation might take place, in fact, in someone who grew up with a parent for whom mistakes were catastrophic. We all know the adult children of such parents: They are so concerned—consciously, yes, but especially

---

[1] See Bromberg (1998, 2006); Davies (1996, 1997, 1998, 1999, 2004); Davies and Frawley (1991, 1994); Flax (1996); Harris (1996); Mitchell (1991); S. Pizer (1998); Slavin (1996); Slavin and Kriegman (1992, 1998); D. B. Stern (1997).

unconsciously—with avoiding the disapproval of critics, inner and outer, that they are virtually incapable of spontaneous experiencing.

What is the ideal situation? The ideal, and one that many of us actually do approximate, in at least some significant portion of our experiencing, is the ongoing and continuous awareness of conflict between self-states, what Bromberg (1998) calls "standing in the spaces." It is only when we can tolerate conflicts between multiple states that we can negotiate the disagreement between them (S. Pizer, 1998). I hasten to add, though, that resolution is not necessarily the *raison d'etre* of negotiation between states of mind. Negotiation is an ongoing, never-finished weighing of the alternatives. If we are willing and able to experience conflicting purposes at the same time, negotiation is the natural stance for us to take toward them. On the other hand, we cannot negotiate until conflict comes about.

If I wish to write something that will be of use to others, for instance, I need to be able to experience simultaneously my illusory critic and my creative side. I need to be able to think creatively at the same time that I think critically *about* thinking creatively. And when differences between these interests crop up, as they do more often than I would like, I need to be able to evaluate each purpose in the light of the other. I must either be able to revise my manuscript or to answer my illusory critic in a way that satisfies him. I need, in other words, to be able to allow myself to create the experience of conflict. If I hole up within one or the other of these self-states and cannot formulate the perspective that would be offered by the other, there is no conflict; I am dissociating.

Dissociated experience, we have learned, does not simply disappear quietly into some hidden corner of the mind. It is enacted.[1] I will "play out" the state of self I cannot tolerate experiencing directly, and I will thereby unconsciously influence those with whom I relate to adopt a variation on the same dangerous response that led me to dissociate the self-state in the first place. In one variety of enactment I embody the traumatized self, in a continuous and futile attempt to make everything happen differently, thereby healing myself; but instead I provoke the other person to experience and behave in ways that, tragically, simply keep retraumatizing me. In the reciprocal version of this enactment, in a similarly unconscious attempt to wrest control of the situation, I traumatize the other just as I have myself been traumatized, but I have little or no appreciation of my

---

[1] See, for example, Aron (2003a, 2003b); Bass (2003); Benjamin (1998); Black (2003); Bromberg (1998, 2006); Davies (1996, 1997, 1998, 1999, 2003); Davies and Frawley (1991, 1994); B. Pizer (2003); S. Pizer (1998).

role in doing so. (And if the trauma has been bad enough, I may not even care [Stein, 2004, 2006].)

We expect the roots of dissociated self-states to be inaccessible; but in an enactment, the reciprocal state called out in the other is as inaccessible to him as my dissociated self-state is to me. My interactive partner is unaware that his role is anything other than his own choice; he is as unaware as I am that he is being nudged into it by a reciprocal pattern to which we both contribute. Each person therefore experiences the other person as instigator, at fault, imposing his will.

For example, if I dissociate my internal auditor, and my work is grandiose, I will be unaware of my overreaching and therefore be unable to appreciate my role in provoking criticism from others. When criticism comes it will surprise me, and I will be either devastated (and will perhaps behave in ways unconsciously designed to inspire guilt) or outraged (how *dare* they!). On the other hand, if I dissociate my risk-taking, creative side, I will be out of touch with the way that the extremity of my self-criticism suggests to others the magnitude of the contribution I secretly (even from myself) expect to make.

We do not insist that Sullivan replace his "illusory critic" metaphor with the description of impersonally defined cognitive processes because it is intuitively and immediately obvious to us what he means by the metaphor. In our imaginations we do not limit the characterization of our various conflicting purposes to the purposes themselves; we characterize our purposes as "parts" of us, as "states" of our selves. We do not simply describe our internal worlds; we people them. We do not understand ourselves as concatenations of affects, cognitions, and conations, however reasonable it may be under some circumstances to describe our minds in these terms. Instead, we sense our fragments as characters. Sullivan's (1954) theory describes the various aspects of personality as "personifications," reflecting his view (he mirrors object relations writers in this one respect) that the elements of our inner landscapes have human characteristics.

And for good reason. Each of these personifications grew up around the relatedness to a particular significant person or around the relatedness to parts of various significant people. When experience is traumatic, the child cannot bear to experience simultaneously states that were created in the presence of safety and others created during the appearance of a dangerous, traumatic person, or part-person ("angry-father," for example). Dissociation is born. The child, and then the adult, enacts the traumatic states and lives his "known" life inside the bearable ones.

Dissociation, Enactment, and the Achievement of Conflict

Everything discussed in the remainder of this chapter is an exploration and expansion of the following proposals about dissociation and enactment. Once I have explored these ideas fully enough, I will return to the question of how the eye sees itself. I will not be better equipped than I am now to answer that unanswerable question, but I will be in a position to make the case that it should be recast, and in that new form it will become a sensible question.

1. Enacted experience, and thus dissociated states as well, cannot be symbolized and therefore do not exist in any other explicit form than enactment itself. Enacted experience is unformulated experience.
2. Dissociated states, because they are unsymbolized, do not and cannot bear a conflictual relationship to the states of mind safe enough for us to identify as "me" and inhabit in a consciously appreciable way.
3. Enactment is the interpersonalization of dissociation: the conflict that cannot be experienced within one mind is experienced *between* or *across* two minds. The state dissociated by the patient is explicitly experienced by the analyst, and the state explicitly experienced by the patient is dissociated in the analyst's mind. Each participant therefore has only a partial appreciation of what is transpiring.
4. Enactment, then, is not the expression of internal conflict. Enactment is the *absence* of internal conflict, though the external conflict, the conflict between the two people in the enactment, may be intense.
5. Enactment ends in the achievement of internal conflict, which occurs when the two dissociated states, one belonging to each participant in the enactment, can be formulated inside the consciousness of one or the other of the two psychoanalytic participants.

I am indebted to Philip Bromberg's (1998, 2006) thinking in the development of these ideas. I might go so far as to say they bear his imprint, because the relationships drawn in this chapter between dissociation, conflict, and enactment also appear in his work. Specifically, Bromberg (1998; see especially 2000, pp. 564–567) believes that enactment is the result of dissociation, that conflict does not exist in enactment, and that enactment dissolves when conflict becomes possible. I have reached these same conclusions, starting from the idea of unformulated experience (D. B. Stern, 1983, 1997), a dissociation-based perspective on the unconscious, and a theory of enactment anchored in that conception (D. B. Stern, 1997; see also this book, Chapters 3 and 5–7).

I have also drawn on the orientation that began in the work of Jody Davies and Mary-Gail Frawley-O'Dea (1991, 1994) and has been developed further in Davies' more recent writings (1996, 1997, 1998, 1999, 2003, 2004): The patient's dissociated experience is routinely enacted, and the analyst's sole route of access to that experience is the analysis of the transference–countertransference. Davies' clinical presentations, especially recently (2004), are eloquent and nuanced illustrations of the problems all psychoanalysts face in finding a way into enactments and the mutual dissociations that underlie them.

In the wide-ranging position articulated by Fonagy et al. (2002), dissociation, splitting, and enactment play prominent roles, just as they do in Bromberg's and Davies' thinking and my own (see especially Fonagy et al., Chapter 10, pp. 373–433). There are interesting, sometimes striking, similarities between the work of this group and the model I present here, and they deserve to be detailed. In Chapter 8 of this book, both the similarities and the differences between these two views are discussed.

Two Background Considerations

Before setting out to explicate the points I have just made, I highlight two background considerations, each of which supplies a portion of the theoretical context or background within which I intend the points I have just listed to be understood.

Sources of Conflict

When I refer to conflict that remains to be created, I am referring to only a small part of the conflict that goes on within subjectivity. I am *not* claiming, for instance, that all conflict emerges from the analysis of the relations of me and not-me, as if conflict had no other source. It goes without saying that a great deal of conflictual experience is well known to the patient prior to any sort of treatment. And a great deal of the conflict the patient eventually comes to appreciate as the treatment unfolds—as a matter of fact, the largest portion of the conflict created during the treatment occurs between what Sullivan refers to as *good-me* and *bad-me*. These phrases are umbrella terms for the self-states that originated in the approval and disapproval of the significant people in our early lives. Together, they make up what each of us feels as me, or self. Conflict between good-me and bad-me, even if it is not initially recognized by the patient, is not terribly difficult to achieve. Because both aspects of the conflict already exist within the self, it is often sufficient simply to point out an inconsistency or a contradiction and ask the patient what it might be about; or perhaps the analyst makes an interpretation. Although conflicts between good-me and bad-me may be unformulated, in other words, the states themselves either are already formulated or are within the range of the patient's capacity to articulate. Even when the separation of good-me and bad-me is represented in an enactment between the patient and the analyst, as happens often enough (the roles of *good* and *bad* may be split between analyst and patient), the quandary is generally negotiable without much difficulty.

The enactments that derive from the separation of me and not-me, though, are much more difficult to negotiate, and often enough intractable.[1] Simple interpretation is just not sufficient, at least if by that we mean the more or less relaxed, professional application of the analyst's mind—his wits and intuition. To work with an enactment, the analyst must actually give himself over to the nonrational, affect-laden parts of the experience, and sometimes for fairly lengthy periods. Not-me dominates the treatment only episodically, though such episodes are not necessarily rare, depending on the particular treatment; but addressing them successfully is perhaps the most important part of the therapeutic action of any treatment, because it is through the incorporation of not-me that the self (i.e., me) expands. And so, while including unformulated conflicts between good-me and bad-me in what I have to say, the enactments I address here are primarily the enactments most significant for psychoanalytic work, those rooted in the relations of me and not-me.

The Analyst's Dissociations

The second background consideration concerns the reciprocal dissociations the patient calls out in the analyst (and that the analyst calls out in the patient, because that, too, can happen). Even though in one significant sense the analyst's reciprocal dissociations are reactive to the patient, they are not implanted in the analyst's mind as if they were alien objects, the way they are frequently conceived in the terms of projective identification.[2] Instead, reciprocal dissociations are inevitably dynamically meaningful

---

[1] I have presented elsewhere comparative clinical examples of the relatively negotiable enactments characteristic of unformulated conflict between good-me and bad-me, and the more severe and troubling enactments—impasses or "deadlocks"—that come about when the patient shifts into not-me. Unformulated conflict between good-me and bad-me is dissociated in what I have elsewhere called the "weak" sense, while unformulated conflict between me and not-me is dissociated in the "strong" sense (D. B. Stern, 1997; see also this book, Chapter 3).

[2] See Chapter 1 for a discussion of these issues.

events in the life of the dissociator. When the analyst participates in an enactment, it is because she dissociates; and when she dissociates, it is because she finds herself in circumstances that make her vulnerable in a way she can manage, for the time being, *only* by dissociating. Enactment takes place between two separate subjectivities, each acting on some kind of combination of her own interests and what she understands to be the interests of the other. The patient cannot provoke such a dissociation if the analyst is not vulnerable to it. The analyst's dissociation is therefore as much a product of her own life as is the patient's; and so the creation of conflict and the negotiation of an enactment requires growth from the analyst in just the way it requires growth from the patient. The analyst's role is not defined by invulnerability, in other words, but by a special (though inconsistent) willingness, and a practiced (though imperfect) capacity, to accept and deal forthrightly with her vulnerability.

These were themes Heinrich Racker (1968) pursued throughout his work. Racker (1957), of course, is the author of the famous aphorism that "'the myth of the analytic situation' is that analysis is an interaction between a sick person and a healthy one" (p. 132). He believed that the analyst routinely develops a "countertransference neurosis," contracted via identifications with the patient's internal objects, and that the fate of the treatment hangs on the analyst's capacity to resolve it. If the analyst characteristically denies his own aggressiveness, for instance, he is unlikely to feel empathic when the patient is feeling aggressive. Instead, the analyst is likely to identify with those of the patient's internal objects that scold or reject the patient for having angry feelings or behaving aggressively. The patient, that is, influences the analyst (at least the analyst who is vulnerable, which is all of us some of the time) to re-create the original interpersonal circumstances that lie behind the creation of the patient's internal object world. It is easy to see that these "complementary" identifications are one well-traveled route to what, in contemporary terms, we call difficult or sticky enactments, or impasses.

Racker did not see impasse as an expectable part of treatment, of course. It was a different time in psychoanalysis. For him, it was the analyst's responsibility to observe and analyze his complementary identifications, thereby restoring his capacity to identify with the patient's ego (concordant identification). Though Racker does not put it this way, we could say that the cure of the countertransference neurosis, and the transference neurosis as well, depends on the analyst's capacity to stretch his identification with the patient's objects and to encompass the patient's self as well. The analyst has to be able to tolerate both perspectives at once. Once we have said that, we have not only restated the thesis of the multiple self but also the idea that the self is healed by the creation of conflict, by bringing together the part that resides in the patient with the part that has been called into existence inside the analyst.

And so, while I owe my greatest debt to writers of the current generation for the ideas I am presenting in this chapter, I am also indebted to the earlier writers from whose work the thinking of the current generation has arisen. Sullivan has been a particularly influential intellectual ancestor. But that is probably more because I have my beginnings in interpersonal psychoanalysis than because Sullivan is the only relevant writer of that era. The object relations writers, and Klein, and Racker, and Bion, and all the writers since Bion who have used Bion's way of thinking about projective identification, are important sources as well. All these writers, in one sense, write about psychoanalysis as a treatment for painfully fragmented subjectivity, as the creation of a new tolerance within the patient for the different parts of his own self. For Racker and Bion, just as for Bromberg and Davies, the estranged parts of the patient's self are called out in the experience of the analyst, and it is from there that they are brought home.

Transcending "Single-Mindedness": Dissociation and Enactment as the Absence of Conflict

The idea that enactments can be conceived not to be the outcome of conflict may surprise analysts unfamiliar with interpersonal theory. Since the work of Sullivan, it has been possible to conceive the foundations of psychopathology (or, in the terminology Sullivan preferred, problems in living) as the absence of internal conflict. Unlike Kohut, who, for very different reasons than Sullivan, explicitly demoted the significance of conflict in his theory, Sullivan did not directly address the question of conflict. However, he did introduce dissociation as the primary defense, and he conceived "real" events as the reason that defenses arise in the first place. "In fact," writes Bromberg (1996), "Sullivan's (1954) theory of interpersonal analysis, reduced to its essentials is, in my view, a theory of the dissociative organization of personality in response to trauma" (p. 215).

Actually, Bromberg's characterization applies more readily to the early Sullivan than to Sullivan's later work. Early in his work, Sullivan (1940) characterizes dissociation very broadly, in a way that suggests for it a formative role in the development of the self. He wrote, for example:

For the expression of all things in the personality other than those which were approved and disapproved by the parent and other significant persons, the self refuses awareness, so to speak. It does not accord awareness, it does not notice; and these impulses, desires, and needs come to exist dissasociated from the self, or "dissociated." (pp. 21–22)

In his later writings, though, Sullivan tended to restrict the range of dissociation, using the concept primarily to define the drastic defensive measures typical of what he called "schizophrenia" (in his hands a much broader diagnostic category than we use today, apparently including many people we would not consider psychotic). Referring back to the book containing the passage I just quoted, Sullivan (1954) wrote, "Dissociation is unfortunately made rather too important in *Conceptions*, in which I did not take enough time to emphasize all the other things that go on besides dissociation" (p. 317, footnote).

When contemporary writers on dissociation link their work to Sullivan, as both Bromberg (1998, 2006) and I (D. B. Stern, 1997) have done quite explicitly, it might be argued that we are really referring primarily to Sullivan's early work. That, at least, would seem to be the position Sullivan himself would take. However, Sullivan did continue in his later work to argue that personality (that is, the self-system) is formed by our efforts not to reexperience what has hurt us before; and for that reason it is quite supportable to argue that the work Sullivan did near the end of his life, along with the early work, remains a model of psychopathology organized by trauma and dissociation, not by conflict. In neither part of his career did Sullivan consider that which is unbearable and dissociated, or not-me, to exist in conflict with the bearable experience that makes up the self (good-me and bad-me). Not-me is global, primitive, unsymbolized experience banished from the self; and in that exiled state, while it threatens to break through when circumstances are right (or rather, wrong), it does not compete with self-experience for conscious representation. (If circumstances become so dire that not-me becomes present and knowable in explicit awareness, the consequences are not good. For the most troubled people they are what Sullivan often called "grave.") There is no drive in this theory, and so there is no urgency for discharge, no press for registration in consciousness, no derivatives, no return of the repressed. Dissociated experience is simply absent, gone, unformulated, unknowable in the ordinary course of things (D. B. Stern, 1989, 1991, 1997, 2002a). Because no one in the 1930s and 1940s had thought yet about the link between dissociation and enactment (the concept of enactment would not be formulated for several decades), the effect of dissociated experience on the psyche, as Sullivan understood it, was silent and invisible under most circumstances. Dissociation determined where experience dared not go without unbearable anxiety. But this psychic prohibition was not codified or symbolized anywhere in the mind. Rather, the personality was structured around it, the way a painting can be structured around unpainted spaces on the canvas. By a kind of reverse tropism requiring no particular expenditure of effort, the self-system simply turned away from the kinds of experience that had been dissociated. As an illustrative metaphor, think of a road through the countryside: If you don't stray from it, you have no reason to suspect the existence of anything you can't see as you walk along it—and no reason to suspect yourself of excluding anything either. That is the effect of the self-system: to keep experience on safe, well-worn, predictable paths. And so, for all intents and purposes, dissociated experience in Sullivan's theory is simply absent.

In Freudian terms, defense grows from unconscious conflict. The purpose of the Freudian defenses is to keep conflict from becoming conscious by allowing only one pole of the conflict to be represented in awareness. In the view that I have developed from Sullivan's work, it remains the case that defense protects us from the experience of conscious conflict, but it does so in a very different way: Conflict is avoided by simply refusing to construct one part of the experience, the part we refer to as dissociated. As Sullivan's theory suggests, that experience just isn't there. It is not that it is "moved" to a hidden location in the mind or changed in such a way that it is unrecognizable—it is simply not allowed to come into being. It remains unsymbolized, unformulated (D. B. Stern, 1983, 1997, 2002a).[1] In that unformulated state, while it does not necessarily threaten to break into consciousness, it does remain a source of trouble because, as we have become all too aware, the price for defensive control over consciousness is that the dissociated experience is enacted. (It is perhaps worth repeating that this point was not available to Sullivan.)

There is another reason than the theoretical, though, to think that dissociated self-states do not exist in conflict with tolerable ones, a reason even better than theory: experience itself. Consider the fact that there is no conscious experience of conflict in enactment. One might even say that the absence of the experience of conflict is enactment's defining aspect.

---

[1] For a fuller theoretical description of the process described in this paragraph, see D. B. Stern (1997) Chapters. 6–7; for clinical accounts of enactments in these terms, see D. B. Stern, (1997) Chapters 10 and 12 and this book, Chapter 3.

Enactment is *the limitation of both participants' experience to one pole of what would otherwise be a conflict*; in enactment, it is precisely the point that we and the patient are each trapped within a single perception of the other. We cannot perceive anew; each of us is "single-minded." We cannot experience a way of understanding the interaction that would conflict with the perception that traps us. Taken together, the patient's and the analyst's explicit experiences comprise a conflict, but this is a fragmented conflict, located across the divide of two minds, not contained within one. *Internal* conflict can be absent, and that absence of conflict, when it is clinically salient, appears as enactment.

The absence of conflict in each participant's experience of enactment continues until one of the two participants, usually (but by no means always) the analyst, is able to simultaneously occupy in consciousness both the tolerable state and the dissociated one. Only when that happens can the conflicting purposes that organize the two states be negotiated. Only then, actually, can the conflict even be constructed within one mind; and therefore, only then can it be directly experienced. The experience of internal conflict by either the analyst or the patient, in other words, is the necessary and sufficient condition for the negotiation of an enactment.

Intrapsychic and Constructivist Conceptions of Dissociation

Consider for heuristic purposes how my participation in my vignette might look from a more traditional intrapsychic perspective on dissociation and the multiple self, what I call the "splitting" hypothesis. In splitting, tolerable and dissociated self-states both exist "in" the mind. The relationship between these two states is conflictual in the traditional psychoanalytic sense, with one state available to consciousness and the other existing out of awareness. Consider the possibility that during the time I was enjoying my patient's superficial show of "progress," I could not bear the conflict between, on the one hand, my desire for narcissistic pleasure and, on the other, my understanding (dissociated but fully formed and present somewhere in my unconscious mind) that I would have to sacrifice it in order to do good work. In this view, I could not tolerate experiencing consciously the conflict that the interaction potentiated in me, and so my solution was to dissociate the intolerable state, which then continued to "be there" in my mind, now conflicting *uncon*sciously with the state I consciously inhabited.

In these intrapsychic terms, the analyst's part of the enactment takes place because of internal dynamics set in motion by interaction with the patient. The patient's corresponding part comes about in the same way. In splitting, enactment is the disavowal, by each participant, of the internal conflicts between their respective dissociated self-states. Both parts of the conflict continue to exist in each person's mind, but they are kept apart; they may sometimes be experienced alternatively, but never simultaneously.

The place held in Freud's theory of repression by the banishment of experience to the unconscious is taken, in the splitting scheme, by the process of creating internal divisions. The shards of subjectivity that result from this splitting then appear in awareness as successive, mutually exclusive states. This is a theory of defense organized along the "horizontal" axis of the psyche (successively experienced states), not in the "vertical" dimension of repression ("down" into the repository of the unconscious). In this one way, the intrapsychic splitting model resembles the model of dissociation and enactment I am proposing here. In all other significant respects, though, the splitting model remains similar to the conception of defense as repression: Dynamics are based on unconscious internal conflict between different parts of the mind, and this conflict is already in place when external events make it immediately relevant. In the splitting model, the interpersonal field is assigned only the role of shifting the balance of forces, of sparking or "setting off" internal events that are already poised to take place, having been given their essential shape in the distant past. Unconsciously motivated events *between* people (enactments), in other words, are understood to be grounded in conflicts *within* them. Unconscious internal conflict therefore *precedes* enactment.

In the conception of enactment I prefer, on the other hand, the experience of conflict *within* people is likely to be the outcome of clarifying the nature of the enactments *between* them. As shorthand, and to emphasize the point that the symbolization of an enactment always remains to be accomplished, I refer to this latter, Interpersonal/Relational model as the *constructivist* conception of dissociation and enactment.

A Comparison of Splitting and the Constructivist Account

Perhaps the most radical tenet of interpersonal theory is that the interpersonal field is a primary influence on the contents of consciousness (Bromberg, 1998, 2006; Levenson, 1972, 1983, 1991; D. B. Stern, 1997;

Sullivan, 1940, 1954). The field contributes both facilitations and limitations of experience, influencing which states of mind or self can be created and occupied by patient and analyst in any particular moment. That is why dissociation, the most significant of these limitations on experiencing, is not conceived in interpersonal theory as disavowed intrapsychic conflict. It is, rather, the subjectivity we never create, the experience we never have.

In splitting, as in repression, we are said to know in one part of ourselves what we don't know in another. We unconsciously refuse to experience what we actually do know in some hidden part of ourselves. In an enactment conceived in constructivist terms, on the other hand, meanings are split, but not between different parts of one mind. They are split, rather, between the psyches of two people: The analyst experiences one part of the meaning and enacts the other; and the patient experiences the part the analyst enacts and enacts the part the analyst experiences. The two minds are mirror images of each other; they fit together like the two halves of a broken plate. What we hope will eventually *become* one person's consciously experienced conflict is played out between two people. In the meantime, analyst and patient are each tempted to conclude that only *she* sees the truth of the situation; only *she* is badly treated by the other.

Think back once more to my clinical illustration. Think of the separation between the part of me that wanted to enjoy my patient's "progress" and the part that felt guilty about sacrificing my capacity to observe and thereby letting my patient down. From the constructivist perspective, the latter self-state (the guilty self-state) *did not exist in symbolic form anywhere in my mind* until that strange affective deadness crept into the sessions and, in making me realize that "something" was there, aroused my dormant curiosity about what was happening. Under the circumstances provoked by affective chafing, the guilty self-state *came into being* (was formulated), and conscious internal conflict was finally possible. My previous "single-mindedness" was not due to the denial of an existing conflict inside me; it was due to an (unconsciously) insistent absence of curiosity on my part, created and fostered by my participation in the enactment.

From a constructivist position the primary defense is the unconsciously motivated refusal to create or articulate experience, a turning away from the possibilities (D. B. Stern, 1983, 1989, 1997, 2002a, 2009). When one does not deploy curiosity, experience goes "unmade" and is therefore literally absent. It is not "parked" or secreted in some corner of the mind; rather, it is never articulated or constructed in the first place. Dissociated self-states, therefore, are *potential* experience, experience that *could* exist if one were able to allow it; but one cannot, and unconsciously will not (D. B. Stern, 1997, 2009; see also this book, Chapters 3 and 5–8).

The interaction of present circumstances with our deepest affects and intentions creates every moment of experience anew. We seldom directly experience what we do to participate in constructing our own experience, though. No matter how intellectually convinced we become of our creative role, our experience—what we actually undergo—has an unbidden quality. The future comes to us; it is "found"; it "arrives."

Because the next moment is unformulated, it may be shaped in many different ways—but not in just any ways at all. There are significant constraints, ranging from tight to loose, on the experience we can construct without lying or succumbing to madness (and even in madness the constraints do not disappear—instead, their expression becomes bizarre). The concept of unformulated experience does not constitute a denial that reality exists; it is, rather, a claim that reality is not a given, but a set of limits on what experience can become without being false. Even tight constraints, though, such as those on our freedom to formulate the meaning of an enactment, still leave plenty of room for multiple interpretations.

Dissociation, then, is the unconscious refusal to consider a certain range of the possibilities that might be articulated or formulated in explicit experience (i.e., the possibilities within the constraints), a shutting down of the curiosity that might have revealed them. The possibilities we are free to construct in any given moment depend on the meanings the interpersonal field of that moment has for us.

The Analyst's Restoration of Self-Tolerance

In my clinical illustration we could say that I *directly experienced* narcissistic pleasure and *enacted* a way of letting down the patient (I accepted too easily that things were going well), while my patient *enacted* his attempt to please me (he did not realize he was encouraging me to feel happy with his "progress") and *directly experienced* what it was like to be let down by a parent/analyst who was all too ready to be fooled into believing things were hunky-dory (that is, at every step of the way, my patient knew better than to believe his own presentation). It was not until I found my way to an awareness of my unconscious participation, the way I actually *was* letting the patient down, and to the guilt that I could then formulate, that I was in a position to experience the conflict and to negotiate it. (But remember that my descriptions of what I was enacting could not have been formulated until the enactment resolved into a conflict within my own mind.)

I knew on the basis of experience, though, that it was far too simple to condemn myself for my unconscious part in the enactment. In fact, if I had succumbed to self-hatred over it, I would simply have been renewing the enactment in a different form. My self-hatred would then have been as rigid and single-minded as my narcissistic pleasure had been before. In order to create the kind of experience within which I could set about trying to negotiate the enactment, I needed to be able to create the joint experience of two conflicting states: my guilt about failing the patient, and my sense that I had done my best.

Over time, I worked my way to a position in which I regained the capacity to feel, in my work with this particular patient, narcissistic pleasure in the exercise of my analytic capacity. In the terms of the problem the patient's family did not solve, we might say that it took time for me to find a way to respect my patient's freedom without giving up the possibility of acting like and feeling like a good parent. Neither his parents nor I had been able to maintain the feeling that, however the patient worried us, we were doing our level best, and that that was all we could do, even if it was not good enough.

It took me time, in other words, to return to a tolerance of myself, to an appreciation of the full measure of my experience. Perhaps we lose and regain that tolerance and appreciation every time our analytic capacity is compromised. Perhaps the analyst's rediscovery of her tolerance of herself is one way to describe the negotiation between the analyst's self-states. In this case, the beginning of a change was my development of a sense that the atmosphere of the sessions was not what it had been. The snags and chafing were hints of an unknown emotional presence, a stirring. It required work, effort, to formulate a feel-able awareness of that presence, one that was describable; and that awareness of what had been absent, in concert with what I already felt and knew, finally came to constitute a conflict. For a while, at the beginning of these events, the snags and affective chafings were the only sign of more going on than met the eye, the sole registration in my awareness of something that could eventually become a conflict. It was my clinical interest in those signs, my everyday devotion to the clinical task, that eventually brought my own dissociation to light and allowed me to experience a conflict where none had been before.

I can now go back and answer a question I posed some time ago. If enactments suck into themselves our capacity to observe them and to know what to do about them, why does the same fate not befall the snags and chafing that hint at their existence? If the eye cannot see itself, why should it be able to see *hints* of itself?

Actually, most hints of this kind probably do escape our detection. But we catch a few of them, and it is our unremarkable devotion to the analytic task that allows those exceptions.[1] Snags and chafing are the nascent signs of a conflict we are in the midst of creating, a conflict that, even if we do not theorize it that way, we know must be directly and consciously experienced if the enactment is to be negotiated.

In my example, becoming able to formulate the state of mind I had dissociated afforded me, for the first time, the opportunity to make a decision about whether to continue the enactment. And of course, once I had the choice, it was obvious. An enactment loses its teeth as soon as one of its participants can imagine an alternative to it. On the other hand, had I not been able to breach my own dissociation and eventually experience conflict, the enactment would simply have continued unabated until it reached some kind of terminus of its own. Perhaps eventually, feeling let down yet again by one to whom he turned for help, the patient would have left treatment.

Pain and the Creation of Freedom

With clinical experience, analysts learn to value uncomfortable affective cues. We value these nuances as alerts to moments of interchange that deserve more thought and study, to experience that we need to feel and know as precisely as we can, and that may eventually allow us to get a foot in an experiential door that we cannot even clearly see yet. Although early in our professional lives these strange promptings may often be merely painful or disturbing, the same interactive hints later become for us intimations of freedom. It is our capacity to be interested in these intuitions, the devotion to our clinical work rooted in our desire for freedom—freedom for the patient, yes, but no less, freedom for ourselves—that motivates us to tolerate the painful experience. Over the course of our careers, previously uncomfortable reminders of the existence of what we do not

---

[1] "Unremarkable devotion to the analytic task," while it is accurate as far as it goes, is also a sanitized expression of what I have in mind. The work of an analyst can be demanding, after all, and no one chooses to do something difficult every day without getting some kind of a charge out of it. Psychoanalysts must be people for whom doing treatment stimulates the kinky and often slightly naughty or guilty satisfaction that Lacan calls *jouissance*.

understand become precious. We come to value freedom more and security less. Or perhaps, with experience, it just takes less to make us secure, so that we can tolerate more easily our desire for freedom. In time, we work toward what Symington (1983) calls "the act of freedom"—the analyst's liberation from the previously unconscious grip of the field—less and less by trying to satisfy the patient's needs or by knowing the truth, more and more by feeling our way into the experience we are having with the patient and the patient with us. I am quite sure, for instance, that in the first years of my practice, though I would have sensed that something was wrong in the treatment I have used as an illustration, I would not have had a very well-developed idea of what to do with this impression. I would have felt it as a warning, not as an opportunity.

In the midst of a relational storm that might otherwise obscure it, the analyst's desire for the patient's freedom and her own sometimes allows her to see, understand, and accept the patient's help.[1] If Searles (1976) is right, this help is not only moving but also mutative. We could say that the analyst's desire to cure the patient allows the analyst to accept the patient's desire to cure *her*.

On some level, in some unformulated, inarticulate way, did my patient want me to notice the subtle change in the atmosphere between us? I suspect that he did. He wanted me to love him enough to feel his subtle withdrawal from me and to care about it without becoming anxious over it. But was he also giving me my own chance for "cure" in the transference, my chance to be a good "parent," by sacrificing my narcissism and coming through for him? Perhaps he was.

Reformulation

To this point, I may have made it seem that it is only one's experience of the dissociated self-state—the formulation of the experience that had been unformulated—that changes as conflict is achieved. But that is not the impression I want to leave. In the resolution of an enactment, one's experience of the safer state, the state that one had more or less comfortably occupied in awareness, changes as well. The conscious and explicit experience one had of oneself and the other during the enactment, that is, also becomes something other than it was.

---

[1] See Aron (1991, 1996); Blechner (1992); Gill (1982); Hoffman (1998); Mitchell (1993, 1997); Searles (1975, 1976); Singer (1971); Tauber (1954, 1979); Wolstein (1983); see also this book, Chapter 3.

As conflict appears and a dissociated self-state comes into aware-ness, the newly formulated experience *recontextualizes* what had been consciously and explicitly experienced before. That recontextualization makes unavoidable the *reformulation* of that experience. Once the older, consciously accessible experience shares awareness with an alternative perception, it simply has to feel and seem different than it did before. Its meaning has to change, at least a little bit, because its context has been rearranged, it is situated differently in the mind. As enactment ends, then, neither the dissociated state nor the (previously) safer, explicitly experi-enced state remains as it was. Each recontextualizes and participates in redefining the other.

In my own case, my easy pleasure in doing the work with my patient, first recontextualized by my dawning awareness that it was narcissis-tic, suddenly seemed unacceptable. I felt it as a symptom of sorts. As time passed and I regained my tolerance of myself, finding it possible to experience guilt and pleasure simultaneously, even if it was not com-fortable, my pleasure was recontextualized yet again, this time by my growing sense that *both* my states—my pleasure and my guilt—were understandable responses to the patient's part of the enactment. And so, though my experience of pleasure was explicit all along, it did not remain the same pleasure: Its meaning and the way it felt to me changed as my previously dissociated state become possible to formulate. What began as naive pleasure first morphed into a symptom of my narcissism and eventually took its place, in my mind, as part of the enactment between the patient and me. The same kind of process went on regard-ing my explicit experience of the patient: I began by accepting his mar-velous progress at face value, feeling encouraged by it, then moved to a position in which his progress appeared false and made me feel like a vain failure and annoyed with him that he had taken me for a ride. In the end, his show of accomplishment, like my pleasure in it, was recontextualized in a way that made it more clinically productive and tolerable for both of us.

Part III: Redefining the Riddle: Single-Mindedness and Internal Conflict

To conceive how the eye sees itself, then, we are drawn back to the origins of psychoanalysis, to its roots in internal conflict. We must renew the hon-ored place of conflict in our theories, but the internal conflict we need to conceive is not conflict as Freud understood it: It is not the conflict between drive and defense, or among the id, the ego, and the superego; and it is not the conflict between consciousness and the unconscious. What we need is a conception of consciously accessible conflict as personal and social meaning, a conflict that goes on simultaneously within us and between us, a conflict of purposes, interests, and desires.[1]

Furthermore, and even more crucially, we must reconsider the assumption that every aspect of subjectivity is subtended by conflict. We need to recast our thinking to reflect the view that, even in circumstances of great emotional pain, internal conflict can be absent, and that its absence can be the source of the pain, a problem that needs to be addressed by creating it anew. The repetition compulsion, in other words, is not necessarily maintained by a rigidly enacted conflict between conscious and unconscious aims, but by the *absence* of the conflict we need to be able to experience if we are to sense the availability of choice. We need to take the point of view, more than a little strange in the terms of traditional psychoanalysis, that, in the case of dissociated self-states, conflict is not a given but a goal. Without denying that every moment of life is conflicted, we must accept that there are times when do not experience *enough* internal conflict, that a significant part of the pain in human relatedness occurs because conflicts that might be actualized within us are not.

Conscious internal conflict is necessary because, if we are to back away far enough from what is happening with the other to create the opportunity for reflection, for "seeing" the events in question, we need more than one perspective. We need an alternative interpretation (an alternative *experience*, I might rather say, though I mean the same thing by the two words), and an alternative interpretation inevitably conflicts with the one we already have. In the terms of dissociation, we can say that the sensing of one's own state of mind requires a second state of mind to serve as a background against which the first can become a figure. Of course, the first also serves as background to the second, so whenever one becomes capable of sensing and reflecting on one state of mind, one is capable of sensing and reflecting on two. Without an alternative perspective to set against one's previous single-mindedness, a new perception is simply impossible to accomplish. And so the achievement of conflict and the articulation of

[1] For example, Bromberg (1998, 2006); Davies (1996, 1997, 1998, 1999); Ehrenberg (1992); Hoffman (1998); Levenkron (2006); Mitchell (1993, 1997); Renik (1993a, 1993b); Slavin and Kriegman (1998).

the meaning of an enactment are, in fact, the same event. The point can be made from either direction: We can say that the alternative perspective of a newly achieved conflict allows the formulation of the unformulated; or we can say that the formulation of the unformulated is, in itself, the creation of the alternative perspective that subtends new conflict.

The creation of internal conflict is also the creation of a sense of initiative. Desire in the absence of a conflicting alternative is nothing more than compulsion, and compulsion negates the feeling that one is choosing one's own life. In deconstructing enactment one therefore escapes a certain kind of psychic slavery. The fact that the motive organizing one's enslavement is frequently the attempt to dominate the other (Benjamin, 1990, 1999, 2000) makes the enslavement no less constricting. In the stark, two-dimensional world of enactment, the dominant take and keep power, but they lose their freedom as surely as the oppressed do. In this sense, enactment as I am portraying it—enactment based in dissociation—takes place along the same lines as what Benjamin refers to as the reversible ("doer–done to") complementarity. Neither the patient nor the analyst is any more capable of experiencing himself creatively than he is of recognizing the other. Both participants fail to appreciate the fullness of *both* of their minds.

The most important outcome of a successful analysis is the firm and unthinking conviction that one's life is one's own, that oneself and no one else is living it. Frequently this feeling that one's life is the creation of one's own mind—which in dryer terminology we can describe as the sense of agency—arises from our access to the experience of conflict, because when we are able to face the necessity for choosing the perspective we will take on the problems that face us, we are able to feel our own hand on the tiller.[1] In enactment, by contrast, experience either feels as if one is helpless to shape or influence it (and one may desperately wish to do just that) or as if it is being imposed by the other. Sometimes it just goes by unnoticed. All these kinds of experience, but especially the sense of being forced, are among the factors most responsible for feelings we all often have in enactments, feelings of powerlessness and lack of ownership of our own minds. We feel enslaved; we feel *made* to live this way, and we feel as if we cannot

---

[1] It bears repeating, though, that the perspectives from which we choose are not constructed on a merely conscious basis. The *availability* of perspectives is a matter of intentionality far deeper than conscious decision making. The range of interpretations (experiences) we allow ourselves is a function of a curiosity that goes beyond what we can decide to be interested in. I want to avoid any implication that agency is *only* a matter of the growth in our capacity to make conscious choices: Our sense of agency also arises from our perception of our freedom to experience, a perception that is often created, ironically enough, by our surprise at what comes to us unbidden (see D. B. Stern, 1991, 1997, 2002a).

help it, as much as we know that that is not so. Dissociation prevents that precious feeling of fully inhabiting life that Winnicott (1960) describes as true self, "the sense of being real" (p. 149).

I began this chapter by setting myself the insoluble riddle of how the eye sees itself. I then promised to reformulate the question in a way that could be answered, and I have done that. It turns out that knowing the countertransference seems impossible only as long we are thinking from the position of single-mindedness. When we are able to create only one state of mind, it seems and feels as if, to observe itself, that mind must somehow twist around and think itself from an impossible elsewhere— the bootstrapping problem. In the achievement of conflict, we create an alternative to the rigid perceptions that have locked us into the status quo; we create multiple consciousness. As single-mindedness is replaced by two or more internal positions, one part of us becomes capable of observing another part without having to perform metaphysical contortions; the mind can feel and reflect on what it could only live out blindly before. And so we do not have to solve the problem of the eye seeing itself after all. What seemed the impossible dilemma of countertransference awareness becomes, instead, the thinkable problem of how we transcend single-mindedness by creating the experience of conflict.

When Does Freedom Happen?

But transcending single-mindedness is more easily said than done. We always hope that thinking new thoughts makes us more available for new experience. I certainly have that hope for the ideas I have introduced here. But as much as new ideas may help to prepare the ground for new experience, no idea, by itself, creates for us new perceptions of the patient as we are sitting there needing those new perceptions (whether we know it or not) so very badly. The problem of clinical freedom has no generic solution.

That is perhaps not so much a bane as a boon. If we believed we knew just what ought to be done, as analysts probably once did feel more often than they do now, if we still had a noncontextual theory of technique, psychoanalysis would eventually become nothing more than practicing the right way—one more instrumental treatment, boilerplate dictated by DSM. Despite the annoyance, frustration, rage, envy, sorrow, guilt, shame, and humiliation that we and our patients feel during enactments, it is a reminder of the mystery of living, and thus of human dignity, that freedom from the grip of the field is beyond our capacity to create by an act of will.

Experience is sufficiently manifold and complex that we find ourselves simply living out most of it as it comes to us. In the overall scheme of things, actually, our capacity and inclination to reflect on experience are the exceptions. And it is not just the unconscious and the dynamics of relatedness that stand in our way of understanding our involvements with others. If we wanted to tot up the difficulties, we would also have to factor in (though of course that is exactly what we cannot do) the (nonrelational) contingency of existence, Lacan's register of the Real, so inconvenient for theories, wreaking havoc with our intentions to create order and regularity. What will happen next? Will the treatment be interrupted by accident, illness, financial reversal? One or both of the participants might even die before they finish their work together. It is simply impossible to predict that, when the knob on the door of my office comes off in my hand as I am trying to let my patient out of the room, she finally and suddenly grasps that I am human. Nor do I have a snowball's chance in hell of understanding why *this* was the event to do the trick. Why could it only be now? Why the doorknob, for heaven's sake? Why didn't the same thing happen when I simply could not wait and had to interrupt the session to go to the bathroom? *That* was pretty undeniably human, was it not? There did not *seem* to be anything essentially different going on between us then, and the symbolic meanings my patient and I can conjure for the episodes, hard as we have tried, do not enlighten us in this respect. In the end, who knows? John Lennon's most famous aphorism comes to mind: Life is what happens while you are making plans. Breaking the grip of the field can be what happens while you think you are up to something else altogether.

Why do we suddenly manage to feel affective snags and chafing *now*? Why *these* snags and chafing and not all those others we must be missing along the way? Why are we able to accept the patient's aid today when we could not yesterday? Sometimes it is possible, either at the time or after the fact, to understand why it was this one moment, or these 2 days, or 3 weeks, that allowed the achievement of conflict. But often it is not possible to know why the grip of the field relaxes when it does. All we can do to create the outcomes we desire is to prepare for them; all we can do is to try to open ourselves to an awareness of whatever affective clues drift our way. But why it is that our preparation, our work, and our best intentions are only sometimes sufficient remains a mystery. We immerse ourselves in the writings of psychoanalysis and in the study of our own experience and that of our analysands, and we practice over the years with the balance of discipline and innovation that seems right to us. In some hours we transcend single-mindedness: The result is good. In other hours we are as mired in enactment as the session ends as we were at the beginning. It is our accomplishment of freedom that makes an hour good, but often enough, as long as we are working to capacity with a deeply involved analysand, we do not really know why freedom comes to us when it does.

5

Partners in Thought
A Clinical Process Theory of Narrative

The Diary of a Castaway

I had been thinking about the problem of narrative in psychoanalysis for some time when I ran across a television screening of *The Incredible Shrinking Man*, a B movie scripted by the science fiction writer Richard Matheson and released in 1957. I had not seen the film for almost 40 years, but I remembered it fondly enough to see if it held up. I imagined that immersing myself again in the atmosphere of one of those awful, innocent 1950s science fiction movies would be nostalgic. Unexpectedly, it was a good deal more than that, and not only because the movie was better than I understood when I first saw it. I had long felt that new narrative in psychoanalysis is not simply the outcome of the analyst's objective interpretation, as Schafer (1983, 1992) and Spence (1982, 1987) portrayed it, but is instead the unbidden outcome of unconscious aspects of clinical process. Oddly enough, by helping to direct and cohere my thoughts on this point, *The Incredible Shrinking Man* jump-started the Interpersonal/ Relational psychoanalytic understanding of narrative construction I offer in this chapter. The understanding I present, though, is based not only in a certain kind of theory; it is also rooted in a personal sense of clinical process. And so the tone I have adopted is personal as well. This chapter should probably be read as a statement of convictions; but I maintain the hope that my convictions will resonate with the reader's own.

The plot of *The Incredible Shrinking Man* rests on an absurd 10-second encounter between a man on his boat and a small radioactive cloud that just happens to be drifting aimlessly around the ocean. During the moments it takes the cloud to approach the boat, envelop it, and pass beyond, the man's wife is inside the cabin, fetching bottles of beer. She returns to find that her husband's chest is speckled with some kind of glitter. In the crazily concrete way of these films, the wife, having been inside, is spared the glitter, along with the later effects the glitter will have on her husband. The man brushes off the sparkly stuff and mumbles something to his wife about some strange fog. There is no further discussion of the matter, but the typically weird music accompanying this inexplicable moment certifies that something mysterious and sinister has come to pass.

That is the set-up for the rest of the movie, in which our hero learns that he is shrinking. Wrenching losses ensue, one after another, until finally, when he has become so small that he lives in a dollhouse, his wife, still dutiful, and a gargantuan in his newly proportioned world, bids him good-bye one day, goes out of the house, and accidentally lets in the cat. In a terrifying scene, the cat wrecks the dollhouse trying to get at the tiny man who, in escaping, manages to shoulder open the door to the basement, but then falls off the side of the steps a full floor down into a basket of laundry. No one knows he is there. In fact, his wife and the rest of the world, to all of whom he has become famous as the Incredible Shrinking Man, believe that the cat got him.

It is only then that the movie hits its stride. It turns out that its improbable beginnings have been nothing more than a means of entry for Matheson, the scriptwriter, who really wants to tell a Robinson Crusoe story. And a great story it is. It is the story of a tiny, abandoned man, thought to be dead, marooned in his own basement with no chance of rescue, horribly alone, living in a matchbox, climbing ordinary stairs, each one now turned into a towering cliff, with equipment fashioned from the materials he finds, feeding on cheese left to catch mice, having to invent ways to cross chasms that are nothing more than the mouths of empty cardboard boxes, prey to a monstrous spider he fights with a needle he has found in a discarded pincushion, and threatened by a flash flood from a leaky boiler. In the end, after these compelling and strangely moving adventures, intricately imagined, and filmed with a notable attention to detail, and special effects surprisingly good for the era, the man becomes so small that he can finally escape into his own backyard through the screen mesh covering the basement window. He is now too small for us to see, but we know he is there. We imagine him standing in a forest of towering grass blades, shrinking to nothing, as he offers us the final lines of his tale. At the very end, in the moments before he winks out altogether, the camera pans upward and the tiny hero, gazing at the star-filled heavens, thinks that the infinitesimal and the infinite are much closer to one another than he has imagined before. Surprisingly enough, it is a moment of serenity, acceptance, and dignity. After the trauma, humiliations, and cynicism he has suffered in the first months of his disease, he has not only returned to himself, he has transcended what has befallen him. It is hardly routine for survivors of trauma to find their suffering a provocation to grow, even if they manage to accept and live with their experiences; and of course the story of the shrinking man is a fiction, and a fantastical one at that. But this fictional little man has grown.

For the most part, the hero tells his own story. Yet during the first part of the film we have no explanation for why we are privy to the tale. We eventually find out that the tale is actually a diary of the events it depicts, written by the hero himself. In the course of his adventures, just prior to the episode with the cat and the dollhouse, the hero, cynical and miserable to the point of desperation, begins to write. This is the line in the movie that made me sit up and take notice: "I was telling the world about my life," the shrinking man reads to us from his diary, "and with the telling it became easier."

It does not require specialized training or experience to recognize the truth in this simple statement. If there is mystery here, it is mystery we are so used to living with that it does not surprise us. The fact that narrative plays a natural role in creating a meaningful life in even a B science fiction movie puts us on firm ground in agreeing with those many writers and scholars who tell us that we shape personal meaning by organizing our experience into meaningful, sequential episodes.[1]

But the intuitively obvious is not enough. What does the diary actually *do* for the shrinking man? Why does it help him to tell his story? *How* does it help him?

The narrative of the strange events of the shrinking man's life supplies him with a coherent and felt experiential order that he has lost in the rush of bizarre happenings. Prior to constructing his tale in the explicit terms of his diary, he has become an object in his own life, a figure suffering chaotic, incomprehensible events for no apparent reason and with little feeling. The emergence of meaning from what has felt to him like senselessness, helplessness, and despair confers agency and therefore dignity. He is once again a subject. After his fall into the laundry basket, the tiny man creates his experiential world, his story of the obstacles he faces and either accepts or overcomes, in such a way that his end has authentic

---

[1] See Bruner (1986, 1990, 2002); Ferro (1999, 2002, 2005, 2006); Polkinghorne (1988); Ricoeur (1977, 1981); Sarbin (1986); Schafer (1983, 1992); Spence (1982).

pathos. After months of a growing sense of chaos and nihilism, he ends his life a deeply thoughtful and affectively alive human being.

In creating his diary, the shrinking man also creates a relationship with imaginary others who then serve as witnesses of what he "tells" them. The movie grips us, despite its flaws, partly because we recognize at some level the help that this witnessing offers him: we ourselves become his witnesses. I turn now to a perspective on what it means to have and to be a witness. I will return to the case of the shrinking man once these ideas are in place.

Witnessing

We first learned about the significance of witnessing from studies of trauma, in which witnessing of some sort is usually considered an essential prerequisite to the capacity to narrate one's own experience. I believe that the need for witnessing became visible first in this context because it was in the impact of trauma that some of the most damaging effects of the *absence* of the witness were first observed: Without a witness, trauma must be dissociated; and once the isolated trauma sufferer gains a witness, the experience of the trauma becomes more possible to know, feel, and think about (e.g., Boulanger, 2007; Brison, 2002; Laub, 1992a, 1992b, 2005; Laub & Auerhahn, 1989; Richman, 2006). I will be discussing witnessing here as a routine part of everyday, nontraumatic experience that I believe begins in the earliest stages of development.

In fact, although Fonagy et al. (2002) do not use the language I am using here, what they tell us about the beginnings of the self can be read as the proposition that the witness precedes us. As they put it, "we fathom ourselves through others" (p. 2). Caretakers identify certain feelings and desires in the infant and treat the infant accordingly. This treatment begins to organize the infant's relatively inchoate world in the terms of narrative, and self-states begin to cohere in and around these earliest stories. In one sense, then, we are called into being by acts of recognition by the other. We learn we are hungry because the other feeds us at a moment when we are having a certain uncomfortable feeling; and so we then have a story that goes with that feeling: "I am hungry." We learn we are sad because the other comforts us at a moment when we are having a different distressing feeling; and so we then begin to have a story that goes with *that* feeling: "I am sad." This is one way we begin to tell and live stories; there are other ways. All the various tributaries to narrative sum to the creation of experience:

Hungry is what you are when you need to be fed; sad is what you are when you need to be comforted. As Harry Stack Sullivan (1940) writes over and over again, we know ourselves via reflected appraisals. Fonagy and his co-writers describe the same thing: "At the core of our selves is the representation of how we were seen" (p. 348); and "At the core of the mature child's self is the other at the moment of reflection" (p. 380).[1]

As development proceeds, we eventually gain the ability to formulate our experience for ourselves, internalizing the capacity that first belonged primarily to our caretakers. But we do not outgrow the need, paraphrasing Winnicott, to see our reflections in our mothers' eyes; the need only becomes more sophisticated. We may no longer need the other actually to show us the meaning of our experience, as we did when we were infants; but if we are to know our own experience in reflective terms, if we are to be able not only to construct narratives, but to be aware of the narratives we construct, we do need to believe that we are known by the other. We need to feel that we exist in the other's mind, and that our existence has a kind of continuity in that mind; and we need to feel that the other in whose mind we exist is emotionally responsive to us, that he or she cares about what we experience and how we feel about it (Bach, 2006; Benjamin, 1988, 1990, 1995). This is what it is, I believe, to have a witness. Without a witness, even an imaginary witness, events either fail to fall into the meaningful pattern of episode that is narrative, or we merely enact our stories blindly, unable to think about them or know what they feel like. Our witness is our partner in thought.[2]

---

[1] Fonagy and his collaborators and Sullivan are among the contributors to what has become an extensive literature describing the structuring of the infant's and young child's world by the relationship with the mother. Some of this literature falls under the rubric of mentalization (Chasseguet-Smirgel, 1990; Fain & David, 1963; Fain, David & Marty, 1964; Green, 1975; Lecours & Bouchard, 1997; Luquet, 1987; Marty, 1990, 1991; MacDougall, 1985). Other work grows from an interest in the recognition of otherness (Benjamin, 1988, 1990; Bion, 1962, 1963; Eigen, 1981; Lacan, 1977; Modell, 1984; Segal, 1957; Winnicott, 1971). A third relevant line of thought is rooted in the study of mother–infant interaction and the growth of the interpersonal field (Beebe & Lachmann, 1988, 1994; Sander, 1962, 1988; D. N. Stern, 1977, 1985; Sullivan, 1940/1953). All of these branches of the literature are part of the context from which grows my interest in witnessing and its place at the roots of personality. Last in this list of citations, but certainly not least, is Poland's (2000) lovely and innovative paper on witnessing in psychoanalysis, in which witnessing is contrasted with interpretation and is characterized as the activity by which otherness is recognized. The influence of Poland's paper is ubiquitous in this chapter.

[2] It has been conclusively demonstrated (if the point actually needed to be demonstrated) that thought and rationality should not be equated. Thought is creative and effective only when thoroughly imbued with feeling (e.g., Damasio, 1994). Although thought and feeling are inseparable in this way, we do not have a single word that allows reference to both. Whenever I refer to "partners in thought," I mean to refer to both thought and feeling. The partnering I am describing is at least as much an affective phenomenon as it is a cognitive one.

The witness, while it may feel like a single presence, may nevertheless be composed of part(s) of one's own mind or of the other's, or of both simultaneously. The witness is the state(s) of self or other who one imagines is best suited to fulfill the partnering purpose at the particular moment in which the need arises. It is not a simple internalization of the historical mothering one. An internalization of a loving parent who has grasped and known one's continuity is probably a necessary condition for the development of the capacity to witness oneself, but it is not sufficient. The witness begins as that kind of internalization but becomes a changing amalgam of history, fantasy, and current reality. It is not a structure of the mind, but a function, or better, a way of being. Its composition is limited by one's experience, of course, but within those limits the witness changes as continuously as the events witnessed; the particular selection of parts of oneself or the other recruited to witness on any one occasion depends on that occasion's context. It is not only the witness who is in flux, however; the one who is witnessed is, as well, since the state of self in need of witnessing also changes with context. However complex it may be to describe the phenomenon in the third person, though, in phenomenological terms the matter is simpler: The witness is the one imagined, consciously or *sub rosa*, to be listening.

To have the ongoing sense that our story exists in someone else's mind (even if that someone else exists within our own mind) we must first (and very often in imagination) continuously "tell" that other person what we are experiencing. We construct what we know of ourselves by identifying with the other and "listening" through his ears to the story we are telling. We know our stories by telling them to ourselves, in other words; but we can do that only by listening to ourselves through the other's ears. Psychoanalysts work in just this way: They listen to patients in the way that allows patients to listen to themselves.[1] To convince yourself of this

---

[1] Some form of this point is widely recognized, probably by dozens of writers. Eshel (2004) describes "I-dentification" as "the analyst's thoroughgoing identificatory experiencing of the patient's most painful and terrifying experiences," which "renders them tolerable, liveable, enables them 'the possibility of being'" (p. 331). Farber (1956) writes, "in listening we speak the other's words. Or, to put it another way, the analyst is able to hear only what he, potentially at least, is able to say" (p. 145). Laub (1992a) says, "The listener has to feel the victim's victories, defeats and silences, know them from within, so that they can assume the form of testimony" (p. 58). And finally, or rather first, there are many passages of this sort from the work of Winnicott. This one is representative: "An example of unintegration phenomena is provided by the very common experience of the patient who proceeds to give every detail of the week-end and feels contented at the end if everything has been said, though the analyst feels that no analytic work has been done. Sometimes we must interpret this as the patient's need to be known in all his bits and pieces by one person, the analyst. To be known means to feel integrated at least in the person of the analyst" (1945, p. 150).

point, just think about how often, during and after your own analysis, you found yourself at odd times during your day imagining that you were telling your analyst something. I remember when I first noticed it happen. Sometime after that I realized how frequent these tellings were and how often they went unattended.

This kind of telling and listening, though, arises much earlier in life than the age at which people typically go into psychotherapy and psychoanalysis. If you have children you remember overhearing them talk to themselves in their cribs, often quite animatedly, after you put them to bed. They are organizing their experience of the day, giving it sense. But to whom are they talking? Not to "themselves," at least not exactly in the sense in which "self" will be a meaningful idea later in life. At this early age self and other are not yet conscious and coherent parts of experience; neither self and other, for instance, can be explicitly reflected on. Besides, why speak out loud if the only audience is oneself? It is plausible to imagine that babies in their cribs are talking to their first witnesses: their parents. But these are their internalized parents, or some of their first internalized objects. These children are imaginatively listening to themselves through their parents' ears and thereby lending their experience a credence, coherence, and depth of feeling it otherwise could not have (Nelson, 1989). As a matter of fact, what we are hearing when we listen to babies creating coherence in those minutes before sleep may very well be part of the process of self-formation.

The diary of the shrinking man, like what patients say to their analysts, is an explicit kind of telling, with the difference, of course, that the shrinking man's audience, like the audience listening to the little child in his crib, is imaginary. Like the child, the shrinking man is writing to some figure in his inner world. Imaginary audiences are very common. But explicit telling is not. Most telling of the sort I am describing here, the kind of telling that allows one to listen to one's own thoughts, is implicit. It goes on hazily, not very specifically, seldom noticed except, in a leftover from our crib days, in the states that take place just before sleep in adult life or at other times when we are alone, when we sometimes notice that we are formulating our thoughts by addressing some ill-defined other. Most of the time, though, it is *as if* we were telling, and *as if* we were being listened to and then listening to ourselves. But the activity is no less crucial for being hazy and imagined. In order for this process to come about in the first place, probably we must be fortunate enough to have had parents who left us able to believe, in at least some states, that there exist others, especially certain imaginary others, who are continuous presences interested in knowing our experience (Bach, 2006; Benjamin, 1988, 1990, 1995).

When life feels arbitrary, senselessly cruel, or meaningless, as it did for the shrinking man before he began his diary, one is liable to be aware of no story at all. Events seem arbitrary and do not fall into narrative order. Affect is flattened or diminished; one may consciously feel only a kind of numbness or deadness. The living, hurt places in one's mind—actually, the injured parts of the *self*, the parts we most need to protect—despite their influence on day-to-day life, go undiscovered until *something happens in ongoing relatedness* that allows us to see that someone else recognizes the pain we ourselves have been unable to know and feel. Our grasp of our own previously dissociated experience through what we imagine to be the eyes and ears of the other is synonymous with the creation of new meaning. As a coherent narrative of the experience falls into place, there is an awakening, including an awakening of pain. In fortunate cases, there is also relief. Both pain and relief illuminate the absence of feeling in what came before.

That was the fate of the shrinking man. Until he began to tell his story, he was losing courage by the day and becoming increasingly angry and cynical. But once he began writing his diary, his imagined readers, who "listened" to him "tell" his tale, seemed to help him contact his dissociated vitality and make it once again part of the mind he felt as "me." That change was enough to bring back his determination to face whatever was in store for him. For now I merely note the following point: imagined witnesses can be as effective as real ones.[1]

All right, I thought, the diary allowed the shrinking man to know his own story. But so what? Why did the character even want to go on living? Why didn't the shrinking man kill himself, or at least think about it? Wouldn't I have thought about it if I were he? Was that omission a failing of the script? The man may as well have been the last human being. He was permanently, completely, hopelessly alone. Wouldn't absolute, inescapable aloneness inevitably lead to despair? Or did the screenwriter know something? Should we consider the hero's perseverance to be a consequence of the value that telling someone his story of isolation brought back to his life?

For another take on the question, I turned to my copy of *Robinson Crusoe* (Defoe, 1957), a story that gripped me as a boy, gripped me earlier and even more deeply than the story of the shrinking man. The first part of the book is a journal of Crusoe's years living alone on a deserted island, the sole survivor of a shipwreck. (Crusoe writes until he runs out of precious ink.) In the usual manner of diaries, the document is written as if

---

[1] I must defer to the future an exploration of the significant differences between imagined witnesses and real ones and between the process of witnessing under these two sets of circumstances.

Crusoe were addressing someone, and you soon fall under the spell: It is as if it is *you* to whom Crusoe is telling what happened to him. I remember feeling an intimacy with Crusoe when I read the book the first time; I felt I was there on that island, just as I felt I was there in that basement with the shrinking man. It was one of the most thrilling reading adventures of my childhood. I remember marveling that Crusoe could live so fully by himself, and now, with the reminder supplied by my recent experience with the shrinking man, I also remember feeling, even as a boy, that the diary must have made Crusoe feel less alone.

By writing their diaries and being able to believe in the interest in their experience held by those imaginary others to whom they wrote, Crusoe and the shrinking man created partners in thought, imaginary others with whom to share life. We all create partners in thought, all the time. In most of life, though, real flesh-and-blood others are so ubiquitous, and the stories of our lives fall together in such an unnoticed way that it is much harder to appreciate both the significance of narrative and the role of witnesses in its creation. The ongoing reciprocal process by which we quite implicitly offer one another the reassurance that we understand well enough to continue to serve as witnesses generally goes unnoticed, just keeps on keeping on, like the Boston Change Process Study Group's (2002, 2005, 2007, 2008; D. N. Stern et al., 1998) "implicit relational knowing," unless or until misattunement interrupts the flow and forces us to attend to the break in our confidence in the other's responsive emotional presence. The very isolation of Crusoe and the shrinking man offers us the opportunity to grasp the role of their narrative creations in giving their lives meaning, and the conception of the witness allows us to understand why writing their diaries helped them as it did.

Although witnessing is mentioned often in the trauma literature, Sophia Richman's (2006) work on "transforming trauma into autobiographical narrative" contributes observations with more pinpoint relevance to what I am trying to say than others I have read. Remember what the shrinking man said about his diary ("I was telling the world about my life, and with the telling it became easier.") and compare it to Richman, who tells us this about autobiography and trauma: "By sharing the creation with the world, there is an opportunity to come out of hiding, to find witnesses to what had been suffered alone, and to begin to overcome the sense of alienation and isolation that are the legacy of trauma survivors" (p. 644). Richman also quotes Joan Didion's observation that writing can make experience coherent and real. Didion made the remark during a television interview with Charlie Rose in which she was talking about the memoir she wrote about the death of her husband: "What helped me to survive was writing this book, because otherwise I wouldn't have been able to understand what I was going through" (p. 648). And finally, Richman agrees that the witness may be imaginary. Here is what she writes about her father's memoir of life in a concentration camp: "I believe that in order to write what he did, he had to conjure up a reader who had an interest in his story and could function as his witness" (p. 646).

Narrative Freedom and Continuous Productive Unfolding

It is as true in the clinical situation as it is anywhere else that, by the time our best stories are spoken, they just seem right, convincing generations of psychoanalysts that it was the content of what they said to their patients—that is, clinical interpretation—that was mutative. I share the view of those who see the matter otherwise. The real work has already been done by the time a new story falls into place.[1] Because they and I are tackling the same problem, I appreciate the work of the many writers who understand the therapeutic action of interpretations as relational. Mitchell (1997), for example, writes, "[I]nterpretations work, when they do, ... [because] the patient experiences them as something new and different, something not encountered before" (p. 52). But that is not the position I am taking here. I am arguing that the appearance in the treatment of mutually accepted new content or newly organized content, which is generally narrative in form, is not usually the instrument of change at all; it is rather the sign that change has taken place. It is true that a new understanding is the fulfillment of possibility; but it is to *the creation of that possibility, not the shape of its fulfillment,* that we must look for the source of change. The important thing about a new understanding—and this applies no matter whether it is the analyst or the patient who offers it—is less its novel content than the new freedom revealed by its appearance in the analytic space, a freedom to feel, relate, see, and say differently than before. This is the likely explanation for the widely recognized observation that former analysands, even those who credit their treatments with saving or renewing their lives, remember few of the interpretations their analysts made. It was not the interpretations, per se, that helped, but the freedom that made

---

[1] For example, Boston Change Process Study Group (2002, 2005, 2007, 2008); Bromberg (1998, 2006); Ghent (1995); Pizer (1998); Russell (1991); 2007, 2008; D. N. Stern (2004); D. N. Stern et al. (1998). See also this volume, Chapters 3, 4, 6 and 8.

the interpretations possible in the first place. What *is* remembered from a successful treatment, as a matter of fact, is much less the analyst's words or ideas than something about the appearance of that freedom, something about what particular important moments *felt* like, something sensory, perceptual, and affective. The new story, then, is not the engine of change but the mark change leaves behind. Or perhaps this is better: The new story does not create change, but shapes the way we represent it to ourselves.

But as much as I agree with that statement, it is also a bit of an overstatement. In the attempt to acknowledge that claims for the mutative effects of narrative interpretations have been overstated, we could find ourselves throwing out the baby with the bathwater. We must admit that each new story along the way is not only the mark of change, but also helps to provoke the next round of curiosity, and thus to open new narrative freedom and the stories that follow. Each new story is simultaneously what change leaves behind and part of what brings about the next generation of clinical events. In fact, we can say this in a stronger form: Each new story *belongs to* the next generation of clinical events.[1]

And so when we observe that patients may not remember the events of their treatments primarily in narrative terms, we must also acknowledge that memory for narrative is not necessarily the best index of narrative's influence. The affective changes that take place in treatment, and that are memorialized in the new narratives that fall into place there, are reflected in our ways of remembering the past, creating the present, and imagining the future. It is in these effects that we see the most profound influence of new stories. Narratives are the architecture of experience, the ever changing structure that gives it form. Without narrative, affect would be chaotic and rudderless, as shapeless as a collapsed tent; and without affect, narrative would be dry and meaningless.

We see in new narrative freedom a deepened capacity of the patient and the analyst to dwell in each other's minds, to collaborate in the analytic task, to serve as each other's partners in thought. Any new understanding in the clinical situation is testimony that these two people have become better able to "tell" each other their stories and to "listen" to their own

---

[1] This emphasis on the creation of new narrative freedom is not meant to suggest that either character or any of the other kinds of continuity in the personality are unimportant. But looking at character in Relational terms does require us to conceive it as multiple, not singular. That is, character must be defined in context: Under thus-and-such circumstances, a particular person's conduct and experience are liable to be defined in a particular way that is at least partly predictable. But we cannot guess what anyone will do or experience if we do not know something about the nature of the interpersonal field in which that person is participating.

tellings through the ears of the other. I mean "tell" and "listen" in the special way that goes on in imagination and that depends both on being able to believe that you have an unshakeable existence for the other and on recognizing yourself in your imagination of the other's picture of you.

The freedom to create a new narrative in the clinical situation, or to find value in a new narrative that has been created by the other, is a specific instance of the general case of narrative freedom. Most of this new grasp of things emerges without conscious effort, unbidden, like implicit relational knowing, from the ongoing relatedness between patient and analyst. As long as there is no obstruction of the capacity of each person to serve as witness to the other, narrative freedom is the expectable state of affairs, and the capacity of analyst and patient to reveal new experience through an ever-renewed curiosity deepens over time as their intimacy grows. There is a sense of continuous productive unfolding. Under these conditions, there is a more or less uninterrupted flow of new affective experience and understanding for both patient and analyst. Old stories hove into view, are destabilized, and dissolve; new stories fall into place. The process is often smooth and pleasurable. This kind of clinical work goes on much of the time with many patients, more often with some patients than others. Although the process may be punctuated with minor difficulties—hesitations, bumps, and snags—the overall nature of the work is an ever richer and more thorough exploration and experience of the tolerable part of both the patient's experience and the analyst's. The analyst generally feels (and is) valued, skilled, and useful, and the patient feels helped. The analyst's unconscious involvement with the patient is present, but seldom problematic. It serves as a contribution, not an obstacle, allowing the analyst to offer a different take on the patient's experience from the one the patient started with, a novel view that is generally experienced as helpful by the patient. There is the satisfying sense of a job well done. Continuous productive unfolding is, in the analyst's mind, what Hoffman (1998) would refer to as the unconstricted interplay of ritual and spontaneity, what Knoblauch (2000) and Ringstrom (2001, 2007) would call improvisation in therapeutic relatedness, and what Winnicott (1971), the font of such thinking, would call play.

Not-Me

This relatively smooth and productive clinical process lasts as long as experience feels tolerable. But a very different, more troubling, and sometimes even destructive kind of relatedness takes place when the experience evoked in the mind of either patient or analyst, or of both, is *not* tolerable—that is, when the state that threatens to emerge into the foreground and shape consciousness is not recognizable as oneself. Such a state of being is *not-me* (Bromberg, 1998, 2006; D. B. Stern, 2003, 2004; Sullivan, 1953/1940), and in ordinary life it exists only in dissociation, apart from what feels like *me*.[1] Not-me has never had access to consciousness, and in its dissociated state it has never been symbolized: It is unformulated (D. B. Stern, 1997), a vaguely defined organization of experience, a primitive, global, nonideational affective state. It does not exist within the self because it has never been allowed to congeal into one of self's states. We can say it this way: Not-me *would be* a self-state if it were to move into the foreground of experience. But if that were to happen, not-me would not *feel* like me. The experience would be intolerable; and so not-me remains dissociated. I *must* not, *cannot* be not-me. The threatened eruption of not-me into awareness jeopardizes my sense of being the person I am. In both my own work on dissociation and the work of Philip Bromberg (1998, 2006), not-me has never been formulated; dissociated experience has that quality in common with conceptions such as Bion's (1962, 1963) *beta* functioning and *beta* elements and Green's (2000) nonrepresentation.[2]

Not-me originates as a response to unbearable fear or humiliation, the experience of having been the object of a powerful other's sadism. It is the sense that one is once again that stricken person: terrorized and terrified, sometimes to the point of immobility or helpless, destructive rage; contemptible, sometimes to the point of a self-loathing that yearns for the destruction of self or other; shamed and horrified, sometimes to the point of losing the desire to live or creating the desire to kill; weak, sometimes to the point of a shameful and utterly helpless surrender that feels as if it can

---

[1] "Me" and "not-me" are ideas more substantial than their colloquial names might suggest to those unfamiliar with their long history in the literature of Interpersonal psychoanalysis. The terms were devised by Harry Stack Sullivan (1940) as a means of representing the parts of the personality that exist within the boundaries of what is accepted as self ("me") and what is dissociated from self ("not-me"). The contemporary literature of dissociation, primarily the last twenty years of work by Philip Bromberg (collected in volumes published in 1998 and 2006; see also Chefetz and Bromberg, 2004), has lent the ideas new life. Recently they have also played a central role in my own thinking. See also this book, Chapters 3, 4, 6–8.

[2] As in the case of beta elements and nonrepresentation, dissociated material cannot be addressed by traditional defensive operations because the dissociated has not attained symbolic form: "Unformulated material is experience which has never been articulated clearly enough to allow application of the traditional defensive operations. One can forget or distort only those experiences which are formed with a certain degree of clarity in the first place. The unformulated has not yet reached the level of differentiation at which terms like memory and distortion are meaningful" (D. B. Stern, 1983, p. 73).

be prevented only by suicide or held at bay only by committing mayhem. One *will* not, *can*not be this person, because when one was, life was not bearable; and yet, if not-me enters consciousness, one *is* that person.

Every personality harbors not-me, although of course the degree of trauma that has been suffered by different people varies enormously. The impact it would have for not-me to emerge into awareness and become "real" depends on the severity of trauma and the consequent degree to which not-me is vicious, loathsome, terrifying, terrified, or abject, and the degree to which the whole personality is unstable and vulnerable. For those who have suffered severe trauma and whose vulnerability is therefore unmanageable, the eruption of not-me can be catastrophic, provoking massive affective dysregulation or psychotic decompensation. For those who are less troubled, the consequence is nevertheless awful enough to be avoided.

Enactment: An Illustration

When not-me is evoked by the events of clinical process, continuous unfolding is replaced by some variety of enactment. In the following example, for heuristic purposes I describe more about both my own experience and the patient's than I knew as the interaction was taking place.

My patient was late, and I was taking advantage of the extra minutes to have a snack. When the patient arrived, I was enjoying what I was eating and wanted to finish it, and it therefore took me a few seconds longer to get to the waiting room than it would have if I had simply been waiting in my chair. The patient was standing there, waiting for me, when I got to the waiting room. He had not sat down, which I took as a sign that he was eager to come in. Perhaps I should not have allowed myself my little delay. I was faced with a small incident of my selfishness. In a defensive attempt to avoid self-criticism (an insight available only in retrospect), I said implicitly to myself, without words, "Well, for heaven's sake, the patient was late. What's wrong with using the time as I see fit?" But I was aware of greeting the patient without my customary warmth.

The patient, because of his relationship with his demanding and easily disappointed father, has an intense vulnerability to humiliation. The experience of being snubbed (my lackluster reception) made him worry (*sub rosa*) that he was a burden or a disappointment to me, thereby threatening the eruption into awareness of not-me. In the patient's mind, my greeting confirmed what he feared: My contempt was leaking; I had tolerated him up to now only because he paid me. The secret was out. He had always had to contend with the danger of being a loathsome, contemptible boy, and he must not, could not, be that boy.

What happens at such a juncture? My patient had to do whatever was possible to avoid the eruption of contemptible not-me in awareness. His usual defensive maneuvers were of no use now; the danger was upon him. In our prior work, I had been quite careful to respect his vulnerabilities, but I had momentarily failed in that respect in greeting him as I had. In the past, the patient had also defended himself by (unconsciously) influencing the relatedness with me, making sure never to disappoint or provoke me, and thereby avoiding any possibility of facing this kind of stark "evidence" of my contempt for him. But his usual ways could not help him now.

The last-ditch defense, when not-me is imminent, is the interpersonalization of the dissociation, or enactment: "*I* am not contemptible, *you* are contemptible." The patient now claimed that most of the time, when I seemed authentically interested, I had been merely pretending. I hadn't really cared—that was now clear for the first time. Other therapists didn't pretend as I had; they really did get to know and care about their patients. My patient began to cite moments from the past that he now believed lent credence to the interpretation that I just was not very good at my job, that I should have chosen a field in which my limitations would not have hurt those I served.

I struggled with my affective response to being the object of contempt, feeling unhappy, hurt, and on the verge of anger. I was feeling the very shame that the patient was so eager to avoid. But I was nowhere near such understanding at this moment, and I said something (I don't remember exactly what it was) that protested my innocence. I knew that I sounded defensive.

This situation could have moved in either of two directions at this point. In one scenario, I come to terms with my own affective reaction to the patient and tolerate it. Under those circumstances, following my defensive reaction, I would grope toward a therapeutically facilitative response to the patient, although such a response probably would not occur immediately after the patient's provocation, because anyone's initial response to an accusation is likely to be defensive. This is actually what happened in this case, and I will tell that part of the story just below. But it is also common in this kind of situation, when the analyst is seriously threatened, for the patient's enactment of a dissociated state to call out a dissociated, or not-me, state *in the analyst*. A *mutual* enactment ensues. With my patient, such a scenario might have looked like this: In the same way the patient has begun to feel that it is not *he* who is contemptible but *I*, I now succumb (even if I "know better," which of course I usually do) to the strongly felt sense that *I* am not doing anything problematic—it's just that *the patient* is impossibly sadistic. I will almost undoubtedly feel uncomfortable in this position, probably guilty about being a bad analyst, but I will see no way out of it for the time being. Mutual enactments, which are not as uncommon as the traditional psychoanalytic literature might be read to suggest, may go on over significant periods and often pose a genuine threat to the treatment (D. B. Stern, 2003, 2004, 2008).

Enactment, Witnessing, and Narrative

Thinking in narrative terms reveals that enactment of either kind—that is, either with or without the dissociative participation of the analyst—is even more than the unconsciously motivated inability of the patient or analyst to see each other clearly and fully. As enactment rigidifies the clinical relatedness, it also interrupts each person's capacity to serve as witness for the other. Even if the analyst does not respond with a reciprocal dissociation, in other words, the patient loses, at least temporarily, the capacity to allow the analyst to be his partner in thought. The patient also temporarily loses the desire, and probably the capacity, to be the analyst's partner. When the analyst *does* respond with a reciprocal dissociation, of course, the situation is both more troubled and more difficult to remedy. In either case, the effortless, unbidden creation of narrative that went on during continuous productive unfolding now grinds to a halt.

One way to define states of self is as narratives: Each state is an ever-changing story. Or rather, as I have already suggested, because self-states are not simply experiences or memories, but aspects of identity, each state is an aspect of self defined by the stories that can be told from within it. Our freedom to tell many self-stories at once—in other words, our freedom to inhabit multiple states of being simultaneously—is what gives to the stories that express the ways we know ourselves and others the plasticity to change with circumstances. The many states that compose "me" not only participate in shaping the circumstances of my life, but are, in the process, themselves reshaped. This continuous interchange and renewal is the hallmark of the self-states that make up "me."

But not-me cannot be told. Not-me remains insistently, stubbornly, defensively unformulated, not yet shaped or storied at all, isolated, existing in dissociation and thereby rendered mute. This is the situation within enactments, both solitary and mutual: neither analyst nor patient knows how to narrate the significance of what is transpiring; neither knows the meaning of the transaction nor the feelings and perceptions that make it up. And so those events remain coded only in procedural terms, in action. If not-me is to come within our capacity to tell, then me, the self of the dissociator, must somehow expand to accommodate or contact it.

I continue now with the events that actually took place with my patient. I felt defensive and ashamed in reaction to the patient's accusations. My defensiveness was apparent to me and, I told myself, probably to my patient; but I did not respond with a reciprocal dissociation of my own. I pulled myself together and said something on this order: "I was taken by surprise by what you said [the patient's accusations against me]—I didn't know where that was coming from. But now I'm asking myself if the way you felt might have to do with something you sensed during the last session, or when you came in today. Did you notice something I said or did? Because I did. This may not be the important thing, but I did notice that I didn't greet you as I usually do." Despite my reaction to the patient's accusations, in other words, I was able to consider the possibility that I might have played a role in setting the patient's complaints in motion. In this context, at least, I was able to conduct an inquiry without succumbing to an answering dissociation and enactment. I did not shut down the narrative possibilities, in other words, as the patient had no choice but to do from within his own dissociative process, but instead returned to being curious, relatively open to whatever emerged in my mind.

Neither the patient's dissociation nor his enactment was particularly rigid as these things go, although the situation certainly might have moved in that direction if I had failed to gain a perspective on my own reaction and remained defensive. But I was fortunate in this case, because, sensing that I was no longer threatened, the patient showed some interest in my foray. But he was still suspicious, and he said, "Well, but then why did you get defensive?" referring to what I said in response to his accusations. I answered, again from within my relocated stability, that I did believe that I had been defensive, and that it is often hard for anyone not to be defensive in the face of strong criticism.

The patient softened and (to my surprise, to tell the truth) seemed to begin to search himself for something that might be responsive to what I had said. He eventually was able to say that my greeting had indeed stung him. The atmosphere cooled further. The patient had little difficulty now in seeing that my defensiveness could be understood, from within my perspective, as a response to his own critical remarks. More important, the patient had now lived through an episode in which his brief certainty that he was a burden to me, and that my caring was inauthentic, was disconfirmed. This was not primarily a cognitive signification for him. The patient could *feel* or *sense* what it was like for me to be with him through the course of his accusations. That was important; but more important yet was that the patient felt for one of the first times the confidence that I had felt hurt or angry with him without losing track of my warm feelings about him (or losing track of them only very temporarily). In a small but crucial way, the patient was now someone other than he had been. Over the following months, other new experiences of this kind opened in front of him because his growing confidence in my openness to his experience and my own made it possible for him to begin to listen imaginatively through my ears to his own feelings of being a burden; and in the process, those experiences gained substance and reality for him, on the one hand, and became less shameful and more bearable, on the other. Stories about these things emerged in his mind with increasing frequency, some of them articulate and others implicit. Over time, not-me became me. For my part, through my experience of my reaction to his stinging criticism, I also became more able to witness the patient; and beyond that, I came to depend in a new way on the patient's capacity to witness me—the way, for example, he eventually accepted my reactions to his criticisms.

Dissociations are not breached by insight, nor are enactments dissolved through verbal understanding. Interpretation is not the analyst's key intervention. Enactments end as a result of a change in affect and relatedness, which provokes a change in each participant's perceptions (and stories) of the other and himself (See Chapters 3, 4, 6, and 8). Insight into this changed state of affairs, when it plays a role, comes later. Historical reconstruction often does take place after the appearance of the new story, and it can be quite helpful. But therapeutic action lies in becoming a different person, usually in a small way, in the here and now. The expansion of the self takes place in the present, in small increments. As enactment recedes, the treatment moves back into continuous productive unfolding, and new narratives once again begin to appear unbidden in the analytic space. The new stories my patient and I have told as the treatment has moved on have been more and more often about the contemptible little boy.

Returning to the Castaways

But if the analyst is so crucial to the patient, how do we understand Robinson Crusoe and the shrinking man? They had no analytic relationship, no relationships of any kind. (Crusoe did eventually have Friday, but that was years into his saga.) Now it may be clearer why I claimed earlier that enforced isolation makes these characters such good illustrations of my thesis. Their creators' suggestion that the characters grew and changed despite their circumstances is not mistaken, nor is it by any means a refutation of the point that we are profoundly social beings. On the contrary, such stories could not demonstrate the necessity of witnessing more clearly than they do. It seems likely, actually, that some kind of imaginary witness is invoked in all tales of enforced isolation, real and imaginary.

In the movie *Cast Away*, the character played by Tom Hanks, alone and shipwrecked on an island, finds a soccer ball floating in the surf, paints a face on it, and begins to talk to it, using the conversation as a kind of ironic commentary to himself on the matter of his own loneliness. He calls the ball "Wilson," after the name of the sporting goods company that made it. But as the years pass, irony turns delusionally earnest, and Wilson eventually becomes the castaway's dear friend, continuous companion, and confidant. Years after that, the shipwrecked man escapes from the island on board a raft he has made himself. In the calm that comes after a storm at sea, and dying of thirst and exposure, he sees that Wilson, whom he had tethered to the mast for protection, has fallen off and is drifting away from him across the swells. The movie's one truly devastating moment comes when the castaway sees that in his weakened state he cannot rescue his "friend" without losing the raft and drowning, and he calls out piteously after the swiftly disappearing Wilson, pleading for forgiveness.

Let me offer one last example, just to put it on the record that factuality reflects castaways' need for a witness just as well as fiction does. I recently read a dreadful story in the *New York Times* (Onishi, 2007) about a man in Tokyo so poor that he had not eaten in weeks and so alone that no one either knew or cared. In his last days he kept a diary. Among the last entries before his death from starvation was his expression of the wish for a rice ball, a snack sold in convenience stores across Japan for about a dollar: "3 a.m. This human being hasn't eaten in 10 days but is still alive. I want to eat rice. I want to eat a rice ball." The very fact that the diarist wrote at all testifies to his imagination of an audience. But note also that he speaks of himself in the third person. Is it credible that he would have done that if he really imagined that he was addressing only himself? Could there be a more eloquent expression of the need to listen through the ears of the other? It was preserved even as this man was dying.

To know what our experience is, to think and feel, we need to tell the stories of our lives, and we need to tell them to someone to whom they matter, listening to ourselves as we do the telling. If we have to make up our audience, so be it. Our need for a witness goes so deep that imaginary witnesses must sometimes suffice.

Witnessing One's Self

We are familiar with the idea of internal conversation between parts of ourselves. If we can hold an internal conversation, can one part of ourselves serve as a witness for another? We have seen that Richman (2006) believes so. Laub (1992a, 1992b, 2005; Laub & Auerhahn, 1989) does too. He suggests that massive psychic trauma, because it damages the processes of association, symbolization, and narrative formation, also leads to an absence of inner dialogue, curiosity, reflection, and self-reflection. And what does Laub believe is responsible for this inner devastation? He says it is the annihilation of the internal good object, the "internal empathic other" (Laub & Auerhahn, 1989), partner in inner dialogue and narrative construction. Laub (1992b) tells the story of Menachem S., a castaway of sorts, a little boy placed in a labor camp who somehow managed to survive the Holocaust and, miraculously, to find his parents afterward. He had spent the war talking and praying to a photograph of his mother that he kept with him. "Mother indeed had promised to come and take him back after the war, and not for a moment did he doubt that promise" (p. 87). But the mother and father he refound, "haggard and emaciated, in striped uniforms, with teeth hanging loose in their gums" (p. 88), were not the parents he had maintained in his memory. Mother was "different, disfigured, not identical to herself" (p. 91). Having survived the war, the boy now fell apart. Laub writes, "I read this story to mean that in regaining his real mother, he inevitably loses the internal witness he had found in her image" (p. 88).

Richman's (2006) experience is once again germane. Here she describes the inner presence to whom she wrote during the time she was working on her own memoir (2002) of her childhood as a hidden child during the Holocaust:

> The internalized other (the projected reader) was an amorphous presence without distinguishing characteristics, but seemed to be an interested observer, a witness, someone who wanted to know more about me and my life. Perhaps the amorphous presence represented my mother, my first reader-listener, who lived to hear my school papers and received my writing with unwavering admiration. (p. 645)

Something on this order is what happened for the castaways I have cited, for the toddlers in their cribs, for all of us, much of the time, day to day. And so we see that the experience of the castaways is hardly unique; it is what we all do routinely. It is the castaways' enforced isolation, as a matter of fact, that throws the process of witnessing into high relief.

But just as Laub's internal empathic other can be destroyed by trauma, we cease to be able to invoke the imaginary internal witness as soon as the experience we must witness touches on parts of us that hurt or scare us too badly to acknowledge, or that are injured in a way so central to our makeup that awareness of them threatens the remainder of the personality. The imaginary internal witness becomes unavailable, in other words, when the one who must be witnessed is not-me. And yet this is precisely the part of us that, if we are to grow, we must somehow learn to bear and to know. In such cases it is crucial to have a witness outside our own minds. In such cases we not only profit from seeing a psychoanalyst, we need one.

Final Thoughts

The psychoanalytic accounts of narrative with which we are most familiar (Schafer, 1983, 1992; Spence, 1982) are written as if the stories themselves are what matter. Problems in living are portrayed as the outcome of telling defensively motivated stories of our lives that deaden or distort experience, or of skewing experience by rigidly selecting one particular account. Therapeutic action revolves around the creation, through objective interpretation based on the analyst's preferred theory, of new and better stories—more inclusive, more coherent, more suited to their purpose. In the accounts of narrative by Schafer and Spence, while there is room for a good deal of flexibility in the way the analyst works, clinical psychoanalysis is defined by its technique, and its technique, in one way or another, is defined by the way interpretation is employed.

Schafer (1992) believes that psychoanalytic clinical work is very much like text interpretation. This "text" is both "interpenetrated" and "cohabited" by patient and analyst. But it remains a text. Consider what the analyst does with the patient who "talks back" (i.e., the patient who tells the analyst what he thinks of the analyst's interpretive offerings):

> [T]he analyst treats the analysand in the same manner that many literary critics treat authors—with interest in what the analysand says about the aims of his or

> her utterances and choices, but with an overall attitude of autonomous critical
> command rather than submission or conventional politeness, and with a readi-
> ness to view these explanatory comments as just so much more prose to be both
> heard as such *and* interpreted. (p. 176)

It is hardly controversial for a psychoanalyst to claim that what the patient says often has meanings that the patient does not know. But there now exists a substantial body of literature that does take issue with the claim that an analyst can *ever* adopt "an overall attitude of autonomous criti-cal command" (e.g., Bromberg, 1998, 2006; Hoffman, 1998; Mitchell, 1993, 1997; Pizer, 1998; Renik, 1993; D. B. Stern, 1997). This large group of writers, most of whom identify themselves as Relational or Interpersonal analysts, takes the position that the relationship of patient and analyst is one of continuous, mutual unconscious influence. Neither the patient *nor* the analyst has privileged access to the meanings of his or her own experience.

This is the broad perspective within which the view developed in this chapter belongs. Although it remains undeniable that refashioned narra-tives change lives, the source of this change is the patient's newfound free-dom to experience, an expansion of the self, created through events of the clinical interaction that are only partially under our conscious control. It is not so much that we learn the truth, but that we become more than we were. Our greatest clinical accomplishments are neither interpreta-tions nor the stories they convey, but the broadening of the range within which analyst and patient become able to serve as each other's witnesses. This new recognition of each by the other is a product of the resolution of enactments and the dissociations that underlie them, and the resulting capacity of analyst and patient to inhabit more fully each other's experi-ence, to listen more frequently through each other's ears. As dissociation and enactment recede, patient and analyst once again become partners in thought, and now the breadth of their partnering has grown.

Instead of thinking of narrative as a consciously purposeful construc-tion, we should recast it as something on the order of a self-organizing system, in which outcomes are unpredictable and nonlinear (e.g., Galatzer-Levy, 2004; Thelen & Smith, 1994). Clinical process is the medium—or to use the language of nonlinear systems theory, the event space—within which narrative stagnates, grows, and changes: The destabilization of old narratives and the emergence of new ones are the outcomes of unpredict-able relational events. I hope I have explained my perspective well enough by now to substantiate the claim I made at the beginning: New narratives in psychoanalysis are the emergent, co-constructed, and unbidden products of clinical process.

Without denying for an instant the necessity for careful conceptualization or clinical discipline, I intend what I have said to serve as an argument against the claim that clinical psychoanalysis can be defined by any specification of technique. Psychoanalysis is, rather, a very particular way that one person can be of use to another, a way that depends on our possession of common practices but also on our awareness that those practices are often inadequate to the experience that makes up our immersion in clinical process. For the analyst who believes that the recognition and resolution of enactments is central to clinical psychoanalysis, the personal is unavoidably linked with the professional, a point that reinforces something we have known at least since the work of Racker (1968): If the patient is to change, the analyst must change as well. In the end we find, as is so often the case, that when the mind is locked, relationship is the key.

6

Shall the Twain Meet? Metaphor, Dissociation, and Co-occurrence

The Meaning of Metaphor

The American Heritage Dictionary (2000) offers this definition of metaphor:

1. A figure of speech in which a word or phrase that ordinarily designates one thing is used to designate another, thus making an implicit comparison, as in *"a sea of troubles"* or *"All the world's a stage"* (Shakespeare).
2. One thing conceived as representing another; a symbol: *"Hollywood has always been an irresistible, prefabricated metaphor for the crass, the materialistic, the shallow, and the craven"* (Neal Gabler, *New York Times Book Review* November 23, 1986).

From this definition, especially from its second part, we might almost conclude that metaphor is synonymous with symbolic function. That is certainly not the meaning most of us were taught in school. We tend to think of metaphor in the terms of the first definition only, the tamer and less expansive of the two: metaphor as a figure of speech, a purely linguistic phenomenon.

But it turns out that matters are not that simple today, not since the claims of Lakoff and Johnson (1980, 1999; see also Modell, 2003, who has done much to bring this work to psychoanalysis), who have revolutionized our understanding of metaphor and its place in cognition. For over 25 years, these writers have been making a strong case for the view that, far from being a mere figure of speech, metaphor lies right at the heart of thought.

Lakoff and Johnson characterize metaphor, surprisingly enough, as a phenomenon of the body. The most basic metaphors, the "primary metaphors" from which all the others are derived, are based in universal bodily experiences, especially those of infancy and childhood. Certain bodily experiences are inevitably linked to certain other experiences best described as affective and cognitive, resulting in "cross-domain conceptual mapping," or the linking of "subjective experience" (thoughts and feelings) with sensorimotor experience.

In Lakoff and Johnson's view, thought begins with the primary metaphors and builds from there, with ever more complex metaphors being constructed on the basis of the metaphor-saturated experience that has come before. Actually, to say that experience is saturated with metaphor is only half the story. It is true as far as it goes; but for Lakoff and Johnson metaphor is also the very structure of experience.

When two thoughts, meanings, or perceptions are identified simultaneously, the possibility of representing or symbolizing one of them by reference to the other comes about. Generally we call this phenomenon association, as in the sense of safety I feel when I think of the scent of anise cookies baking in my grandmother's kitchen. Thereafter, without any thought of my grandmother, the smell of anise provokes the same feelings. Anise, that is, comes to represent comfort and safety. Lakoff and Johnson (1999) write that the meaning (comfort and safety) is *mapped onto* the sensual experience (the smell of anise), forever thereafter lending meaning to the odor. This mapping is generally unidirectional, though: Although I inevitably feel safety and comfort when I smell anise, the feeling of safety or comfort makes me think of the scent of anise only if attention is drawn to the connection (e.g., "When you think of that feeling of safety, is there any particular scent that comes to mind?").

Lakoff and Johnson's explanation for the rise of the most basic metaphors, which they believe are universal and body-based and arise very early in the lives of all people, regardless of culture, rests on the same kind of simultaneity of the metaphor's terms that, in my own smaller and more personal context, made the smell of anise a metaphor for comfort. Consider just two of the primary metaphors (here summarized and paraphrased from Lakoff and Johnson [1999, p. 50]):

1. Affection is warmth: The subjective judgment of affection is repeatedly paired with the sensorimotor judgment of warmth because babies feel warm while being held affectionately. The affective experience is mapped onto the sensorimotor event, so that it makes sense for us to say "They greeted me warmly," for instance.

2. Important is big: The subjective judgment of importance or significance is repeatedly paired with the sensorimotor judgment of size because babies and children find "that big things, e.g., parents, are important and can exert major forces on you and dominate your visual experience," so that it makes sense, for instance, to say that, "Tomorrow is a big day." That is, when we think of important, we think of big.

Notice that in these examples, as in my example, the affect (what Lakoff and Johnson call the subjective judgment) is mapped onto an experience in the sensorimotor domain, resulting in a unidirectional symbolic process. The feeling of affection evokes the feeling of warmth, and the sense of importance evokes the perception of size, but the reverse does not occur: Large size does not automatically evoke the sense of importance, and higher temperatures do not evoke the feeling of affection.[1]

Transfer and Transference

Here is what we read about the etymology of the word "metaphor," from the same definition in *The American Heritage Dictionary*:

> Middle English *methaphor*, from Old French *metaphore*, from Latin *metaphora*, from Greek, transference, metaphor, from *metapherein*, to transfer : *meta-*, meta- + *pherein*, to carry.

---

[1] The work of Lakoff and Johnson is important for psychoanalysts for a number of reasons, only one of which has to do with a reevaluation of the significance of metaphor. Another contribution made by these authors is to offer a way of theorizing all experience to be based in the body (the title of their 1999 book is *Philosophy in the Flesh: The Embodied Mind and Its Challenge to Western Thought*) without resorting to a drive concept. However, as much as I appreciate their thinking and its potential contribution to psychoanalysis, I do not share their epistemological stance. It is true, in one respect, that Lakoff and Johnson do away with objectivism. They take the position that truth cannot exist in objective form in the world outside our minds because much of what we call truth, even most of it, is created in the shapes of the metaphors that we think with. The mind therefore has at least as much to do with shaping what we take to be truth as the "objective world" does. In fact, it does not make sense to refer to "the world outside our minds," because mind and world are a unity. This far I can go, and even appreciate. I am thoroughly in agreement with Lakoff and Johnson's critique of Cartesianism. But Lakoff and Johnson end up replacing one objectivism with another. They present their theory of metaphor as the new objective truth, one more theory meant to supplant those that have gone before. The problem of endlessly overturning one "objective truth" and substituting another is precisely what inspired the insights of hermeneutics and postmodernism. Given their presentation of their theory of metaphor as the new truth, it is not surprising that Lakoff and Johnson explicitly challenge postmodern, constructivist views.

It seems that "metaphor" has come full circle. We learn from this definition that the origins of the word lie in the transfer or the "carrying" of meaning; if we listen to Lakoff and Johnson, it has arrived back at those origins. Isn't the mapping of one meaning onto another a kind of transfer, or carrying over? "Mapping" has a certain precision in Lakoff and Johnson's usage, but for psychoanalytic purposes, because "transfer" evokes "transference," I prefer it to "mapping," as in "a metaphor is created when the substance of one meaning is transferred to another."

It seems to me that there exists a very interesting relationship between transference and metaphor. Think of what we used to refer to as "psychotic transference," which is not a symbolic or metaphorical process at all, but an insistence that two people are identical and therefore interchangeable: My analyst *is* my father; no other interpretation will do. Clinical relatedness is much more viable, of course, if the transference is (again in the old-school term) "neurotic": I feel that my analyst is *like* my father, but I continue to recognize that analyst and father are separate. Transference is clinically useful when its meaning is metaphorical; transference is problematic, on the other hand, when it is a literal equivalence. This point seems straightforward enough, but it breaks down into greater complexity when it is closely examined.

In order to feel *as if* my father is my analyst, I must feel that the two people are alike in some key respect. In other words, the as-if kind of transference requires me to have created a *category* in which father and analyst both belong. But the creation of a category is based on more than the identification of similarities between its items; a category is also defined by its items' differences from one another. Without differences to separate the members of a category, the grouping would not be a category at all, but would instead simply collapse back into equivalences. The differences between the items in a category serve as the context that makes their similarities meaningful. It seems that metaphor and category bear a significant relationship to each other.

Modell on Metaphor and Category

Arnold Modell (1990, 2003), who has made a pioneering effort in bringing contemporary thought about metaphor into psychoanalysis, recognized the relationship between metaphor and category in the course of thinking through a new way of understanding the old idea of complexes. "A 'complex,'" he wrote in 2003, looking back at his earlier work of 1990, "can be defined as an organized group of ideas and memories of great affective force that are either partly or totally unconscious." Modell took the position that it is metaphor that "organizes emotional memory. Inasmuch as category formation is an aspect of memory, metaphor provides the link between emotional memory and current perceptions" (2003, p. 41). There occurs the recognition, in other words, that something in the past bears a meaningful relationship to something in the present. This link creates what is essentially a category. Then comes the linchpin of the argument:

> A similarity based on a metaphoric correspondence is the means through which emotional categories are formed. Unconscious emotional memories exist as *potential* categories, which, in the process of retrieval, are associatively linked to events in the here and now by means of metaphor and metonymy. (pp. 41–42)[1]

We know from Lakoff and Johnson (1999) that metaphor—one meaning standing for another—is created by the simultaneity of two experiences. When a memory and a present experience occur simultaneously in our minds, a meaningful link may be established between them. It is in this way that metaphoric correspondence is at the same time the creation of an emotional category.

Modell also tells us that trauma can make it impossible for the sufferer to situate memories of the traumatic past in the context of the present, resulting in the familiar concreteness or literalness about the past that clinicians see every day in the experience of those who have been traumatized and in the inability of these people to integrate past and present. Modell writes that, in the experience of many trauma sufferers, "*It can be said that the metaphoric process was foreclosed or frozen*" (p. 41; emphasis in the original). In trauma, that is, the past exists as a concrete record and cannot be contextualized in the present. Note that this drains meaning from the present because the present cannot be enriched by association

---

[1] Metaphor and metonymy are two forms of symbolic representation. In metaphor, one object or concept stands for another. It is immaterial whether the two items bore any meaningful relation to each other prior to being incorporated in the metaphor, and so, if one does not know why the two terms came together, metaphor often appears arbitrary, like anise and comfort. Metonymy differs from metaphor in that the two experiences, objects, or concepts are meaningfully related prior to becoming part of the metonym. Usually the thing that is symbolized subsumes the thing that serves as the symbol, as in "Soldiers serve the flag" (a national flag stands for the entire country); or "The king has the scepter" (scepter stands for sovereignty). Metonymic relations result in categories in the same way that metaphoric ones do, but because their terms must bear a prior relationship to one another, metonymy is a less flexible means of symbolization. The mere temporal coincidence of the terms, what I will call "co-occurrence" later in this chapter, is sufficient to create the potential for metaphor.

with some portion of the past. But the foreclosing of metaphor also drains meaning from the past—or rather, from the reconstructions of the past we undertake on the basis of what we learn and experience in the present, a process analogous to what Freud (1895, 1918) called deferred action, or *Nachträglichkeit*. The "frozen" (Modell's word) metaphoric process, that is, dooms the past to be frozen, as well, because a frozen aspect of the past cannot be reformulated in a way that allows it to serve present purposes. A frozen memory in that sense is a "thing-in-itself," a concretization that cannot contribute to future meaning, rather like what Bion means by a *beta* element.

I take Modell's "unconscious emotional memories," which he describes as "potential emotional categories," to be exactly the kind of experience we see in psychotic transference. Such experience remains isolated. It cannot become part of a category. And so one cannot relate to it in a way that would make it possible to know it; one cannot reflect on it. In order to know or reflect, one must be able to feel something that would be put into words as some version of, "Oh, yes, that was one of the times that I felt (or did or thought, etc.) …" or "Oh, yes, that was like the feeling I had when …". To relate to an experience as an experience of a certain *kind*, a member of a certain emotionally defined category, in other words, is what allows us to *reflect on* that experience. As in the case of transference, the very belongingness of the experience to the category allows us to appreciate its uniqueness. If an experience cannot belong to a category, as trauma cannot, if it must exist in isolation, as a concretization, a "singularity," it must remain a thing-in-itself and cannot be cognized, known, or felt. It seems, then, that the process of creating associative links between otherwise separate experiences is crucial to psychic growth.

Metaphor and Witness

If a tree falls in the forest with no one to hear, does it make a sound? It creates vibrations in the air, yes, but to make a sound it must be heard; and it cannot be heard unless there is a witness to hear it.

The same is true in the rest of life: Without a witness, no experience can be "heard." We are familiar with this point in the case of trauma: Before she herself can feel trauma as real experience, the traumatized person either needs another person to know what she has gone through and care about it, or needs to be able to imagine such a person (e.g.,

Felman & Laub, 1992; Laub, 1995). To be truly alone with experience, to be able to imagine no one who cares about it, is to be unable to make emotional sense of it.

But one can be truly alone in the presence of another, even in the presence of one willing and able to witness. We cannot allow someone to witness unless we feel safe enough in their presence (again, the presence may be real or imagined—see Chapter 5) to be able to allow a relationship between different parts of ourselves. We must be able to take two vantage points at once, one of them the traumatic experience and the other something else, another kind of experience that relates to the trauma, but that is nevertheless different. We must be able to contextualize the traumatic experience, in other words, either with other memories with which it has something in common or with aspects of the present that resonate with it. The trauma must become part of a metaphor or an item in a category. Only when we know the experience as our own in this way, which requires that the interpersonal field feel emotionally safe and responsive enough that we can let ourselves *think*, and think freely, can the other successfully witness the experience and thereby help us make it real. And this, of course, is the problem with some survivors of trauma: How can they find their way to safety in the presence of the other? The other's willing responsiveness is necessary, but not necessarily sufficient, and the traumatized often have no idea how to make it so. For that matter, the traumatized often have little reason to *want* to make it so.

When trauma becomes part of metaphor, we become able to sense it as a figure against a ground. To begin to feel trauma as our own and to know it as part of our lives, we must be able to see it against parts of life similar enough to be recognizable, yet different enough to remain separate. If we cannot do this, we remain distant from the pain and the meaning. We may be able to offer a factual account of the events, but the feelings and the part they play in our story remain unformulated, unconscious.

Witnessing is prevented by the enactments that take place in any treatment, such as the one in the clinical vignette presented below, because the emotional atmosphere of enactments, by definition, does not feel safe. The participants in an enactment are unlikely to be emotionally responsive to one another in the way witnessing requires. The rigidities of enactment, we shall see, can be defined as singularities, each participant locked into a particular set of perceptions of the other and himself. Enactment is not only a rigid kind of relatedness but also the absence of metaphorical thought.

Metaphor and Dissociation

Metaphor and category do not come ready-made; they are products. What comprises their raw material then? Where do metaphors come from? Why, in other words, do associative links happen at all?

I have already mentioned Lakoff and Johnson's (1999) simple answer: simultaneity. Whenever two experiences take place at the same time, there is the potential for the meaning of one to be mapped onto, or transferred to, the meaning of the other, as in "The scent of anise reminds me of safety and comfort."

I have been making the point for many years (D. B. Stern, 1983, 1989, 1991, 1997) that the experience that feels most as if it belongs to us arrives in our minds unbidden. Even if we know better, it feels as if we do not create the unbidden. It feels more as if we allow it—and even then, this "allowing" is not something we can become aware of doing. We feel instead as if we are conduits for the unbidden. We do not know what we do to make it happen, but we do learn (when we believe that we can bear whatever will come to us) to stay out of the way of its creation. Lakoff and Johnson's simultaneity account dovetails nicely with this bit of phenomenology. Simultaneity, like unbidden experience, is something that happens *to* us, after all. It is like high tide, depositing in our minds collections of things that we might never otherwise think to put together.[1] To the degree that we are able to allow our minds freedom—that is, to the extent that we are, in the deepest sense, curious—we mine this flotsam, mostly nonconsciously, for useful co-occurrences of meaning, and then we allow those to percolate and develop into experience that it becomes appropriate to call metaphor.

Lakoff and Johnson do not try to address the active, nonconscious imagination that selects only the most meaningful co-occurrences. Nor do they address the possibility that this selection process ought to be as effective in *rejecting* our awareness of co-occurrences as it is in accepting it.

---

[1] This expression is an approximation. Although we cannot control what our minds do, we can prepare ourselves by immersing ourselves in our field of study or practice, thereby making it more likely that the co-occurrences available to our minds are relevant to the problems we face.

In fact we know that the rejection of an awareness of co-occurrences, along with the potential metaphorical experience that could have developed from them, is routine. Think of what happens in the minds of trauma sufferers. Do we really think that the co-occurrences that would allow the past to be contextualized in the present do not happen in the lives of these people? Do we believe that these people never have the *opportunity* to link their traumatic memories with the present? Of course not. The co-occurrences happen all the time. What does not happen is *awareness* of these co-occurrences—metaphor. (Remember Modell's words: in the experience of trauma sufferers, "*the metaphoric process* [is] *foreclosed or frozen.*") Metaphor, in other words, is the actualization of the potential made available in co-occurrence.[1]

We need a word here to represent the prevention of actualization, the stunting or blocking of the process by which co-occurrence enters awareness and becomes metaphor. We do not have far to look. What we are describing is the prevention of the conscious connection, linking, or association of two experiences. The word we are looking for is *dissociation*.

Dissociation is conceived in more than one way. In the field of traumatology, starting with Pierre Janet (Ellenberger, 1970), dissociation represents the mind's fall-back operation, a desperation move that takes place automatically when all else fails, a nonvolitional shutdown that protects the mind from coming apart. In this usage, which is no doubt still the most widespread, dissociation is not employed actively, as an unconscious defensive operation. It happens to people; they suffer it passively.

The other contemporary usage of the term was inspired by the intersection of the first meaning with psychoanalysis. In this model, dissociation is an unconscious defensive process, an active process and not a passive one, and used in a much wider range of situations than those that are generally considered traumatic.2 In fact, from this perspective dissociation has supplanted repression as the primary defensive operation. The mind is therefore theorized not as a vertical organization of consciousness and unconsciousness, but as a horizontally organized collection of self-states, states of being, or states of mind, each in dynamic relation to the others.

---

[1] Metonymy, therefore, because it does not originate in co-occurrence, is apparently irrelevant to the line of thought I am developing about metaphor (see footnote 2).

[2] This line of work was pioneered by Harry Stack Sullivan (1940, 1954, 1956) and developed into a psychoanalytic perspective by Philip Bromberg (1998, 2006) and others (Bucci, 2007a, 2007b; Davies, 1996, 1997, 1998, 1999, 2004; Davies & Frawley, 1991, 1994; Howell, 2005; Mitchell, 1993; D. B. Stern, 1997, 2003, 2004, 2009).

Some states coexist comfortably—that is, from within some states, I can bear to feel that certain other states are also "me." From within a comfortable, self-assured state of being, for instance, although I may not like having to accept the part of me that tends to feel envious of others under certain circumstances, I can at least tolerate knowing and feeling that both are me. If I could not tolerate that knowing and feeling, the states would be dissociated, which would mean that they could not be experienced simultaneously and would remain sequestered from each other. From within the parts of my experience that I accept as me, the rejected part of my experience is alien to me. I cannot and will not tolerate its presence within what feels like it is mine. It is *not* me, or, in Sullivan's (1953/1940) term, "not-me." I am safe as long as that state is isolated and disconnected from the multitude of experiences that invoke *me*.[1]

And so when the actualization of co-occurences is blocked or prevented and metaphor does not emerge, it is not because a central, unitary self is unable to know the experience that would result if the metaphor came to life. The situation is more complicated than that. The reason metaphor is rejected is that the two experiences in question invoke states of self that are dissociated from each other. To accept the metaphor would require simultaneously accepting me and not-me. I would have to accept that I am what I cannot be, what I refuse to be. What is rejected, then, when metaphor is blocked, is not memory but a certain experience of who I am.

Clinical Illustration

Now I return to the topic of transference and countertransference and, as promised, to enactment. I present a long case vignette to illustrate the points I have made.

Two years ago, I began working with an unusually attractive, charming, socially adept, intelligent, and well-educated woman who, despite always having assumed that she would marry and have children, could not seem

---

[1] I have defined two kinds of dissociation: dissociation in the strong sense; and dissociation in the weak sense, passive dissociation, or narrative rigidity. For definitions of these terms, see D. B. Stern (1997, 2009) and this book, Chapter 1. In this chapter, I am using dissociation only in the first, "strong" sense. That usage means that what is defended against is actively and unconsciously rejected; it is specifically selected to remain unformulated for defensive reasons. In dissociation in the weak or passive sense, on the other hand, psychic material goes unformulated because we are so attached to creating our lives along the lines of a particular narrative that alternative meanings simply go unconsidered.

to make relationships take that direction. Now approaching the age of 40, she was worried about her future. To begin with, I was baffled at her lack of success, and despite myself, I began to wonder if perhaps her problem was that her positive attributes threatened most of the men she met. (I did not yet understand that she threatened me.) But this explanation did not seem to me to be a very good explanation, because it seemed unlikely that she could have threatened *all* the men she met. And besides, that interpretation would ignore whatever her own contribution might be. At this point, though, I could do no more than refer to "her contribution" in the abstract. Nevertheless, I pointed out to her, somewhat dutifully, that only if she could discover ways in which she was unconsciously creating and maintaining her own distress would there be realistic hope that she could change this part of her life.

Abstract principles hardly motivate people to enter psychoanalysis. That is doubly true for those patients, such as this woman, whose capacity for self-observation is limited. (I was later to find, happily, that this impression needed to be revised.) The analyst needs to be able to cite a concrete example of some way in which the patient unconsciously undermines herself. More than that, the analyst needs to believe the example he cites. With this woman, I could neither cite nor believe. I was struggling with the thoroughly nonrational perception that she was flawless. I knew better, of course. I was even able to refer back to the example of her lack of psychological mindedness as an illustration; but, unsurprisingly, I could not convince myself: The perception that dogged me was a feeling, not a reasonable perception. I did not yet see that her perfection was itself the point: She was like the perfect princess who lived at the top of the glass mountain. Like the suitors who tried to ride their horses up the mountain to reach the princess, I could find no point of purchase, no way to talk to her that would create some kind of sense of relatedness with her. It was easy for me to feel inadequate in her presence.

I was reduced to hashing and rehashing with her the end of the relationship that had finally brought her into treatment. She was in genuine pain about this, and she appreciated my suggestion that her pain was less about the man himself than about her worry that her hopes for the future were dimming fast. But this idea was hardly sufficient to carry the treatment. I could sense that, unless I found a way to help her deepen the work—which is to say, unless I found a way into a discussion of the less than perfect parts of her experience, but without shaming her about them—the treatment was going to end shortly. She would feel better, at least temporarily; and if I had nothing more to offer, she would leave.

I had ceased anticipating this patient's visits with pleasure soon after we had started meeting, and at this juncture, 2 or 3 months in, I was becoming quite familiar with the feeling that I was not a very competent analyst for her. My rehashing of her recent relationship seemed vapid, superficial, and intellectualized to me; and while it was not difficult for me to connect my feelings of inadequacy with her impenetrability, I also imagined, with moderate discomfort, that she agreed with my assessment of my efforts.

Actually, it is not true to say that I could observe nothing beyond this woman's perfection. I have mentioned being impressed with her impenetrability. I had also noticed the defensive quality of her continuous, brittle good cheer. She could cry about her pain, and she could be angry, but only if some objective situation in the outside world merited it. I had the sense that sadness or anger under any other circumstances would feel unjustifiable to her and would probably represent a weakness in her eyes. It would shame her. She could not be vulnerable to me, in other words, and I felt sure that I was not the only one with whom she felt this way. As a matter of fact, I imagined that this might be exactly the problem she was encountering in maintaining a romantic relationship. I could not just offer the patient that observation, though, not unless I had something to say that would help her make use of it in a way that did not potentiate the shame I could sense in the wings.

Time was running out. This was not a person who could discuss her frustration with the treatment or with me in a productive way. To do so would seem unacceptably hostile to her, rather like criticizing her marvelous parents (one of many attitudes that had made it difficult to get the treatment moving). Or rather, even if she *were* able and willing to talk about her frustration, it would do her no good unless I could say something that would give that frustration a different or broader meaning than it had now, something that would bring some life into the work for her. If I could not do that, then talking about her frustration would simply be a prelude to her departure.

And so one day, having failed to come up with the perfect (!) interpretation and with the time left in the treatment swiftly draining away, I took a deep breath and stumbled into an attempt to say something authentic to this woman about my reaction to her presentation of herself. I did not know where I was going or exactly what I would say when I got there. I talked to her for a couple of minutes about feeling that there must be parts of her that she was not pleased about, that maybe she didn't even like, because everyone has parts like that. Yet (I told her), I didn't seem to be able to get to know her that way. I told her that I felt she was having a very hard time being vulnerable with me, letting me really know her. I told her that, while vulnerability could be uncomfortable for anyone, I thought it must be particularly uncomfortable for her. I could see, I said, that unless we were able to move what we were doing in the direction of me getting to know her in a way that would no doubt make her feel vulnerable, the treatment was going to end, because she was going to cease seeing any value in it. I told her I knew how frustrated she must be with what we were doing, and, like me, how little she must be able to figure out how to make things different between us.

These thoughts did not come smoothly, nor did I express them that way. I struggled with them. And of course I was watching her reaction. She seemed interested in what I had to say about vulnerability, and she agreed outright with my estimation of her frustration. These things were good; but still I could not see how I was going to identify something in her experience, something that she could see at least as well as I could, that would open what we were doing into a psychoanalytic treatment.

At some moment, as I was talking, she appeared to me to change. It was quite subtle. She seemed softer and more open. That description, though, "softer and more open," was not available to me in the moment, only later on, when I thought back on it. In fact, I was not even aware of the presence of my new perception of her until, in retrospect, I tried to understand what had happened in the moments before I finally found myself able to say what occurred to me next, which was something new about her experience, something that I thought she would recognize and that might just help us into a more analytic kind of relatedness. The thought formed itself as I was speaking. Actually, I am quite sure that its possibility was created by the prior subtle change in my perception of her, which was, in turn, created by some change in her own affective state. As I spoke, I think that my novel perception was also helped along by my patient's facial expressions, through which she expressed a frank, friendly, and inquisitive interest in what I was saying.

But I am describing these moments with more precision than I experienced at the time. The truth is that I surprised myself—I didn't know what was coming until I was in the process of uttering it. I said, "I think you must be lonely. I think you must always have been lonely." Seeing her shock and recognition and the tears welling in her eyes, I was encouraged to continue: "I wonder if you have ever felt really known by anyone."

She wept, but this was not the hard crying that had accompanied her angry descriptions of the way her boyfriend had treated her. She hid her face in her hands. After a minute or two of silence she looked up at me and said simply and sadly, "I *am* lonely. I've always been lonely." After another silence, she confirmed that, indeed, she had never felt that anyone had known her, not even her parents, who were so very proud of everything she had accomplished, but equally eager not to know more than that about her. Her mother had actually physically turned away from her, she told me, on the few occasions when the patient had tried to talk to her about less than sunny matters. (Over the next months she revealed, unsurprisingly, that there actually had been quite a few unsunny matters.)

The session ended. It was obvious to both of us that we had started to do something quite different. As she walked in the door for her next session, she said as she sat down and smiled at me, "Now we have something to talk about." It was unnecessary to say it.

In later sessions, although she sometimes returned to her previous presentation of herself, my patient also found her way surprisingly often to moments of vulnerability and authenticity. She is one of those people who had no idea that it was even possible to talk in the way that successful psychoanalytic treatment demands. She had more capacity to think about herself than I had seen before. In fact, she had more capacity of that kind than she had known about herself. I began to know her differently, and I have grown quite fond of her.

It is worth noting that at the same moment that I saw her loneliness, I suddenly regained my sense of competence. Immediately I had the feeling that things were going to be all right in this treatment, and I regained my customary clinical confidence. These were the signs, from within my experience (we already know the signs from within hers), that a mutual unconscious enactment had dissolved, an enactment in which she was perfect and I was badly flawed.

Dissociation and Enactment

Over the past few years I have been theorizing links between dissociation and enactment, reported in other chapters of this book. Enactments require that the patient, or both the patient and the analyst fall into a mutual dissociation. It is generally not important (and not a good idea to try to establish, either) who begins the process. In any case, one participant treats the other in a way that threatens to force acknowledgment of not-me. Whenever that happens, in treatment or any other part of life, the response is enactment: in effect, one's behavior says "*I'm* not x; *you're* x," where "x" is some not-me aspect of one's personality. In this case, let us say for heuristic purposes (that is, I am starting with the patient's contribution only for the sake of simplicity; I could just as well start with the analyst) that the patient, prone to the concern that treatment would reveal her unacceptable imperfections, felt threatened with unbearable shame, which for her was not-me. She could not tolerate that possibility, and so she began enacting the dissociation by presenting to me her well-honed perfect persona and thereby made *me* feel the shame of imperfection.

I do not conceive the analyst's part of an enactment to be the outcome of having been colonized by an alien part projected by the patient, as in projective identification. Each participant's dissociation emerges instead from the interaction of her own private motives with the unconscious influence of the other. When both participants are vulnerable to the same themes, a state of affairs that is obviously not routine but which nevertheless takes place with great frequency, the result is a reciprocal enactment of the same themes.

I was for a time vulnerable enough to the way my patient treated me—which is to say that to some degree this kind of shame had to be not-me for me as well—to take on the shame unthinkingly and without being able to deal with her veiled contempt. My experience was, like hers, a singularity, a concretization that I could not use in my mind, which remained a thing-in-itself and therefore could not be felt or known. And of course my singularity was reciprocal to her own. We fit each other like a hand and a glove, or better, in a metaphor I am fond of and have used before, like the two halves of a broken plate.

On the other hand, my shame was not intense enough to push me toward responding with a countervailing unconscious enactment of the intention to make *her* feel ashamed. That happens often enough between analysts and patients (see, for example, the case of Hannah in Chapter 3), and it would have been easy with this woman. The analyst who must feel competent at all times, in other words, might have dealt with this woman by revealing her insecurity or the brittleness of her good cheer.

Dissociation and the enactment are both breached when either participant develops a new perception of the other, a new perception that, in coming into being, makes it possible to experience the other (and therefore, herself as well) in more than one way (see Chapter 4). In this case, that moment came when I suddenly saw my patient as softer and more open.

In the terms I have been exploring in this chapter, the new perception makes it possible to attend to co-occurrences that had always come and gone but had never been allowed to percolate and grow. The moment I saw my patient in this new way, I was able to contextualize her pursuit of perfection differently, more poignantly, and of course that changed the nature of our relatedness. I am quite sure that there had been opportunities (co-occurrences) for me to recontextualize her treatment of me (i.e., see her treatment of me metaphorically) before this, but I had been blind to them. The new perception is evidence that the potential in certain key co-occurrences has become available for actualization, often for the first time, and the result is metaphor or category where neither had been before. The past can be contextualized in the present. In response to my new perception of her and the difference that that new perception quite automatically made in my treatment of her (from the moment you see the other differently, you just cannot treat him or her the way you had the moment before), my patient's experience of shame about her imperfections, which had been not-me, frozen in an unchanging world, could begin to be metaphorized, to be situated in a present context that could be compared to the past, a new context in which imperfection no longer had to mean the same thing.

I want to reemphasize that it was not some particular *memory* that the patient had been unconsciously unwilling to encounter. What she was avoiding was the perception of herself as a *certain kind of person*, a person whose imperfections frightened her, a person who needed the love of her parents but who questioned whether she would be loved if she could not fulfill their image of her. The transference, while it had not been psychotic, had certainly qualified as a singularity, existing apart from her capacity to think. In order to dwell exclusively in the self-state of perfection and banish the state in which her imperfections had to be acknowledged, the transference *had* to be a singularity. Only singularity would do. Now she could question the nature of her relatedness to me. The transference became metaphorical, and as such, became clinically viable. (The countertransference, of course, went through the same sequence of changes.) Multiple images supplanted singularity. And finally, as her dissociation (and mine) was breached (over and over, but never as dramatically as the first time) and her sense of self expanded, I could finally become my patient's witness.

7

Opening What Has Been Closed, Relaxing What Has Been Clenched

Dissociation and Enactment Over Time in Committed Relationships

People who want to be in long-term romantic relationships, but who have trouble maintaining loving, sexual feelings toward their lovers, have two kinds of problems. One kind of problem has to do with preserving loving, sexual feelings long enough to get into such a relationship in the first place; the other difficulty, suffered by those who are already in long-term romantic relationships, concerns keeping loving, sexual feelings alive.[1]

The first kind of problem is a consistent, rigid inhibition. One's capacity to stay sexually and intimately connected to a lover does not rise and fall according to context, as these parts of relatedness do in a long-term relationship. One is simply interested until one is not, and then the passion is over and gone; and because of that, because of the rigidity of this kind of problem, its structural quality, its (relative) lack of responsiveness to context, it is especially easy to fall into thinking about such difficulties in what can seem one-person terms. These people stay at such a distance from the unavoidable and continuous oedipal themes in their relationships with their lovers that they do not really engage in the struggle.

---

[1] Virginia Goldner (2004, 2006) organized her discussion of the first chapter of Stephen Mitchell's (2002) book, *Can Love Last?*, around the observation that Mitchell's portrayal of romantic love, surprisingly enough, seemed more one-person than two-person. That is, Mitchell's description of the difficulties of romantic love seemed to Goldner to have an inadvertently intrapsychic cast. Mitchell's chapter and Goldner's discussion then became the basis of an online colloquium organized by the International Association of Relational Psychoanalysis and Psychotherapy, held in 2005 and called "What Happens When Love Lasts? An Exploration of Intimacy and Erotic Life." On the basis of their postings, some of those who participated in the colloquium were invited by the organizers, Margaret Crastnopol, Ph.D. and Randy Sorenson, Ph.D., to contribute articles to a collection (*Psychoanalytic Dialogues, 16*(6)) that addressed the same subject. An earlier version of this chapter was written for that collection of articles.

In referring to "oedipal themes" and "struggle," I am thinking about a paper by Davies (2003) in which the successful outcome of the oedipal situation is conceived not just as the acceptance that one can never win, but as the acceptance that one will both lose *and* win. The oedipal conflict is not successfully resolved by accepting defeat, that is, but by becoming strong and self-respecting enough to accept instead a lifelong and vitalizing engagement in the themes of love and rejection.[1] The child who knows that she is loved by a parent who often or even usually chooses his spouse—but who sometimes chooses the child, too—grows up to be a relationship partner able to thrive within admiration and love and to tolerate rejection and narcissistic wounds without being badly thrown. These are the lucky people who "remember" that they are loved even when love is not immediately present. Love is the background condition for them, the affective atmosphere within which the most important relationships take place. When their partners are rejecting, they are disappointed and hurt, but they are not left in suspense about the future. That is, unlike the less fortunate—those who cannot get into long-term romantic relationships in the first place—people who are actually in relationships, at least those in relationships that are not in what Goldner (2004) expressively refers to as "defensive lockdown," find their way through this oedipal terrain. Over and over again they find their way to and fro between intimacy and sexual desire, on the one hand, and distance, hurt, and relative lack of interest, on the other. In different ways at different times, they struggle with the other person as old and new object, as parent and lover.

We know from life, of course, and we see once again from this brief description, that having problems *in* a committed relationship can be a quite different kind of problem than being unable to get into such a relationship in the first place. Within successful existing relationships, partners find a way to continue their engagement over love and sex, whereas those who cannot find their way into a relationship at all very often avoid the struggle altogether, giving up the ghost as soon as the conflict appears. Is it perhaps a mistake to place both the engagement of struggle and the avoidance of it under the same rubric? The back and forth of engagement tends to be more existential and contextual than avoidance is, and habitual avoidance tends to be more neurotic, rigid, and stereotyped than engagement is.

---

[1] See also Stuart Pizer (2004), who uses Davies' ideas to invent a concept he calls "the paradoxical analytic triangle," a tool to use in thinking about the interrelatedness of the loving feelings and rejections in a very long treatment.

The problem I set for myself in this chapter is this: How can we think, in two-person terms—in Interpersonal or Relational terms, that is—about both kinds of problems, about both the rigidities of those people who cannot find their way into relationships and the changing issues between couples who are already in them? Is there a single frame of reference that encompasses desire both as fluid and contextual and as structural and relatively unchanging? Given the theme of this book, it will not be surprising that, in thinking about this question, I find myself drawn to the subject of dissociation.

Bad-Me, Good-Me, Not-Me

It seems to me that both kinds of difficulties—the struggles of engagement and the ongoing status quo of individual characterological inhibition—relate closely to how broad or deep an experience of self one can tolerate. The language that suits this kind of thinking is the language of self-states, which I introduced in the earlier chapters. We might say that both the emotional oscillation of engagement and the defensive lockdown of habitual avoidance can be described in terms of the degree to which one has the freedom to move about between states of mind.

In what Bromberg (1998) calls "normal" dissociation, and what I call narrative rigidity or dissociation in the weak sense (D. B. Stern, 1997; this book, Chapters 1 and 3), other people's participation interacts with one's own tendencies, predilections, and inner life in such a way that access between self-states that are otherwise simultaneously present in the mind is temporarily disrupted. This is what might happen, for instance, when someone unexpectedly shames us for something with which we are usually quite familiar in ourselves, but which we do not particularly like. Taken by surprise, we might react with heat, attributing the disliked characteristic to the other person and feeling wrongly accused. Or, in even more everyday terms, perhaps we frequently walk around with a fairly good opinion of ourselves, our good points in the foreground of our minds, our less savory aspects outside immediate awareness. But when called upon to acknowledge what we do not like about ourselves, it is relatively easy for us to do so. It may require a spouse's irritation, or an analyst's confrontation, and we may be grudging about it, but we do know these things about ourselves, or can stand knowing them. We can tolerate them. Normal dissociation is relative and often situational. The unconscious defensive need for it is not urgent. Normal dissociation makes life more comfortable, that's all. These mild dissociations are therefore remedied with relative ease, sometimes simply by a shift in the circumstances that provoked them in the first place (for a clinical example, see Chapter 3, the case of Daniel).

In the terms of Harry Stack Sullivan's (1954) that I have been using in this book, we could say that normal dissociation, or dissociation in the weak sense, takes place when the part of me that I have come to feel as "bad," or bad-me, is not experienced simultaneously with the part of me I feel as "good"—good-me. Bad-me is the part of myself I associate with the criticism, punishment, and rejection of my caretakers in childhood (at a certain point, Sullivan says the child characterizes these caretakers collectively as *bad-mother*); and good-me is the part of me that was loved, valued, accepted, and praised (by all those parts of caretakers characterized collectively as *good-mother*). Even if I don't like being bad-me or am worried about the consequences (a drop in self-esteem, or security, according to Sullivan; but we can broaden the range to include other kinds of less than pleasant outcomes), I do feel that I am being myself when I am either good-me or bad-me; and so even if I am reluctant to experience good-me and bad-me simultaneously, I have little difficulty doing so.

It is not as rewarding to be bad-me, of course; it may even be unpleasant. I may resent the circumstances in which I seem to have no choice but to be particularly aware of being bad-me, and at times I may feel that the pain of acknowledging this side of me is more than I will accept. But my unconscious defensive refusal to acknowledge being bad-me (which amounts to insisting I am only good-me) is usually temporary, and if it lasts longer, it is easily breached—because bad-me does still feel like me. Dissociations between bad-me and good-me are frequent, but they are hardly crucial to the continued, secure existence of the personality, and so they are easily destabilized.

Now, if you add to these ideas the relatively uncontroversial clinical observation that dissociated states tend to be enacted (e.g., Bromberg, 1998, 2006; Davies & Frawley, 1994; see also the earlier chapters in this book), you can see that dissociations between good-me and bad me are generally translated into treatment of the other that conveys something like this: "I am not bad-me, I am only good-me. *You* are bad, not me."

If we then translate this scenario into the contemporary oedipal terms used by Davies (2003), Goldner (2004, 2006), and S. Pizer (2004), we find ourselves, when we temporarily cannot accept rejection from the other, treating the other in a way that conveys something like the following: "I am the loving, generous, reasonable, intelligent, attractive boy my mother adored, not the selfish, angry, unreasonable, stupid, ugly boy (or the inadequate boy who mother thought was 'less' than father) from whom she turned away. No, the bad one is *you—you* are the selfish, angry, etc. one, the inadequate one, the outrageous one, not *me*."

I know that this set of ideas immediately brings to mind projective identification. I have addressed this point Chapters 1 and elsewhere (D. B. Stern, 2001, 2005; see also Mitchell, 1997, Chap. 4). But let me digress briefly here to add a bit more about the matter.

The differences between my views and those of the contemporary Kleinians are due, from my perspective, to the different origins of our views. Psychoanalytic theories of dissociation are rooted in Interpersonal and Relational psychoanalysis. From those perspectives, dissociation can only be enacted if the roles that constitute it are relevant in the psychic lives of *both* participants. The contemporary Kleinian analyst is often expected to be able to experience the impact of the patient's projections while simultaneously maintaining a purposeful, conscious analytic stance toward them. The analyst, that is, however understandable it may be for him to lapse in this respect, is believed to be capable of not becoming lost or embedded in the countertransference.[1] From Interpersonal and Relational perspectives, on the other hand, it is acknowledged from the outset that the analyst's task is to learn the nature of his quite thorough, and quite personal, unconscious involvement, which has always already taken place. There is no consistently maintained "analyst part" that somehow exists above the fray, separate from the subjective aspects of the analyst's personality.

Analogously, from an Interpersonal or Relational vantage point, there can be no consistently maintained parts of the personalities of persons in romantic relationships that exist apart from their relatedness from one another. The analysis of analytic relatedness and of problems in romantic relationships, at least when such understandings are sought by the participants themselves, are both examples of what Mitchell (1997) calls "bootstrap operations."

Now I return to the minor dissociations that go on within ongoing romantic relationships. Although intimate sex is not well served by these minor dissociations, it is also not likely to be precluded for too long at a time either. As we wend our way back and forth from simplified, wishful, and often angry characterizations of ourselves and our lovers to more complex and tolerant observations, we first avoid the bedroom and then slip back into it. These are the ups and downs of sex and love in long relationships. The crucial thing that allows us to return to intimacy each time

---

[1] See Chapter 4, footnote 6.

is our reclaiming of the capacity to tolerate the experience of good-me and bad-me simultaneously, which amounts to accepting the conflict between these two portrayals of ourselves (I am neither as good as I want to be nor as bad as I sometimes fear I am). Of course, it is only when we can tolerate conflicting aspects of ourselves in this way that we can, in turn, tolerate conflicting perceptions of the other. And so it follows that the acceptance of our own conflicting self-states is what allows us to recapture a fuller, warts-and-all perception of the other.

The terms Sullivan invents to describe the aspects of ourselves that we like and dislike are very simple. But their simplicity is deceptive. Consider the degree of complexity introduced as soon as we admit into the picture the fact that all dissociations are conditional, in the sense that they are continuously preserved or challenged by the interpersonal context in which they take place. That is, if the other is able to sense nondefensively his or her response to being treated as bad and then bring it to mutual attention, the interaction will not turn into a mutual enactment.

But if one's partner in the relationship is vulnerable to a reciprocal, answering dissociation ("You think *I'm* bad? No way, it's *you* who's bad"), a mutual enactment is off and running, in just the same way that I have described in Chapters 3–6 for the analytic relationship. The enactment will end only when one partner or the other can find a way back to an internal experience of the conflict between what she feels is good and bad about herself. Once she is capable of that conflict again, she quite automatically treats the other person differently, because he no longer has to control the other's perception. At that point, the dissociation, with its accompanying enactment, which was mild in the first place, vanishes, at least for the time being.

But in the case of "pathological dissociation" (Bromberg, 1998) or "dissociation in the strong sense" (D. B. Stern, 1997; this book, Chapters 1 and 3), the consequences for the relationship are much greater. This is the dissociation that comes into play when certain kinds of experience are specifically and continuously disallowed or rejected; this is dissociation used as an unconscious defensive operation. In instances demanding "strong" or "pathological" dissociation, the disallowed experience is so intolerable that, despite its presence within the very broad bounds of subjectivity, it is not acknowledged as part of the self (it is not me) and therefore cannot be articulated in awareness. It cannot be felt as one's own experience without fairly severe, disruptive consequences. This is neither good-me nor bad-me; this is what Sullivan called not-me, and it is just as disruptive in romantic relationships outside the consulting room as it is in the analytic situation.

Now, this point is key: Unlike relatedness between parts of me, there is no experience of conflict between me and not-me (see Chapter 4.) Good-me and bad-me, remember, can be experienced simultaneously because they are both parts of the self, and so they can be experienced to conflict with each other. Not-me, though, must simply be absent from one's sense of oneself, forever unsymbolized—that is, unformulated. Because it cannot be experienced in symbolic form at all, not-me certainly cannot be experienced to conflict with me.

In the experience of especially vulnerable people, whose defenses are notably rigid, this absence of simultaneous experience of me and not-me is sometimes absolute; if not-me emerges in consciousness, requiring the recognition that I am what I cannot and must not be, the self is so seriously threatened and destabilized that experience can become psychotic. The emergence of not-me in consciousness does not carry the same degree of danger for more stable and flexible personalities, of course, but even they are unable to access or symbolize that part of their subjectivity at will; and for them, too, it therefore can be strange (Sullivan's word was "uncanny"), even excruciating, to find themselves faced with not-me.

Children, we know, develop their capacity to digest experience slowly, over time. It takes many years of continuous, loving care for a child to develop a sophisticated enough capacity for experiencing that he is no longer continuously vulnerable to being overwhelmed by events of everyday life that will eventually become routine. Prior to the development of that degree of resilience, and especially in infancy, the child is dependent on his caretakers to contain and symbolize experience for him (Fonagy et al., 2002). In those early years, experience is traumatic to the precise extent that the child's caretakers cannot bear it, cannot let themselves consciously and fully experience it. The child is vulnerable to trauma, that is, whenever the parent is forced to confront not-me. When the parent cannot stand to feel the experience, the child, who only knows what his own experience is if the caretaker is capable of bearing it (feeling it, knowing it), is deprived of what he needs if he is to create his own mind; and so, over time, this kind of experience becomes as dissociated for the child as it has been for the caregiver. This is not the kind of dissociation that comes and goes, like the temporary and relatively mild dissociations between good-me and bad-me; this is a stable, foundational kind of dissociation around which the personality comes to be shaped. This is the transmission of psychic pain and damage across generations.

We hope, of course, that parents manage to experience their most uncomfortable moments, their moments of not-me, without anxiety so overwhelming that it prevents their symbolization of experience, because then the child herself will eventually be able to take on the same capacity. In those fortunate instances, the experience ends up feeling to the child like "mine," and what could have become not-me becomes me instead. Childhood is an apprenticeship in the creation of mind, and one's caretakers are the masters of the guild.[1]

The (pathological) dissociation between me and not-me is maintained in the same way as the (normal) dissociation between good-me and bad-me: by enactment. But because the dissociation of me and not-me is continuous and absolute, not contextual and relative, and because one's sense of basic security in the world depends on maintaining these dissociations, the enactments that derive from the separations between me and not-me are more rigid, intense, urgent, and less amenable to change or resolution than the enactments that support the dissociation of good-me and bad-me.

Enactment, Dependence, and Knowing Your Partner

In an ongoing love relationship, what is the nature of our dependence on our partner? Don't we come to rely on that person (among other things) to be the same as he or she has been, to deal with us in the ways with which we are accustomed, ways that perhaps we have come to need? Why might we need this familiarity? Might not our lover's familiarity allow us to preserve our own? Might not it be the case, as Benjamin (1988, 1995, 1998) tells us, that we need our lovers to recognize in us what we recognize in ourselves (and to leave unrecognized in us what we prefer not to see)?

---

[1] This description is more or less consistent with the thinking of Winnicott and Bion, but it probably has most in common with (besides Sullivan) Fonagy et al (2002), whose work might serve as a detailed exegesis of Sullivan's (1953/1940) developmental theory of infancy and childhood. In the model proposed by Fonagy et al., mind is conceived to be created by the interaction of the infant's inborn potentials (the "primary" or "constitutional" self) with caregivers' provision of a sensitive mirroring response to what they believe they can understand of the infant's affects and intentions. It is the caretakers' mirroring that structures the infant's inborn somatosensory experience into the experience of affects and eventually into the capacity for a deeper and more thorough reflective processing (mentalization) of the causal mind states (affects and intentions) that lie behind the infant's own behavior and the behavior of other people. The distinctive aspect of this way of thinking is its jettisoning of the Cartesian privileging of internal experience. In most models of the development of self, mind is assumed and inborn, and so the development of mental representations of self and others and the ego structures that make representation possible in the first place are an expansion of this inborn capacity. The radical aspect of the model proposed by Fonagy et al., and the aspect that makes it especially relevant here, is that mind is not assumed and inborn: It is created from the outside in. The mind that results is sophisticated to the degree that early caretakers' mirroring responses correspond to the structures of the constitutional self.

Might not that recognition from the other give us the reassurance that we are who we want to believe we are, and that we will continue to be—and that we are *not* who we prefer *not* to be? Might not our lover's sameness, in other words, allow us predictable, reliable experiences of good-me and bad-me? Might not we be involved, that is, in long-term enactments of good-me and bad-me, enactments that preserve the stability and comfort of both partners? And might not our familiarity with our lovers, in just the same way, reinforce *their* sense of who *they* are and aren't, *their* sense of self?

Of course, even if this portrayal makes sense, it still leaves each member of any couple in the position of sometimes having to put up with certain rather predictable discomforts. It may make us feel and act angry, for instance, when, in the face of our insistence that we are innocent and it is wrong to accuse us, our partner refuses to acknowledge being in the wrong. We may suspect that our partner has a point, which may be uncomfortable, making us feel guilty. We may, in fact, blame our partner for that guilt, too, right along with blaming him for his unwillingness to acknowledge responsibility for being wrong. But even all this discomfort is a small price to pay for having a reliable means of reassuring ourselves of being good-me. (Even if you refuse to acknowledge the truth, I can still believe that *I'm* not bad, *you* are.)

These enactments take time to fall into place and become habitual, which is one reason for the immense sense of freedom and excitement we experience at the beginning of a new relationship. We are raw and open at the beginning, and the themes of oedipal struggle occupy us fully, intensely, and spontaneously. The relatedness is not yet patterned, as it will be. (I think she likes me! She's incredibly exciting, and it's so wonderful that she seems excited by me! Does she like my hair? Is she angry with me? Does she love me? Maybe she really wants to be with *him*.)

The hopes, fears, exultations, and despairs at the beginning of a relationship have a special intensity; but as painful as those first weeks and months can be, they are also one of the most exciting parts of life. Lovers are less intimate at the beginning than they will be later on, but ironically, they also can be less defended. Their openness to being affected by hurt or admiration (for instance) may be greater than it will become. They are freer to be completely delighted with each other. They know each less well, love each other much less deeply, and yet in certain respects are perhaps most thoroughly available to each other.

But what happens to that ongoing struggle, to involvement and change and engagement, as we come to depend on sameness, on the enactments that develop over time? Struggle dims. There is less and less change, life stays closer to the baseline. We reassure ourselves that the other's mind is completely mapped. We become locked into patterns of enactment.

Of course, this is an extreme characterization. In most relationships, the struggle does go on, even as it dims, and there may be as many moments of spontaneity as there are pallid repetitions of the familiar. The point I want to make is that, to the extent that we become dependent on characteristic enactments of good-me and bad-me, the vitality of the struggle and the excitement it generates diminish over time.

Of course, if these points make sense for good-me and bad-me, how much more must they be true for me and not-me? How much more dependent must we be on our partners and spouses to maintain the enactments that protect us from an exposure to what we cannot bear to be, *must* not be? The least fortunate people, whose personalities are the most rigid, because they must protect themselves from the experience of the uncanny, from the eruption of not-me, defend themselves by creating and tolerating relationships that will contribute to their crucial dissociations. These people, in order to keep not-me at bay, tolerate relationships that feel continuously dead and boring or hateful and destructive. The more urgent the need to isolate one's own not-me in the other, the more hateful and intensely sadistic the enactments necessary to accomplish the task. All enactments, especially those of not-me but even including bad-me, are adversarial; but it is much more likely, in enactments that protect one from having to bear the unbearable, for the relatedness to degenerate into violence, physical or emotional. There is no reason to hold back when the consequences of the enactment's failure (i.e., when a particularly virulent not-me threatens to come home to roost) are worse than any outcome of the interpersonalization of the dissociation. The dread of not-me can be compelling enough to lead to murder, sometimes of a virtual stranger, sometimes of a spouse or other family member, as Stein (2006) shows in cases culled from Federal Bureau of Investigation files of violent crime. Fonagy and his collaborators (2002) describe patients, incapable of mentalization, who are reduced to protecting themselves from an outer world that, because the patient operates in the mode of psychic equivalence, seems as literally dangerous as their inner world of fantasy. In other cases, as Fonagy et al. tell us simply, "The child who recognizes the hatred or murderousness implied by the parent's acts of abuse is forced to see himself as worthless or unlovable" (p. 353). If not-me is hated, worthless, unlovable, the outcome can be the enactment of the perception that it is instead *you* (the other) who deserves to be treated murderously.

It seems reasonable to say that relationships in defensive lockdown are more likely than others to be cemented and maintained by enactments of pathological dissociation, those in which the relationship must stay exactly the same if the me's of its participants are to remain safely isolated from their not-me's. Relationships in which the oedipal struggle is alive and kicking (probably the majority), on the other hand, are at least partly maintained by the security offered by habitual enactments of normal dissociation. It is primarily these relationships we would expect to be most open to change, to giving up the old ways, because breaking up their enactments should lead to nothing more dire than discomfort.

Locked Out of Relationships

But what about the people who can't get into relationships in the first place, people who start relationships with great excitement and passion, but who can sustain those feelings only temporarily? What about Stephen Mitchell's (2002) case of Brett, for example, who was the immediate impetus for the original version of these remarks (D. B. Stern, 2006)? I have seen a number of people like Brett, who, at some point in the first few months of a relationship, typically lose their passion for their lovers and then begin to want to see other prospective lovers, who are often emotionally unavailable. Typically, the first relationship then ends, sometimes with great guilt on the part of the restless partner, who is tortured by the unmistakable pattern, but helpless to feel otherwise.

With the background of dissociation theory, I would now say that these are not actually people who cannot get into relationships. People like Brett get into them all the time! The problem, rather, is that the Bretts of this world can allow relationships to take only one course: They are stuck in a rigid pattern with their partners, and the particular nature of this pattern, in which, for one reason or another (differing with the person concerned), intimacy threatens the eruption of not-me, makes relationships too dangerous to maintain once a certain level of intimacy is reached. (I turn to an example of such a pattern in a moment.) Brett was so distressed and helpless about this kind of problem that it was his primary motive to enter treatment.

That degree of distress and that sense of helplessness about the problem are not uncommon among people who know they cannot tolerate romantic intimacy; and so we can speculate with a degree of confidence that what lies behind this relationship pattern is not the avoidance of bad-me but rather the avoidance of not-me. If individuals with this kind of problem were able to bear experiencing whatever stops them from taking relationships any further than they do, they would have done that, even if it caused discomfort, because they very often badly want the problem to change. If, in terminating relationships at such an early point, they were turning away from experience that belongs to the self (bad-me), it seems likely that their motivation to change the problem would have allowed them to feel and own both sides of the conflict. They would have been able to disrupt the enactments that had maintained the dissociations, because the worst consequence would have been the experience of parts of themselves that they did not like. The fact that these people cannot seem to manage to disrupt the enactment, though, as badly as they often wish to do so, encourages us to believe that it is something more than bad-me that feels more dreadful and that they are keeping at bay, something that does not feel to them like themselves at all.

Perhaps, for the sake of illustration (I will use the example of a heterosexual man), a fictional patient's mother was intensely exciting to her little boy, but felt so terrorized by her own loving feelings that our patient's infantile expressions of love and his need for her love for him simply fell outside her range of perception, off the radar. The patient's mother, that is, dissociates tender feeling. We could say that our patient has a version of what André Green (1976) calls a "dead mother," one in whose eyes and mind the baby is unable to find himself. The mother's dissociation of loving feelings, and her enactment of the same deadness to love that she herself (let us say) experienced as a baby and child, provokes our patient's own dissociation. The patient feels unlovable—not hated, as in Fonagy's case, but not answered with love either. No child can grasp his love and his need for it in the absence of a response to it. To feel love for someone else becomes humiliating because one anticipates that one's needs will not be responded to; and to want the love of the other is debasing for the same reason. Over time, the child becomes as dead to love as the mother.

Our patient's loving feelings and his desire to be loved become not-me. As an adult, he perpetually looks for his exciting mother, and he finds her over and over in his lustful adventures; but these new mother-women face him with the dilemma that they often *can* love, and they provoke our patient's inchoate affection for them. These loving women awaken the patient's desire for the return of this feeling, for what his mother could neither experience in her own life nor offer to him. But the long-dead desire, if the patient found himself experiencing it now, would fall into the realm of the uncanny—dreadful, frightening, or even loathsome.

As soon as this patient begins to feel, probably without awareness, slight stirrings of affection for the women he meets, or the whiff of a desire for their love of him, he loses interest, begins to characterize his women friends as dull, and feels like moving on. His growing feeling that they are dull and boring dampens whatever affection they might have been in the process of developing, thereby closing the circle and giving him that much more reason to be afraid of arousing love the next time around.

If this man is to find his way into a relationship that lasts, one with mutual love, it seems likely that it will only be through the repeated appearance and transcendence of just this kind of enactment between him and his analyst. Such an accomplishment would probably require the patient to experience dread and at least the danger of humiliation (and perhaps the real thing); and in the course of the enactments that would have to take place, the analyst would no doubt be the object of feelings ranging from deadness to rejection to contempt. In a treatment of great success, the patient would eventually become more able to experience simultaneously the states in which he loves and the states in which he fears loving, thereby tolerating a conscious internal conflict over how he feels and what he will do about it. But of course there is always the very real danger that the enactments will either result in the treatment ending or that the treatment will endure, but with the deadness that the patient experiences with his ex-girlfriends. In such an outcome, in other words, love and the desire for love would remain not-me. And we can hardly blame the patient for that. Until the conflict is tolerable to him, no other outcome makes emotional sense.

The only difference between our fictional patient and the unfortunate souls I referred to earlier who maintain relationships of the most hateful and destructive kinds is that the enactments our fictional patient gets into do not lock him *into* relationships; they *end* relationships. Remember the question I set for myself at the beginning of this chapter: How can we think, in two-person terms, about both kinds of problems people have in making love last: (1) the rigidities of those people who cannot find their ways into relationships, and (2) the changing issues between couples who are already in them? In answer to this question, we can link these two kinds of problems through dissociation and enactment: The problems in basically loving and satisfying relationships often derive from the enactment of mutual dissociations of good-me and bad-me; but problems such as my fictional patient's problem, and the problems of those damaging relationships that seem to be maintained on some other basis than love, are likely to be the outcomes of the enactment of mutual pathological dissociation, or dissociation in the strong sense—that is, the mutual dissociative sequestering of me and not-me.

One final caveat, however. I do not want to leave the impression that in long-term relationships the healing of pathology is the only route to a broadening or deepening of the relationship over time. There is also such a thing as courage: courage to challenge the status quo in the interest of "more life" (Corbett, 2001), courage to formulate and think about the stories we are always implicitly telling ourselves about our lives, courage to imagine all those other stories about our partners and ourselves that, merely because we are so attached to the stories we do tell, we are continuously in the process of occluding. The danger accompanying this kind of open and accepting experiencing is the danger of sacrificing security; and it is true more often than not that, over time, security does trump desire. But it is not always that way. And when it is not, when freedom and desire win, it is because we are willing to put ourselves at risk by experiencing more readily and deeply than before what we do not like about ourselves—or, in the most significant instances, what we have not until that uncomfortable moment even been able to imagine *is* ourselves.

8

On Having to Find What You Don't Know How to Look For
Two Views of Reflective Function

One of the most influential views of reflective function in the history of psychoanalysis, and clearly the most influential view of that subject in the current literature, is that of Fonagy and his collaborators (2002). Their work has reignited interest in reflection and reinvigorated its study. Since the beginnings of our field, self-reflection has lost a great deal of ground to relational effects in our theories of therapeutic action. That is as it should be, and Fonagy et al. would be the first to agree. In fact, perhaps their most significant theoretical contribution has been their detailed proposal that the development of mind, including reflective function, is itself thoroughly relational. Reflective function is a relational event, with relational roots. As a result of this work, reflection is no longer a dusty subject on the back of the shelf. It is now as fascinating as it was long ago, and it is back in the center of psychoanalytic interest. The work of Fonagy et al. has deeply affected my own work, a fact reflected in the frequent citations of mentalization theory in this book. Their description of the process of mentalization and their observations about how it develops are with me whenever I sit down with patients. I use their observations and their conceptions every single day.

I, too, have devoted a good deal of attention to the place of reflective function in clinical work.[1] My interest in reflection has focused on the formulation of newly explicit experience from its unformulated origins. Like Fonagy et al., I have understood the process of formulation as a relational event. But unlike Fonagy et al., and, for that matter, unlike most writers on

---

[1] These writings have appeared over the past 25 years. The first of these, from the early 1980s into the early 1990s, were revised and collected in my earlier book (D. B. Stern, 1997). Other articles have appeared since that book and are reprinted as chapters in this book.

the subject, I believe we do not and cannot control reflection, at least not the instances of reflection that matter the most clinically. The important reflections in a treatment come upon us; we do not have the simple choice to create them. They arrive of their own accord.[1] I shall explore one aspect of my views in this chapter and compare those views with the perspective offered by Fonagy et al.

Socrates and the Inebriate

I begin, though, far from psychoanalysis, with Plato's (1956) famous report of Socrates' dialogue with Meno, often known as Meno's Paradox.

> Meno: But how will you look for something when you don't in the least know what it is? How on earth are you going to set up something you don't know as the object of your search? To put it another way, even if you come right up against it, how will you know that what you have found is the thing you didn't know?
> Socrates: I know what you mean. Do you realize that what you are bringing up is the trick argument that a man cannot try to discover either what he knows or what he does not know? He would not seek what he knows, for since he knows it there is not need of the inquiry, nor what he does not know, for in that case he does not even know what he is to look for.
> Meno: Well, do you think it is a good argument? (pp. 128–129)

Socrates says he does not. Neither do psychoanalysts, who search all the time for what they do not know how to describe. (The fact that we do not know what to look for has never stopped *us*!)

Socrates' reasons for adopting this view are not literally relevant to modern readers, although the dialogue, interpreted metaphorically, is often cited in discussions of the contributions of memory to thought in the present. (Socrates' argument centers on certain consequences for pedagogy that follow from the doctrine that souls are immortal and spend eternity being reborn into one new life after another.) But whatever Socrates' reasons for it, his conclusion is the same one that would be reached by most readers of this chapter: We do somehow manage to find what we don't know how to look for. Of course, the conclusion is the easy part. The trick is how to do it and how to think about it.

Here we can take a hint from a much less lofty source: The venerable joke about the man who has had too much to drink and who, on his way

---

[1] I have given these points particular emphasis in Chapter 12 of *Unformulated Experience* (D. B. Stern, 1997) and in thiis book, Chapter 5.

home in the middle of the night, accidentally drops his house key in the street. A passerby comes upon the man, who is on his hands and knees searching under a streetlight. The passerby begins to help look. After a few minutes without success, the Good Samaritan asks whether our main character can be any more specific about where he might have dropped the key. The man points off into the darkness. Astonished, the passerby asks why, in that case, the two of them aren't searching over there; and the answer, delivered with a roll of the eyes, as if it ought to be totally obvious, is, "Well, *that* wouldn't do any good, would it? It's *dark* over there."

And so I begin with two claims, both of which I think are familiar to all clinicians: (1) In psychoanalysis and psychotherapy, although often enough we do eventually find what we most need, for long periods we have no idea what that is or even how to recognize it; and (2) This means that we have to learn how to search where we are least able to see—in the dark places. I would go so far as to say that to be a psychoanalyst is to love the dark places and the recalcitrant meanings that lurk there—to love even the way that those meanings evade us. Of course, we, like those with whom we work, are often tempted to avoid the dark. But with another part of ourselves, we also develop a certain calm in the dark—a comfort with the discomfort, if you will, an acceptance—because we have come to have the confidence that what we need will eventually somehow emerge from this part of our experience.

By "dark places" I mean to refer to those parts of experience we cannot access. It is not just that we cannot understand darkened meanings. Unlike the unfortunate man searching for his keys, who knew what he was looking for, psychoanalysts and other psychotherapists often have to wait long periods to learn what it is we seek. Our problem is therefore more difficult than being faced with an impenetrable meaning. The experience we need is actually absent. In the most literal sense, we really don't know what we're looking for. And yet we try to keep ourselves continuously ready to find it.

Let me put this in the terms of reflective function: We have the confidence that our capacity to think about ourselves and other people will eventually come in very handy; but most of the time, before the fact, we just cannot imagine when and how the opportunity to think productively in this way is likely to occur. And even when the opportunity arises, it does not arise planfully. At such moments, we are not able to *decide* to think; instead, we find that we have already *thought*. This position, I think, may be different from the position taken about reflective function by most contemporary analysts, including Fonagy et al., in whose thinking the analyst generally seems able to call at will upon her powers of reflection. I will have to cover a good deal of preparatory ground before I will be in a position to discuss this difference. I will return to it later, after introducing mentalization theory.

Mentalization Theory and Relational Dissociation Theory: Commonalities

In their important 2002 book, Fonagy et al. tell us that it is their intention to link psychic development and philosophy of mind, "to capture and specify the process by which infants fathom the minds of others and eventually their own minds." That is, "we fathom ourselves through others" (p. 2). Mind is created, not inborn, and it is created by the interaction of the baby with the parenting ones. Mind is an interpersonal construction, a product of a certain very particular kind of reflected appraisal.

This is music to my ears, with my roots in the interpersonal developmental thinking of Harry Stack Sullivan. As a matter of fact, the account by Fonagy et al. is remarkably similar to Sullivan's; and where it differs, it frequently could serve as a creative specification and elaboration of Sullivan's thinking.

There are many other areas where the work of Fonagy et al. overlaps with my own views. They argue for the continuing centrality of verbal meanings in psychoanalysis, for instance, while simultaneously making it abundantly clear that a large proportion of the most important events in psychoanalysis takes place outside the reach of verbal language and may never be brought within it. This is also a position I favor (see especially Chapter 4). We all also agree that mind or self is inevitably fragmented. Bromberg (1998, 2006; Chefetz & Bromberg, 2004) and I (D. B. Stern, 1997; see also Chapters 6–10 of this book) each express that point with an updated version of Sullivan's (1954) personifications, me and not-me. Fonagy et al. prefer a different set of terms: "Self," which refers to the part of one's sense of who one is that, because it connects to inborn potentials, is authentic and real; and "alien self," a sense of oneself as "other" that comes about because it is not connected to the inborn potentials of the constitutional self. The basic affinity of our two perspectives is unmistakable.

But I also may differ with mentalization theory. This chapter was written partly to think through the question of whether those differences are real, and if they are, how to characterize them. I am going to take the view that it is at precisely the moments when the analyst is most in need of her capacity to mentalize that she has least access to it. These moments are mutual enactments, and Fonagy et al. agree with me that the analyst's ability to mentalize is often compromised at such times. What we may or may not agree about is: (1) the degree to which the analyst's capacity to mentalize is absent at such times; and (2) the eventual clinical value of these mutual unconscious entanglements with our patients.

Fonagy et al. are highly sympathetic to the plight of the analyst who participates in an enactment, and they accept that some enactments, even rather distressing ones, are unavoidable, especially when working with borderline patients. But in my reading of their work, these writers also believe that mutual enactments are problematic and regrettable. For me, on the other hand, while the potentially damaging aspects of the analyst's unconsciously motivated participation are obviously regrettable, it is also the case that enactment is not only inevitable, but also often constitutes the therapist's most important clinical opportunity. Before I present my own view, though, I will shape what I think is the relevant underlying issue here as a problem in therapeutic action, and then present my understanding of the view offered by the authors of mentalization theory.

Chicken-and-Egg in Therapeutic Action

We have known for many decades that it is too simple to ask whether therapeutic action is based on insight (or reflective function) or relational effects, because the two ingredients interact with each other. For the present purpose, I will consider the issue a chicken-and-egg dilemma. Like all such dilemmas, this one has no absolute solution. But there are differences of emphasis in the two approaches to the problem, and they are important. Here is the dilemma: *Does mentalization pave the way for a shift in the relationship, or must relational effects precede mentalization?* I begin the exploration of this problem by summarizing what Fonagy et al. tell us, in their 2002 book, about the role of mentalization in therapeutic action.

Therapeutic Action in Mentalization Theory

The authors write that "An important aim of psychotherapy, if not its central aim, is the extension of mentalization" (p. 14). This aim is achieved in a number of ways, but all of them depend on the analyst's *own* capacity to mentalize. It is the analyst's more or less continuous capacity to mentalize, say Fonagy et al., that eventually has the effect, via internalization, of extending the patient's capacity to mentalize. The analyst's mentalization is available to the patient whenever the analyst reflects on the patient's experience, or even when the analyst merely labels the patient's experience or describes it. For some patients, such moments are among the first times they have thought about what they think or feel. These are people for whom it is not habitual, at least under certain circumstances, to reflect on their own experience or the experience of others. Assuming that the patient experiences the analyst as trying to be useful or helpful, it sometimes does not even matter if the analyst's reflection is wrong. These instances, like those other moments when the analyst is right, show the patient what it is like to treat experience, especially the experience of affects and intentions, as symbolic representations, not as concrete or literal copies of the world. A symbolic representation is understood to be a subjective rendering, and therefore open to modification; an experience understood as a literal copy of the world, on the other hand, is a direct avenue to the truth that can be modified only by lies or distortion.

The patient also takes in the analyst's reflective function when the analyst deals with the patient on the basis of the analyst's mentalization of her *own* experience, as in, "Oh, now I see. I thought you meant 'X,' but now I see you meant 'Y.'" In saying things like this, the therapist is once again showing the patient that she (the therapist) is treating experience as a representation. Experience can change on its own without a corresponding change in the world; it can be negotiated. Each time the analyst mentalizes with the patient, the patient is just a bit more able to treat his own experience that way, as well as the experience of others in his world. He is more often able to transcend the mode of psychic equivalence, in which experience is perceived and treated as a slavish copy of the outside, and the outside as a copy of the inside. In psychic equivalence, the inside of oneself and the outside, experience and world, are identical, so that frightening fantasies are just as threatening as frightening realities, and frightening external situations cannot be differentiated from the state of one's own mind.

With the capacity for mentalization, experience is no longer a photocopy, but a picture of the world, a picture that we know could have been constructed differently, even if we may not have immediate access to alternatives. Patients who can mentalize, for example, know that their perceptions of their analysts, however ironclad those perceptions may seem, may very well not be the only ways their analysts could be seen. Patients in the mode of psychic equivalence, on the other hand, have what we used to call "psychotic transferences": As far as these people are concerned, their analysts simply *are* what they are perceived to be. There is no ability to create the "as-if" quality.

Once we understand that we can make many different pictures of the same reality, and that all of them have their own validity, the inner and the outer worlds become more and more independent of each other. As the process goes on, experience less frequently feels to the patient as if it were merely imposed on him. He feels less helpless and victimized, and also less omnipotent. His sense of his own limits, the limits of others, and most of all, his sense of agency, of living his own life, are facilitated, and he realizes that life can be chosen, rejected, negotiated, and discussed much more often than he had understood.

Mentalization, or reflective function, is an undeniably significant part of therapeutic action. I don't imagine anyone believes otherwise. The question I want to raise is not *whether* reflective function is important; rather, I want to focus on *when* analysts are capable of responding this way, and why. Can analysts *always* mentalize?

We cannot; everyone also agrees on this point. When analysts are blindly involved in enactments, they can mentalize neither their own experience nor their patients'. The term mutual enactment might just as well be defined, as a matter of fact, as the mutual inability of patient and therapist to mentalize.

During an enactment, from the perspective of mentalization theory, because the analyst reacts directly to the patient's projective identification, the patient's expectation that the inside and the outside worlds must be the same—that is, psychic equivalence—is reinforced. If, on the other hand, the analyst is able to accept the patient's projective identification without reacting directly to it, and especially if the analyst can convert it into a mentalization that can then be given back to the patient, a mutual enactment does not take place. (In my own way of thinking, an enactment takes place, but it is not mutual.) The patient is encouraged to move just a bit further from psychic equivalence toward the beginning of reflective function.

Now, what I am about to say is crucial to the point I am trying to reach: In this theoretical scheme, no matter how understandable mutual enactments may be, and no matter how sympathetic we are to the analyst's role in them (and Fonagy et al. are very sympathetic), they are regrettable to the extent that they interrupt the analyst's capacity to mentalize.

Let me offer illustrations of these views, in two brief quotations from the 2002 book.

> [I]t is necessary to accept that in order for the patient to stay in mental proxim-
> ity, the therapist *must occasionally allow herself* to become the vehicle for the
> alien part within his self. If she is to be of any use to him, she has to become what
> he needs her to be. Yet if she becomes that person fully, she can be of no help
> to him. She *aims for a state of equipoise* between these two positions—*allowing
> herself to do as required yet trying to retain in her mind as clear and coherent an
> image of the state of his mind as she is able to achieve.* (p. 370; emphasis added)

The therapist is portrayed to be in control of the enactment: she "must
occasionally *allow* herself to become the vehicle for the alien part within
his self." This is not something that is portrayed to be happening *to* the
analyst; she "allows" it. It seems to be assumed in this passage that the
therapist has the ability to select the clinical stance toward the patient that
she thinks is best. In this "state of equipoise," she allows "herself to do as
required yet [tries] to retain in her mind" a clear and coherent image of
the mind of the patient.

And now consider this passage:

> Some enactments on the part of both therapist and patient are an inevitable
> part of this work, since the patient cannot remain psychologically close to the
> therapist without externalizing the alien parts of the self. It is at these moments,
> when the therapist is enacting the split-off parts of the patient's experience, that
> the patient's true self may be most accurately observed. *Sadly, almost invariably
> the therapist will have extreme difficulty in communicating insight and under-
> standing at such times. It is far more likely, in the middle of such turmoil, that
> the therapist's rage or terror or both will obscure her vision of the patient.* (p. 14;
> emphasis added)

In this description, the analyst's participation in an enactment of the
patient's alien self is clearly regrettable. Participating in an enactment,
however inevitable or unavoidable it may sometimes be, deprives the analyst of the tools she needs to be useful to the patient.

There exist in our field two broad ways of understanding the relationship of mind and clinical interaction. In the first, older perspective, held
by many contemporary Freudian and Kleinian analysts, but also by some
Interpersonalists, there are parts of the mind, especially the analyst's
mind, that usually (though not always) exist apart from the unconscious
influence of the mind of the other. In the analyst's case, there exists an
internal "perch" (Modell, 1991) from which the analyst can expect to be
able to observe the interaction more or less objectively. This certainly does
not mean that the analyst is not affected by the countertransference. But
even when she *is* affectively moved by the transference, she should usually
be able to observe her own disturbed affective state from this other part

of her own mind, and then use this disturbance as vital information in shaping her understanding and interventions. The analyst, that is, should usually be able to observe and reflect not only on the transference, but also the countertransference.

It should go without saying that many analysts who work from some variety of this position are nevertheless quite tolerant of those times when the analyst's capacity to mentalize her own countertransference fails. These analysts know that, at times, they will be blindly involved in enactments—especially, of course, with more disturbed patients. Fonagy et al. are at the head of this humane group. Their writing is replete with examples of enactments that are presented in a way deeply sympathetic to therapists who find themselves participating in interactions shaped by various disavowed aspects of their patients' minds. Along with many others, Fonagy et al. understand these enactments to be the effects of the patient's projective identifications, a familiar defense employed periodically by almost everyone, but the habitual defense of those with borderline personality organization.

Mentalization theory adds a detailed and original understanding of how the predilection for projective identification begins and what sustains it. I find especially compelling the descriptions of how parental affect mirroring can go awry and the dire consequences that ensue: the absence of a firm boundary between self and other; the intolerable and continuous threat of being dominated by the alien self; and the inability to construct the secondary representations required to process experience, especially affect, to the depth at which it would be manageable (that is, the interruption of capacity to mentalize). When people can't mentalize, it means they can't convert threatening experience—again, especially affect—into a form in which it can be tolerated and thought about. If you can't think about it, the only solution is to get rid of it, and projective identification is the way to do that. In the face of this onslaught, this attempt by the patient to lodge unwanted aspects of his mind in the therapist's mind, the therapist is understandably drawn into reacting, often quite dramatically. Today we know to encourage therapists who are otherwise capable and committed to their work not to feel too self-punitive about their participation in these episodes.

But note that, no matter how accepting the attitude about being drawn into enactments may be, from this point of view such enactments must be understood as failures—entirely understandable failures, yes, but failures nonetheless. They must be seen as failures because the analyst has not been able to use the part of his mind that, in a better or less challenging world, *could* have been used to maintain his capacity for more or less objective observation.

Now hearken back to the questions I asked a few minutes ago: "Does reflective function pave the way for relational change? Or must relational effects precede reflective function?" The position Fonagy et al. emphasize seems to be that mentalization comes first. The analyst must be able to mentalize if the patient is to relate differently, because a change in relatedness requires the new depth of processing that only mentalization provides. We might also state this position by saying that, in concert with the way psychoanalysis is usually written, internalization (in this case, internalization of the analyst's ability to mentalize) precedes behavioral change.

In making these points, I certainly do not mean to deny that there is plenty of room in mentalization work for the productive use of enactments. If a patient stays in treatment following a mutual emotional storm, the mentalization of the experience behind the enactment, especially the affect, would be the most important and immediate clinical goal for any analytic therapist. The point I want to emphasize is that the therapist's unconscious (relatively) uncontrolled affective involvement with the patient, very often reflected in less than fully controlled clinical conduct, is not itself understood to be productive and desirable. It may be necessary, but it is a necessary misfortune, not an opportunity.

Therapeutic Action in Relational Theory

I mentioned above that there exist in our field two ways of understanding the relationship of mind and clinical interaction. You already may have guessed that, in my view, Relational theory is the alternative understanding. From most Relational perspectives, the analyst is continuously involved in an unconscious way with the patient. There is no part of the mind that exists apart from the influence of the other. Every one of the analyst's thoughts and feelings, and all of her conduct, are constructed by her and are therefore personal and open to the patient's unconscious influence. Even those parts of the analyst's conduct that she selects or constructs on the basis of a theory of technique are personal, because of course every choice could have been made otherwise, and no theory of technique prescribes what we actually do from one moment to the next in any more than a very loose way. Whatever content is being discussed is also being played out in some way in the therapeutic relatedness; and this means that, if analysts assume that their interpretations are nothing more than what they appear to be at face value, they are liable to be participating in ways that do not illuminate the transference but reinforce it instead. And so, without realizing it, it happens that the analyst of a masochistic patient makes sadistic interpretations of masochism; the analyst of a seductive patient who is nevertheless fearful of sexuality makes seductive interpretations of the patient's fear; the analyst of a narcissistically vulnerable patient interprets the narcissism in a way that wounds the patient's self-regard. (This seminal observation was first made by Edgar Levenson [1972, 1983].)

But this is only half the point. Just as inevitably as the patient unconsciously affects the analyst, the analyst unconsciously influences the patient. From this point of view, the relationship is understood to take place between two unconsciously intertwined subjectivities. There is no refuge in the analyst's mind from the patient's influence, no socially isolated perch from which to observe.

One point that becomes immediately apparent for analysts working from this perspective is that the motivation for mentalizing with patients is liable to be just as complicated as the motivation for any other intervention and just as likely to be part of mutual unconscious process, visible or not. Telling a patient he seems angry, sad, or pleased about something, for instance, can serve any number of purposes, many of them the analyst's own purposes, developed at least partially, and unconsciously, in reaction to the patient. And it is not only the *content* of the analyst's reflection that may be an unconscious participation in an ongoing enactment, of course, it's even more likely to be the *manner* in which the content is delivered, which may occur entirely outside the analyst's awareness. Or, for whatever reason, the analyst's perception of his manner may be quite different from the patient's. And when it comes to mentalizing one's *own* reactions and sharing the process with the patient, even if one's reactions seem innocuous at face value, the situation is even more fraught with complication. Think of my earlier example: The analyst says to the patient, "Oh, I thought you meant Y, but now I see you meant X." Innocuous at face value, isn't it? But can't we imagine these words taking on many different emotional resonances, depending on the context within which they are spoken and the expressive qualities with which they are given voice? There may be a corrective to the patient embedded in what is meant to pass as acceptance; or the analyst's tone of voice may be subtly patronizing, signifying that "X" is a less interesting meaning than "Y" would have been. And so on. The exercise of the analyst's reflective function can never be assumed to be a simple or straightforward matter.

I should add, too, that, although it is certainly the case that these ongoing mutual enactments are liable to be most dramatic and disturbing in the treatment of borderline patients, I do not mean my remarks to be specific to work with those patients. What I am saying is meant to apply to all treatments. It is likely that the clinical difficulty for the therapist, and her level of discomfort, declines with milder psychopathology, but the principles are the same. The therapist can certainly *hope*, in other words, that her interventions have a particular impact on the patient; but she can never rely on her conscious intentions alone. She must always be asking herself *what else* than what she knows might she be doing or saying? *How else* might she be involved with the patient than she has considered? What role might her seemingly neutral clinical conduct be playing in that involvement? From a Relational perspective, it is as crucial for the therapist to be continuously curious about the unconscious meanings in her own experience as it is for her to be curious about those in the patient's.

The Interpersonal Field

The mutual influence I have described tends to lock the two participants into certain reciprocal patterns of experience and conduct. It does not matter to me what term we use for the field of influence comprised by the interrelation of these two subjectivities. Sullivan's (1940) term was "the interpersonal field," although he meant something slightly different from what we mean today; Mitchell (1988) called it "the relational matrix"; Wolstein (1959) referred to "the transference/countertransference interlock." There are others. Whichever term we choose, the point is that the clinical situation is mutually constructed and conducted, though asymmetrical (Aron, 1996). That is, while maintaining roles that differ in expertise, clinical experience, power, and so on, patients and therapists also relate in a mutual way, as two human beings. Even if they wanted to, they could not do otherwise. For this reason, the patient's transference tends to draw the analyst into a certain kind of countertransference; and the analyst's transference has the same effect on the patient. Sometimes, over time, these meaningfully related interactive patterns, when they are motivated by both parties' dissociations, become mutual enactments. Both parties play roles in maintaining rigid patterns of this kind.

It follows from this point of view that the therapist's expertise cannot be rooted in invulnerability to the patient's influence or in the ability to grasp the nature of the patient's influence and resist being transformed by it. Sometimes therapists indeed are invulnerable, but that is not necessarily a state to be desired. We need our vulnerabilities. And sometimes therapists do sense the patient's influence before responding to it. That, too, though, is not inevitably a good thing, because it can sometimes deprive patients of their habitual ways of making relationships, what Feiner (1982) has called their "ticket of admission."

The analytic expertise that allows us to practice over many decades without burning out grows from a special kind of *acceptance* of our vulnerability and a consequent ability to observe how we *have already been* influenced. To reach something new, we must usually find a way to transcend or deconstruct the old; and to do that requires, often or even usually, that, without our awareness, we create the old in the therapeutic relatedness and then make it visible, available for reflection by both patient and analyst. To articulate the old *is* to create the new. Like water rushing in to fill an empty space, the new comes about by itself, in a way we may not even be able to imagine, when room is made for it by our reflection on the old (see the theory of narrative proposed in Chapter 5).

If this is so, then the most important question is what happens to make it possible to reflect on the old, on what has been invisible. What makes it possible, that is, for the new to leap into being? Whatever this is, it is seldom reflection. Reflection is usually an outcome. By the time you can reflect on the old, it has already lost its bite. New reflection opens up other areas for consideration and change, and in that way the process of change proceeds outward, in ripples. It is often, but not always, the case that taking advantage of the therapeutic potential of new perceptions *requires* their mentalization. But the process usually begins in something that comes before reflection. The process begins in something that makes reflection possible.

My candidate for this "something" is the development of a new perception of the other (see Chapters 3–6). I am not alone in taking this position (see Bromberg, 1998, 2006). The new perception in question may be the analyst's new perception of the patient, or it may the patient's new perception of the analyst. That happens, too. Most often, as in the example I will offer you in a moment, it is difficult to say who had the new perception first. But whatever the origin of a new perception of the other, once you have it, especially when the affective tone of that perception is different from the tone of the previous relatedness, you can't *help* relating to the other in a new way. You couldn't relate in the old way if you tried—at least, not authentically. Among other freedoms that become available at such a moment is the freedom to mentalize what is newly visible and therefore first accessible to mentalization. The new perception itself remains to be mentalized, of course; but it is also now possible to reflect on the unseen bonds that had constricted the therapeutic relatedness into the patterns of the preceding enactment.

Although I do believe that the "new perception" is key to the dissolution of enactments, I do not want to leave the impression that I believe insight to be inconsequential or nothing more than an epiphenomenon. Insight about a new perception necessarily follows the events it describes; but once understanding does arise, it is involved in the creation of the next generation of clinical events, which would have been different if the new understanding had not come about in the first place. And so, in the end, reflective function and new perception have continuous, reciprocal parts to play in therapeutic action.

Illustration

I had met with a very bright middle-aged professional man three times a week for a year and a half. Ron was enthusiastic about beginning an analysis. He hoped to reignite his career, which had been spectacular, but was now sputtering. Although I had expected to enjoy working with him, shortly after we started I found myself dreading Ron's sessions. He was seldom openly angry or dissatisfied, but he frequently told me that my skill was inadequate and that I was not warm enough in manner. He made these observations very politely, but I felt the bite of them; and he treated me in a way that conveyed his criticisms even when he wasn't making them. He told me repeatedly that his primary interest in life was to be as generous and kind as possible to his wife and children. He also participated, apart from the family, in numerous personal and political activities. I often admired the commitment behind many of these activities, familial and extrafamilial alike; but what struck me most regularly and forcefully about them was his presentation of each one as another evidence of his virtue. There was a continuous and subtle suggestion that his virtue was notable, especially when compared to others—and I felt that "others" in this case certainly included me.

Any attempt on my part to point out things in his experience that might complicate this picture (for example, less positive effects) was met with a rueful smile and a demurral. Ron really wished he could identify what I saw in his experience, he would say, but he just could not. In the meantime, his wife, who seemed quite unreasonable to me when Ron began treatment, flew into daily, seemingly unprovoked rages at him. It was not long before I thought I understood how she felt. Ron's virtue, and especially his advertisement of it, most particularly his smiling "patience" in the face of others' frustration with him, was itself a provocation.

Ron's critical observations of me were perfectly accurate, of course, because my reaction to the way he treated me was to feel irritated with him. I felt that way much of the time I was with him. I was often cool and distant, and I was certainly unsuccessful in the pursuit of what he called his "feelings," which, as far as I could see, were limited to two registers: warm, loving, and appreciative; or mournful and sad, a reaction to the regrettable absence of warmth, love, and appreciation in others. I did not know which I disliked more, him with me or me with him. And yet, of course, I also felt that I should be finding a way of working with this state of affairs. I felt interested in whatever I could learn about what was happening between us; but I also felt guilty and self-critical.

I knew that my patient's reactions and my own were interlocked. But as is usually the case, knowing this in the abstract was not enough to help me out of the field's grip. I talked with Ron many times about his dissatisfaction with me and about the kind of relatedness that had come to exist between us. I told him that we needed to find a new way to see what was transpiring between us. Naturally, he asked how we should do that. I did my best to answer the question, but nothing I said seemed to set us on a new path. Ron did begin to tell me, though, that this kind of relatedness had taken place elsewhere in his life, including in his relationship with his wife. He usually dealt with it by ending the relationship, he said, although, for various reasons, he had not done that in his marriage. He spoke often about leaving treatment, but he agreed that it would be better not to do that if instead we could find a way to come out the other side of what was going on between us.

At least now we were sometimes agreeing that we had a mutual problem. Sometimes, Ron could accept that it was possible that his wife and I were not merely unreasonable and persecutory. He was willing to go this far, I think, because he saw that I took his distress seriously, even though he also still felt that I was culpable. But we did not have a convincing way to characterize this problem, which therefore remained mutual in only a hypothetical way. It was clear to me that, without getting some traction in real experience, even the glimmerings of collaboration between us about the issue were not going to keep the treatment going for long.

The beginning of a break in the deadlock came about one day when Ron was once again talking about his doubts about continuing in treatment.

This time, though, he did not say it with anger, but with regret. He looked different to me, helpless, despairing. He said he did not want the same thing to happen yet again: another relationship abandoned because of his dissatisfaction with it. In response, I said something to him that I had said more than once before: I told him I felt sure that our relationship was somehow mirroring a significant relationship from his past, though I did not know which one. But this time, responding (I think) to Ron's changed demeanor, I made the point more softly and with my own feelings of regret. I added that I, too, must be involved in maintaining what was transpiring between us, that I could not imagine how it could be otherwise.

Before I had spoken I had gauged that Ron would understand and accept what I said as an expression of my regret, not as a statement of my willingness to talk about my past. It turned out I was right. But when I say that I "gauged" Ron's response, I do not mean that I actually formulated this meaning in my mind. Nor did I formulate until a few minutes later the part of this moment that surprised me most: my confidence that I could trust Ron not to use what I said as one more reason to criticize me. This was a new perception of Ron, and I would not have had it unless he had somehow treated me differently, in some small way I could not specify. And so it seems likely that he had also perceived me differently. Something between us had shifted.

At this point, Ron began telling me more about his relationship with his father than I had yet heard. His father had been much more continuously and severely critical, unnecessarily brutal really, than Ron had let me know to that point. Ron told me that his hatred and fear of his father had therefore been more intense, and more troubling to him, than he had related before. Within a few minutes it was clear to me that my patient had suffered much more than I had understood.

Later, I asked Ron what he knew about why he had not told me more about this aspect of his relationship with his father. He said he had not been aware of hiding it, but that when it began to come out of him, he realized that he had always been ashamed of having been treated this way, and that it was his shame that had kept him silent about it. I was glad Ron mentalized this shame because it was better coming from him. But if he had not described it, I would have, because the feeling had been palpable in the room.

It was not long before his shame and rage at having been humiliated by his father could be linked to the way he felt I treated him and the way he treated me. Having been so ashamed, he had wanted to shame me—and he had—by making it clear that he was more decent and loving than I was. He would not descend to his father's overt sadism; but it was not long before he appreciated the irony that his "goodness" was its own form of sadism. For Ron, of course, I had been his father; and for me, he had been a member of my own family. As is often the case in emotionally intense enactments, our dissociations had been reciprocal.

This session and those that came after it indicated to me that the treatment would probably not founder, and it did not. We moved on to Ron's longings for his father (and for me), longings that his rage and humiliation had always obscured.

I am going to leave my account at this point, because my intention is only to illustrate my contention that shifts in relatedness precede mentalization. I will not take up here the crucial question of *why* the new perceptions became available to Ron and me when they did. I have addressed that matter in Chapters 3–6, though. It is a very knotty problem. I believe that, while there are indeed some significant things that can be said about the reasons for new perceptions, there is a mystery at the heart of the matter. Seldom if ever do we really know exactly why new perceptions and the interactive freedom they herald arrive when they do.

It is not clear to me whose new perception of the other came first. I suspect, actually, that any attempt to establish priority is doomed to failure, because you can follow the interaction back through any number of episodes, all of which led up to the present moment. There is no marker that tells you that you have reached the source; and that is probably because the events cannot realistically be said to have sprung from a single moment. This is the best account I can offer: Ron would not have spoken to me with the regret he showed if he were seeing me, at that moment, as the sadistic father. I responded immediately to this new feeling on his part, and a new perception of *him* also awakened in *my* mind. It would be true to say that, prior to my new ways of seeing Ron, I wanted badly to be able to treat him differently. But that desire was born less of an empathic grasp of Ron's need for a different response than it was of the narcissistic injury I was suffering of being a bad analyst.

Once I perceived Ron differently, whether I *wanted* to treat him differently or not was immaterial. You might say I was *drawn* to treat him differently; or you might even say I *had* to. I certainly no longer would have been able to treat him as I had just a few minutes earlier; nor could I have rid myself of my sudden empathic appreciation of Ron's situation, even if I had wanted to—which, of course, I did not. This is the kind of moment that inspired the title of this chapter: I found what I had not known how to look for. I did not make it happen; I was taken by it. In my experience, that is how all enactments end. We must put ourselves in the best position we can, which we do by not giving up our attempt to do analytic work; but after that, we can only wait for freedom to arrive.

Of course, only a small proportion of our opportunities for reflection with our patients grow from the breach of a mutual enactment. It is nevertheless worth noting that there are very often moments when it becomes possible for us to say something new to our patients, something we could not have said a few minutes before. Many of the best interpretations arise in this way. I think the principle governing the appearance of novelty in the experience of either the patient or the analyst is always the same, whether we are talking about the new perceptions that break up intense enactments or the everyday appearance in the analyst's mind of reflections she has not had before: To *say* something new requires that you *be* something new. Sometimes you must change considerably, as I had to with Ron; and sometimes the changes are so subtle that we do not even notice them. We are always in the position of having to find what we do not know how to look for, even when we do not know it. And so I believe that I probably differ with the writers of mentalization theory over the relative emphases to place on the alternative answers to the question about therapeutic action with which I began. To me, it more often seems that a shift in relatedness opens the possibility for new mentalization rather than that mentalization creates the opportunity for new relatedness. In the other set of terms I have used, the point can be put this way: Internalization of the analyst's ability to mentalize seldom catalyzes relational change; more frequently, it seems to me, a shift in relatedness allows the processing of the dissociated aspects of the social environment to a new depth. But of course we must also admit that clinical process can move in both these directions.

Was my unconscious involvement with Ron regrettable? Was there a better way to learn about his humiliation and longing? As far as I am concerned, this part of Ron's experience might very well not have come to light if it had not been enacted. I am not the least bit flippant about the gravity of the issue of the analyst's unconscious involvement. I feel quite serious about it; I recognize that it can injure treatments—and patients. But I also believe that continuous unconscious involvement is consistent with some of the most significant kinds of analytic discipline. Keep in mind that I was able to build and maintain enough of a collaboration with Ron that he stayed until we were able to do the work I have described.

I wish pain on neither patients nor myself, and I do what I can, within the limits of my job, to avoid arousing unnecessary pain and to relieve it when it has become unavoidable. But emotional pain comes with the territory. We all know this, but I think the point is especially clear if you believe, as I do, that dissociated experience is unformulated experience. Dissociated experience cannot be represented, consciously or unconsciously; it has yet to attain a shape articulated or realized clearly enough to allow representation. Mutual enactments are our only route of access to these parts of our patients' minds; as enactments end, the experience can finally be formulated. The idea that enacted experience is unformulated is what led me, at the beginning of this chapter, to claim not only that we must find what we do not know how to look for, but that what we are looking for does not exist until we find it.

The therapist has no recourse to being personally involved. Patients cannot directly experience their dissociated parts, but their therapists can. In fact, therapists have no choice but to experience their patient's dissociated pain; that is what it means, from the therapist's vantage point, to be involved in a mutual enactment. Therapists must experience the version of the patient's pain that is brought to life in their own psyches. In the process, therapists suffer a good deal of discomfort. In fact, with clinical experience, we come to recognize what we can sense about such discomforts as opportunities, as what I have referred to in Chapters 3 and 4 as "emotional snags and chafing" and as "intimations of freedom."

We must respect the danger posed by mutual enactments. I know that things with Ron could have gone differently; he could have left treatment in despair. In situations such as this one, we work on the razor's edge. This is one time that the old saw is true: If enactments don't kill you, they make you stronger.

I hope I have managed to convey that the most important instances of reflective function inevitably surprise us. The parts of life we can already point at, that lack only a name, are not the places of mystery within which the most significant change occurs. The mentalization of experience is unquestionably critical, especially with sicker patients. But to name a part of experience that you already know is an operation that you can tell someone else how to carry out. It is basically a technical procedure: Name it, so that the patient begins to be able to represent it symbolically. Clinically speaking, if you can already point at something, if you know it is there, then naming it is not a particularly creative act. Naming experiences we already know is not what excites us about our work. We eventually find what we most need in what we begin by not knowing how to experience. We have to find a part of our subjectivity that was not even a presence in our minds until it was created in unconscious reciprocity with the patient.

Coda

What exactly can we say, then, about the significance of reflective function? What I believe is this: Socrates was right, although he was right for the wrong reasons. We psychoanalysts often do find what we do not know how to look for. And the unfortunate inebriate was wrong: We do not waste our time looking only in the light. We try to locate the places of mystery, the parts of our relatedness with the patient that we just cannot seem to find words for, that (to begin with) we may not even be able to shape into a coherent set of events; and we do that even when, or even especially when, those parts of relatedness are uncomfortable. We immerse ourselves in this discomfort, feeling it so thoroughly that we know it from the inside. We try to deny ourselves no part of it; we try to allow ourselves to become saturated with its effects. And then, eventually, at least when we are fortunate, we find ourselves surprised by a new perception of the other, of ourselves, of the two of us together. Something has released, and we are both more free than we were the moment before.

To my mind, this is not what most psychoanalytic writers mean by insight—that is, I do not believe that this is what such writers usually understand to be the way reflective function is used in treatment. Does that group of writers include Fonagy et al.? I started out, as I wrote this chapter, believing that the answer to that question was probably yes. That is, I believed that Fonagy et al. held a different view of insight than I do, and that is the conclusion that I have offered.

But after discussions with both Fonagy and Target at the conference on mentalization at which this chapter was first presented as a paper, I am less sure of the answer to the question. Fonagy and Target each told me, independently, that they saw their views and mine as consonant. They both said they found nothing to disagree with in my position that it is a new perception of the patient by the analyst, or of the analyst by the patient, that eventually makes it possible to mentalize the frozen events of a mutual unconscious enactment. Fonagy did emphasize, though, that we must continue to think about enactments as problematic, and therefore unwelcome.

We cannot deny that enactments can be problematic, even destructive; and it is certainly true that the repair of the relationship after an enactment, even if that repair is a crucial therapeutic result, implies that we (the analyst) have participated in damaging it; and damage is obviously not what we intend to accomplish. And so we must say, from this point of view, that enactments are unwelcome.

On the other hand, the material represented via enactment very often simply cannot be accessed or represented in any other way. I have already made the points I will offer in the remainder of this paragraph and the one to follow; but it is worth giving these matters particular emphasis, because they are the heart of the matter. Dissociated experience is unformulated. It is a global, nonideational affective state. It is not until this material appears in the relational world as enactment that it even becomes *possible* to mentalize it; and often enough, of course, mentalization remains prohibitively difficult under even these more favorable circumstances.

Dissociated material in the patient's mind frequently first "shows up" or "becomes visible" via the analyst's participation in enactments, participation that begins as unconscious. The analyst's participation in enactments is a significant part of what Sandler (1976) called the analyst's free-floating "role responsiveness." The analyst must participate in this deeply affective, nonconscious way, and then struggle, over time, to grasp the nature of that involvement. And even then—even when it becomes possible for the analyst to grasp his own involvement—the analyst cannot consciously choose to engage in the thinking that makes that grasp possible. Instead, the thinking *arrives* in the analyst's mind. It is unbidden. That is the only route to the mentalization of dissociated material.

It is from within this perspective that I welcome enactments. The freedom we are seeking requires us to plunge into the maelstrom. And so, while we suffer real pain and sometimes racking self-criticism over the myriad ways that enactment compromises us as analysts, we also welcome the opportunities that the necessity to suffer this pain brings us.

If there is a genuine difference between my views and mentalization theory, it has to do with the degree of centrality we assign to the nature of the analyst's experience in enactments and the kind of clinical use we make of that experience. It has to do with the consistency with which we understand the content of the session to be an outcome of clinical process, a process that is inevitably interactive and contextual and in which both analyst and patient are continuously involved in an unconscious way. If there is a difference, it is not a difference in kind, but in emphasis, in the degree to which we espouse the view that unconscious, interactive process precedes content in clinical work. But I am also impressed with how much we share. Few psychoanalytic writers hold views about dissociation and clinical process as close as those of the mentalization theorists, on one hand, and of Relational dissociation theorists, on the other.

9

"One Never Knows, Do One?"
The Relation of the Work of the Boston
Change Process Study Group and
Relational Dissociation Theory

I have been reading and teaching the papers of theBoston Change Process
Study Group since the first one appeared (D.N. Stern, et al., 1998). My
enthusiasm for this body of work is due to the basic sympathy between
their views and my own. I begin by detailing some of those agreements,
and then go on, later in the chapter, to take issue with some of BCPSG's
positions. Because we have so much in common, I want to contextualize
our disagreements within the substantial degree of similarity of our views
in many other respects. The points I discuss bear on all the papers in the
series to date (D. N. Stern, et al., 1998; BCPSG, 2002, 2003, 2207, 2008).

Agreements

First comes the focus BCPSG and I share on the clinical situation, especially on the details of clinical process, and a certain democratic attitude
toward what transpires in the consulting room, well expressed in Lew
Aron's (1996) observation that, while therapeutic roles are necessarily
asymmetrical, the human mutuality that lies at the heart of treatment is
not. The democratic attitude and focus on detailed clinical process that is
so characteristic of BCPSG's work also defined the ground of my training
as an Interpersonal psychoanalyst; and the same attitudes came to shape
the Relational perspective, the second half of my psychoanalytic identity.
Another general point of agreement is the attitude shared by BCPSG and
Relational analysts, including me, that psychotherapy and psychoanalysis are simultaneously social and intrapsychic enterprises, meaning that

their contents and processes are inevitably and continuously mutually constructed.

BCPSG and I share many more specific psychoanalytic positions as well. We have similar conceptions of what it means to describe something as unconscious. Here is a representative quotation (BCPSG, 2008):

> In spontaneous speech, there is something in mind that wants expressing. Let us call this "something in mind" an image, in the broadest sense of the term. The image can be an idea, a movement, a gesture, an affect, a vitality affect, a background feeling. None of these are presently in verbal form.

A nonverbal "something in mind" is reminiscent of what I mean by "unformulated experience" (D. B. Stern, 1983, 1997). Furthermore, BCPSG agrees with me that language does not come about by matching words to the "something in mind." Instead they tell us, just after the description I have just quoted, "Now comes the messy work, especially in spontaneous dialogue. There is an intention (with its goal and structure) to link the image with words. For almost each phrase, the intention enters into a dynamic process with the existent repertoire of pieces of language to find the best fits." About these "fits," they write later, "it doesn't matter if there is a 'right' fit. None such exists. It only has to be good enough for effective communication." Compare that with my view (D. B. Stern, 1983, 1997) that the meaning in a particular unformulated experience may take any one of the more precise formulated meanings toward which it moves. Meaning, that is, becomes creation, not discovery. "Insight into an unconscious wish," says Herbert Fingarette (1963), "is like noticing a well-formed 'ship' in the cloud instead of a poorly formed 'rabbit.' On the other hand, insight is not like discovering an animal which has been hiding in the bushes" (p 80).

Years later, in discussing Fingarette's point, I wrote: "We can now add that the cloud itself changes with the passage of time, and so the ship inevitably disappears; and even before it does, if one keeps looking, perhaps one sees a tree in the cloud that is even better formed than a ship" (D. B. Stern, 1997, p. 176). It seems that my views and those of BCPSG accord concerning the nature of the fit between an expression in the verbal-reflective domain and its implicit referent.

Another similarity: although BCPSG does say that the verbal-reflective "emerges from" the implicit, they also make it clear that they do not intend to characterize the verbal-reflective as a "higher" form of thinking or experiencing. Instead, they understand these two domains to be in a relation of continuous mutual influence. Referring to the verbal-reflective and the implicit, they say this: "it is not a duet of separate instruments. Instead one voice emerges and is derivative of the other." BCPSG cites Merleau-Ponty in support of this position, as I do repeatedly through my work. For a long time (D. B. Stern, 1997), and especially in the recent past (D. B. Stern, 2002a), I have been presenting the verbal and the nonverbal as the most significant contexts for each other. Each defines the possibilities of the other. This view and the view of BCPSG also seem to coincide.

BCPSG and I also seem to agree that a substantial part of therapeutic action takes place in the realm of the implicit. In discussions, several members of BCPSG and I have sometimes disagreed over the degree to which, after unconscious mutual enactments end, they must be described in language in order to be mutative. I generally felt more strongly than they did that the meaning embodied in an enactment must be formulated in language to be clinically useful, at least often; but it was very clear that BCPSG and I were on the same page in focusing our primary attention on the nonverbal negotiation of relatedness (e.g., S. Pizer, 1998) in the treatment situation.

I am stretching a point to call the meaning of unconscious mutual enactment implicit. It is perhaps closer to my view to say that such meanings are dynamically unconscious, by which I mean two things: (1) they do not exist relative to verbal language, but apart from it; (2) they are specifically (that is, defensively) excluded from awareness. Implicit meanings, in my frame of reference, are those that can be directly represented in language; dynamically unconscious ones, on the other hand, cannot be. Dynamically unconscious meanings are what Fourcher (1992) calls the "absolute unconscious." BCPSG's "implicit relational knowing" (IRK) is not dynamically unconscious, either in BCPSG's view or in mine, because IRK is not specifically excluded from awareness; but because of its nature, IRK cannot necessarily be verbally represented either. It therefore lies, for me, on the border between the implicit and the absolute unconscious.

And finally, BCPSG and I agree on the following closely related matters: the emergent quality of meaning; meaning as process, not structure; and meaning-making as continuous. We can summarize this position as the view that meaning is a continuous emergent process. As significant as all our other similarities may be, this may be the most important of them. In fact, I think that this position is one of the most significant links between BCPSG and most, perhaps even all, Relational analysts.

I will explain later how BCPSG and I differ over the source of meaning's emergent quality—that is, over the question of epistemology. But we certainly do agree about the presence of this emergent quality. BCPSG's work, rooted as it is in nonlinear dynamic systems theory, grows from the claim that the events of psychotherapy and psychoanalysis, and IRK in particular, are unpredictable, nonlinear, and emergent. The analyst's task is therefore participation in, and sometimes the discovery of, the involvement that is in the process of developing. For BCPSG, as for Relational analysts, the clinician is not in a position to grasp this involvement and offer interpretations of it as it transpires, because the involvement is always in the process of becoming. Knowing must lag behind participation, that is, if knowing develops at all. Therapeutic action does not rest on the analyst's revelation of the truth but rather on participation in an unfolding, emergent process, what BCPSG started out calling "the 'something more' than interpretation" (D. N. Stern, et al., 1998; BCPSG, 2005). All of this is very congenial to most Relational analysts, including me.

I like very much the BCPSG idea, derived from the work of Louis Sander, that intentions are the basic units of psychological meaning, and that sequences of intentions "give motivated human behavior its psychological existence, coherence and finally its meaning" (BCPSG, 2008, p. 129). Furthermore, I agree that the "intention unfolding process" (p. 129) occurs implicitly. This "silence" in the process helps us to understand why so much of what we identify as "me" occurs unwittingly and yet feels so much as if it is our own. I have pursued for years the themes that we often find ourselves in possession of intentions that we did not know we had, and that what feels most like our own is experience that we have no consciousness of having created (e.g., D. B. Stern, 1983, 1990, 1997). The intention unfolding process is one of the few conceptions I have come across that begins to help us think through this common and compelling phenomenon. The idea allows us to theorize the continuity across the implicit and verbal-reflective domains that we intuitively know is there, and that results in our sense of identity. The intention unfolding process "acts as the referent to identity ... creating a common coinage across levels" (BCPSG, 2008, p. 130). The process takes place, of course, outside the realm of conscious will, which is why what we most deeply intend nevertheless has the capacity sometimes to surprise us. We are very often in the position, BCPSG suggests, of discovering our intentions, not consciously creating them. Of course, this insight corresponds to a cornerstone of psychoanalytic treatment: We must not assume that we always know what we desire, but instead must observe (feel our way into) the desires that already exist, in some ways just as we observe them in others. Only later, when we are better acquainted with them and with our previously unconscious reluctances to allow them to be "me," will we be able to sense them directly.

How the intention unfolding process, in its definition as a "referent to identity ... creating a common coinage across levels," applies to the conception of the multiple self piques my interest. Can the intention unfolding process be paired with the idea of multiple self-states in a way that would further the understanding of how, at least in fortunate cases, people have the capacity to feel like one person while being many, or as Bromberg (1998) puts it, how we "stand in the spaces" between self-states?

In the BCPSG (2008) discussion of intention, I like the way that the marvelously expressive word "chunk" allows a description of continuity across streams of otherwise disparate-seeming modes of experience, as in, "The intention unfolding process arises from a fundamental psychological process that chunks the flow of motivated human behavior into intentions" (p. 129). I have trouble with the word "fundamental" in this sentence and elsewhere, though, and also with such phrases as "innate mental tendency," used to describe the intention unfolding process a couple of sentences later—but I defer discussion of this point until I address the question of epistemology.

One last note here: Most psychoanalysts are well aware of the work of Fonagy and his colleagues (2002) on mentalization. Mentalization theory links firmly with the thinking that BCPSG has done and makes both bodies of work that much more compelling. There seems to be an increasingly wide recognition of the significance in psychological life of inferring intentions, both others' and our own.

These are at least some of the similarities between my views and those of BCPSG. But I have also developed questions as I have read the BCPSG papers, questions that are that much more important to me because of our agreement on so many other matters. The first two of these questions, one concerning enactment and the other about the use of nonlinear dynamic systems theory, may very well be negotiable. The last question, which concerns science and social construction, probably represents an enduring disagreement. My discussion of all three questions, though, presents the thoughts of a friend and fellow traveler.

The Question of Enactment

We have already seen that BCPSG goes this far: They accept that the analyst is inevitably involved with the patient on both conscious and unconscious levels; and that it is not possible for the analyst to observe his or her own involvement until after it has taken place—that is, observation must always be at least a step behind participation. I do not have the sense across the work of BCPSG, though, that they have emphasized the significance of the analyst as a particular personality as much as I and most other Relational analysts do. And (partly) because of that, BCPSG does not give unconscious mutual enactment the place in their views that it holds in most of ours.

BCPSG has not taken the step into conceiving the analytic relationship to be fully personal, with all the problems that an intensive personal relationship inevitably has. Granted, the personal relationship of analyst and patient is very strange because it is also a very particular kind of professional relationship, with firm boundaries of a professional kind. But it *is* a personal relationship. BCPSG's clinical illustrations do not reveal anything like the kind of enactments that are routine in the Relational literature. There are minor difficulties between analysts and patients, but these are not intense personal entanglements. I do not remember an example from these papers in which either the patient or the analyst felt that the conduct of the other was more than negligibly problematic.

I suspect that the absence of mutual enactment in the work of BCPSG has to do, ironically enough, with the source of BCPSG's conviction about the inevitability of unconscious mutual influence—a conviction that is one of the most significant points of agreement between BCPSG and Relational psychoanalysis. BCPSG seems to take their version of this conviction from the longstanding involvement of a number of its members in some of the first and most innovative mother–infant observation research.[1] In that context, inevitable mutual unconscious influence is generally conceived under the rubric of mutual regulation.[2] In the recent past, those processes of mutual regulation have begun to be described, by some of the same writers, between patient and therapist (D. N. Stern, et al., 1998; BCPSG, 2002, 2005, 2007, 2008; Beebe & Lachmann, 2002; Lachmann & Beebe, 1996; D. N. Stern, 2004). For the most part, mutual regulation, whether between mother and infant or patient and analyst, is a continuous sequence of relatively small, mutual, and nonconscious accommodations and adjustments.

Relational psychoanalysis, on the other hand, emphasizes interpersonal disjunctions and resolutions that take place on a larger and more con-

---

[1] For example, Lyons-Ruth (1991, 2003); Lyons-Ruth, Connell, Zoll, and Stahl, (1987); Lyons-Ruth et al. (1998); Nahum (1994, 2000); Sander (1962); D. N. Stern (1971, 1977, 1985, 1995).
[2] See Beebe and Lachmann (1988, 1994); Gianino and Tronick (1988); Jaffe, Beebe, Feldstein, and Crown (2001); D. N. Stern (1985, 1995); Tronick (1989, 1998); Tronick and Weinberg (1997).

flictual scale.[1] There exists no counterpart in the mother–infant observation literature to this larger-scale kind of enactment; and therefore, it is
perhaps because BCPSG has such deep roots in that part of the field that
the Relational interest in large-scale enactment has not flowed as naturally
into their thinking.[2]

From an Interpersonal or Relational perspective, interaction between
patient and analyst is a sequence of successes and failures, like any human
relationship. It is a familiar Relational theme that mutual unconscious
enactment is more an opportunity than a detriment. That is because it is
the part of the patient that the patient does not and will not know (in the
sense that this part of the patient's experience is dissociated, not available
to consciousness) that has brought the patient into treatment, the part of
the person that, after Sullivan (1954), several of us (Chefetz & Bromberg,
2004; D. B. Stern, 2003, 2004, 2006), notably Bromberg (1998, 2006), call
not-me, exists only as unformulated experience. Because not-me cannot
be given symbolic form (it is defensively maintained in an unformulated
state [D. B. Stern, 1997]), it can enter the treatment *only* via enactment
(Bromberg, 1998, 2006; see also Chapters 1 and 3–6 in this book). Some
of these enactments do not reach the analyst in a way that provokes the
analyst's own dissociations (and thus also provoke the answering part
of a mutual enactment); but some of the patient's enactments do reach
the analyst in that way, setting in motion a mutual enactment. Whether
mutual enactment is the outcome or not, the opportunities offered by the
arousal of the not-me part of the patient's personality can only be actualized if the unconscious parts of the interaction, which can sometimes be
deeply distressing and unpleasant for both parties, become possible for
analyst and patient to "know." Not-me, that is, must become me for both
participants. Non-self must become self. In the case of mutual enactment, quite common in Relational annals, the analyst must grow, not
only the patient (for a detailed presentation of this process, see Chapter
4).

I do not see in the work of BCPSG an acknowledgment of this part
of the work, which to me lies at its heart. BCPSG might answer that

---

[1] See Aron (2003a, 2003b); Bass (2003); Benjamin (1998); Black (2003); Bromberg (1998, 2006);
Davies (1997, 1999, 2003, 2004); Davies and Frawley (1994); B. Pizer (2003); S. Pizer (1998); D. B.
Stern (2003, 2004).

[2] Beebe and Lachmann (2005; Lachmann & Beebe, 1996) write about what they call the sequence
of disruption and repair, a much larger-scale kind of mutual regulation that bears an interesting
relationship to the concept of mutual unconscious enactment. Considering the issues raised by
these writers would take me too far from the thrust of this chapter.

the analyst's personality and his or her unconscious participation is an unmistakable part of the concept of IRK. I agree with this point. IRK is a joint, emergent, and unpredictable production of therapist and patient, and it depends on the contribution of each—and, from the analyst's position, the personal contribution as well as the professional one. The issue for me is the *degree* and *depth* to which the influence of the analyst's personal contribution is acknowledged. Despite the inclusion of the analyst's personhood in IRK, I do not see in the work of BCPSG a place for either the "affective snags and chafings" (see Chapters 3 and 4) that alert the analyst to his unconscious involvement and reactivity, or for the sometimes intensely difficulty entanglements that relational analysts, especially those writing about dissociation, have made the focus of clinical and theoretical attention. To say this is not to claim that BCPSG cannot accommodate these ideas and phenomena, only to point out that, up to now, they have not done so. As a matter of fact, I see no reason why these central relational concerns cannot be brought into the kind of theory BCPSG is developing.

Nonlinear Dynamic Systems Theory

It has always seemed to me that psychoanalysis needed to look beyond its own backyard for inspiration. Nonlinear dynamic systems theory (NDST), which originated in mathematics and the hard sciences, seems to hold great promise for many fields, and a growing number of psychoanalysts, BCPSG prominent among them, feel that the list of those fields should include our own. If you add to BCPSG's use of NDST their application of Lakoff and Johnson's (1999) seminal work on metaphor, you must conclude that the body of BCPSG's work exemplifies the interdisciplinary ideal. I subscribe to this ideal myself and admire it in the work of others.

NDST is a way of understanding the simultaneous interaction of a multitude of events and influences—hundreds, thousands, even more. It is a way of grasping how events of almost unimaginable complexity come into being. And of course this multitude of influences does not merely sum to an outcome; the influences also interact with one another along the way. The degree of complexity is astonishing. It is also unpredictable and nonlinear (i.e., changes do not necessarily take place in an orderly way as the result of an accumulation of influence, and may actually be quite sudden). What often appears to be chaos on the surface of things is, if we look closely enough, the manifestation of very complex kinds of order. That is why NDST is also known as chaos theory or complexity theory. NDST is a growing body of ideas about the rules that govern these kinds of phenomena, which are much more common in our world than we used to believe. This is the kind of description and explanation NDST offers, and that is what stirs me about it.

Yet I am uncertain about whether NDST is useful when applied to relational events. I mean "uncertain" literally, not as a euphemism for disagreement. I can present my reservation only by offering a little preliminary explication.

Arguably, Esther Thelen (who died only a couple of years ago, tragically, in her early 60s) and her collaborator, Linda B. Smith, researchers in developmental psychology, have done more to bring NDST to the study of psychology, and through that application, to psychoanalysis, than any other writers (Smith & Thelen, 1993; Thelen & Smith, 1994). Their book on cognition and action (Thelen & Smith, 1994) proposes a theory that accounts for enormously complex phenomena. Yet as speculative as this work is, Thelen and Smith are rooted in very detailed examinations of such phenomena as infant locomotion (it turns out that, if you examine the development of locomotion on the level of minute detail, infants vary enormously in how they progress toward the common endpoint of walking) and infant reaching toward objects ("from the messy details of real time ... global order can emerge" [p. 247]). In fact, most research using NDST in developmental psychology has focused on the study of simple actions—behaviors in space—because what is needed for research from the NDST perspective is a vast number of the most minute kinds of observations, enough to reveal underlying, complex patterns invisible at most levels of understanding, and for that you need very fine-grained measurement, the kind of measurement that is available by mapping points in space (Fischer & Rose, 1999). And therefore, action is vastly more practical to investigate using nonlinear dynamics than more complex parts of human life such as cognition and affect—to say nothing of the unimaginable degree of complexity introduced by considering the interaction of *two* of these nonlinear systems (two human beings, for instance). It seems to me, admittedly a layperson in these matters, that the interaction of two systems of enormous complexity must increase the number of relevant influences on the outcome one is studying by a factor that is geometric, not arithmetic.

That is hardly a reason not to use NDST in psychoanalysis. But it may be a reason to be cautious. The classical systems theorists—von

Bertalanffy (1968) and Bronfenbrenner (1979), for instance,[1] spent many years criticizing the narrowness and simple-mindedness of most explanatory theory and research in the social sciences, including psychology. But they were hindered in taking their work further by the fact that, unlike NDST, classical systems theory did not have clear enough implications for the development of new theory and research methodologies. That older generation of systems theorists could only lament the absence of a more sophisticated appreciation of complexity.

And that is what I worry about today. Are we really able to do more than acknowledge what we all know is the reality of emergent process and multitudinous influences on experience and interaction in the consulting room? Are we able to do more than point at it? Exactly how *does* NDST illuminate data for BCPSG that would have been invisible or seemed irrelevant otherwise? What specific findings or theory would not have developed if BCPSG had limited themselves to classical systems theory, for instance, and had simply said to themselves, "Well, the clinical setting continuously generates conduct and experience in and between its participants that is obviously enormously complex. What will we come up with if we take that view as a starting point and then interpret detailed clinical process as the continuously emerging outcome of this enormously complex set of processes?" Would BCPSG have been able to create their compelling views of the therapeutic situation using just this much theory, or would their views have been impossible without specific NDST propositions? If the answer is that NDST propositions have indeed been essential to the theory creation of BCPSG, which propositions are they?

We know that BCPSG, like other researchers in our field who use NDST, do not collect the voluminous data that comprise NDST studies in (for instance) developmental psychology. In other words, NDST in

---

[1] I am writing here about academic psychology, but if I were writing about classical systems theory in psychoanalysis and psychotherapy, I would have to mention the contributions of Interpersonal psychoanalysts and family therapists. Salvador Minuchin wrote that Harry Stack Sullivan was instrumental in bringing information and communication theory to psychoanalysis, and thus to family therapy. Many of the most important of the family systems theorists also acknowledge this influence: Don Jackson's training included supervision by a number of Interpersonalists, including Sullivan; Jay Haley reports Sullivan's influence on him; and Minuchin was actually trained as an Interpersonal psychoanalyst and writes that he is clear how central that experience was to his thinking as a family therapist. Ivan Boszorrmenyi-Nagy and Murray Bowen, two other influential family therapists, were also heavily influenced by Interpersonal psychoanalysis. I am depending here on a valuable article detailing the connections between these two groups by Richard Gartner (1995). Eventually, Edgar Levenson (1972, 1983), in Kavanagh's (1995) words, took the position, influenced by von Bertalanffy and other early systems theorists and amazingly prescient in the context of the later development of NDST, that "the world is a complex, organismically related set of events in which there is great order but not of the simple cause-and-effect kind" (p. 587).

psychoanalysis is not used to generate research. That is not necessarily a problem, of course; NDST can just as validly be used for theory construction or model making as for the generation of new quantitative research. But if this is the way it is being used, a question arises: Is NDST being used *literally* among psychoanalysts, as it is in mathematics or developmental psychology? Or are we using NDST *metaphorically*, leaving aside the details of the theory (which are heavily mathematical)? It may be quite helpful to use NDST metaphorically. I do it myself (see Chapter 5). But it would be desirable to be clear that the ideas are being used that way, rather than in the way they are used in research fields in which quantitative studies of NDST are more practical.

Science and Social Construction

NDST is the source of the concept of emergent meaning in the work of BCPSG, which I have described as one of the most substantial areas of agreement between BCPSG and Relational psychoanalysis. But NDST is also a scientific theory, which means that it rests on an objectivist epistemology. Here we reach the discussion of the points of epistemological difference between my thinking and that of BCPSG that I promised to undertake earlier in this chapter.

I am not setting out to take issue with science. I am not even setting out to take issue with science in psychotherapy and psychoanalysis. That would be tilting at windmills, but without the nobility of Don Quixote; it would just be wrongheaded. I take issue only with the privileging of systematic, quantitative empirical research in the investigation of psychotherapy process and outcome. The word "privileging" is important here: I have no argument with the use of such research as *one* source of information about psychotherapy process and outcome.

There are many questions in our field for which science probably *should* have a privileged status: the biology of trauma, for instance; or the genetics of schizophrenia and disorders on the pervasive developmental disorders (PDD) spectrum; or the chemistry of severe depression. I even accept the desirability of quantitative outcome studies of psychotherapy and psychoanalysis, for three reasons: (1) that kind of research is couched in a language that the wider culture understands; (2) empirical research may identify certain ideas that clinicians need to reconsider, such as primary autism or the schizophrenogenic mother; (3) good clinical ideas sometimes come from such research (a prime example is the behavioral treatment of phobia, which may not have originated in quantitative research, but which was widely adopted largely because of the confirmatory outcomes of such studies). The problem is that quantitative research on psychotherapy process and outcome has seldom been able to reflect the subtlety and sophistication of psychoanalytic clinical work (there are significant exceptions). One reason for this state of affairs is that the simplest treatment methods and measures are the easiest to quantify. Increasingly, it is exactly these studies, which often do not even study procedures that would be recognized as psychotherapy by psychoanalytically trained clinicians, that are used to validate methods for insurance reimbursement. I appreciate the frustration over clinicians' resistance to quantitative empirical research by those in our field who feel that such research must be done but who also believe that scientific study is just one source of information. I do not sympathize, though, with those who accept *only* quantitative data as evidence of treatment validity and effectiveness. In fact, I do not sympathize with any position of dependence on quantitative data for these purposes.

To say that, of course, immediately brings up the question of how we *should* think about treatment effectiveness, which is a can of worms that I don't want to open here. Suffice it to say that I disagree in the strongest terms with the movement called "evidence-based treatment." I do not believe that quantitative research should determine how we conduct psychoanalytic treatment (see Hoffman [2006] for an excellent discussion of the issues).

I have said something about these general problems in order to be able now to make it clear that I do *not* include BCPSG in the category of those I have just described critically. NDST is indeed science and therefore rests on an objectivist epistemology. But NDST is also about the necessity to accept unpredictable and unexpected outcomes, which means to me that the work of BCPSG would be very hard, if not impossible, to use to "scientize" psychoanalytic practice. More important, it is not BCPSG's *intention* to do that. For BCPSG, as for Relational psychoanalysts, you cannot know exactly what you are going to do as an analyst until you come upon the circumstances that will contextualize your intervention. For all the order we give our time and fee schedules, when it comes to transactional events we are often flying by the (highly educated and seasoned) seat of our pants. After my own heart, the motto of BCPSG could be Fats Waller's famous aphorism: "One never knows, do one?"

And yet the science of the BCPSG approach to clinical process is uncomfortable for me, and I want to try to say why. This is the most difficult part of my reaction to BCPSG's work for me to capture, because the use of NDST, with its encouragement for us not just to study the nonlinear and the unexpected, but to expect them, makes irrelevant all of the most hard-edged of the disagreements between a scientific approach to psychotherapy and views such as mine. It is possible that what I have to say will be a surprise to BCPSG, because, in addition to doing away with linearity and conventional notions of orderly processes of therapeutic change, they align themselves with the contemporary critique of Cartesianism, thereby taking a philosophical position that they may believe is inconsistent with objectivism. Yet it is hard to see how NDST, when it is used literally and not metaphorically, can be understood as anything other than objectivism. The general outline of the argument I will make is based on a broadly conceived philosophy of social construction.[1]

In describing philosopher Charles Taylor's view of language, Timothy Zeddies (2002) speaks for me:

> [T]he web of language comprises a broad experiential and preexperiential background that does not completely dominate [and is not dominated] by individual human subjects. The language we speak is not an individual possession but something that is shared by an entire speech community. Touching any piece reflects only a miniscule portion of an immeasurable web of common meanings, practices, and understandings that define and inform a particular speech community. Articulated speech (spoken or written) reflects only a miniscule portion of an immeasurable web of common meanings, practices, and understandings that define and inform a particular speech community. What is actually spoken or written depends on and is possible because of the vast web of unexpressed and unarticulated meanings, practices, and understandings that remain in the background of explicit awareness and immediate experience. (p. 17)

Taylor is only one of many writers to take the position that the verbal and the nonverbal are inextricably entangled with each other. All the writers who have participated in the "linguistic turn" in the humanities and the social sciences take the position that what we say is not only shot through, but made possible, by what we cannot or will not say. To the extent that the thinking of all these writers emphasizes the continuous interrelationship of the verbal reflective and the implicit, BCPSG is right there on the same page with them.

---

[1] I refer to my social constructionism as broadly conceived because I am not limiting myself to a Foucauldian analysis of knowledge as a social product and the relations of power, but am also including modern ontological hermeneutics. Hermeneutics is often equated with constructivism, but *social* constructionism is a term that usually seems to refer more specifically to Foucault and analyses based on his approach.

But Taylor and company are saying more than that. They are also say-ing that language is used in socially defined circumstances. The people who use any particular language, or any local variant of it, or even just people who live in a particular place, constitute a community of language users who define how and for what purposes they speak, write, and read. And so language is not only used in socially defined circumstances—lan-guage is itself a social product. But that is not all. The whole of life, in this philosophical perspective, is a social product, the implicit right along with language—any human activity you can think of. This vast accumulation of social products, which sums to what we know as culture, is in con-tinuous flux; and it is we who are changing it. But because such change is often (though not always) slow, and because taking an independent stance toward our own culture is like the eye seeing itself (the instrument is part of the object of study), we often do not notice the changes as they occur (as we make them). As the wise man said, "I don't know who discovered water, but it sure as hell wasn't a fish." Therein lies the potential for a kind of enslavement, because ideology—the unseen values that shape a sub-stantial part of our participation in the world—thrives on invisibility.

How we behave with one another, how we feel, how we think, what we believe—all of this is a social product. All of it is a creation in context, and it takes its meaning from that context. There is reason to question whether our understanding of any taken-for-granted phenomenon we might choose to examine—the verbal, the nonverbal, the whole kit and caboodle—would be the same if our subjects came from different cultures or lived in different periods of the history of our own culture. The point gains in complexity, of course, when we acknowledge the significance of subject positions. "Our culture" is hardly the same for a gay African American man of limited means, for instance, as it is for a wealthy, straight Latina. Even if we set out with what we believe is the intention to under-stand the other, we know how commonly we run roughshod over cultural differences, ironing them out into facsimiles of what is familiar. Frederic Bartlett (1932) offers what may be the classic examples of this phenom-enon, which he calls "conventionalisation," in his study of the memories over time of Cambridge undergraduates for a Native American story that, of course, contained much that made little sense in upper crust England. After startlingly brief periods, the unfamiliar details and plot elements remembered by the undergraduates were distorted to fit cultural expecta-tion or simply disappeared.

Reading any anthropological study of what it is to be a person, or how people think, or the nature of psychopathology, or any of a thousand other topics, will convince you (at least they convinced me) that people are simply not the same everywhere. Let me cite just one example, one I use in teaching all the time: In a few astonishing pages, Clifford Geertz (1974), the eminent anthropologist, describes what it is to be a person in three different cultures: Java, Bali, and Morocco. To a Westerner, these peoples' understandings of self may as well be from Mars. I won't go into the details. I cite the paper to support the familiar social-constructivist contention that just because something seems to us like part of the natural world does not mean that it is. In fact, the parts of human life that are objectified in this way thereby cease being questionable and, for that reason alone, become precisely the parts of life that most need to be questioned. Here is Geertz's conclusion, which has had wide currency since the publication of his essay:

> The Western conception of the person as a bounded, unique, more or less integrated motivational and cognitive universe, a dynamic center of awareness, emotion, judgment, and action organized into a distinctive whole and set contrastively both against other such wholes and against its social and natural background, is, however incorrigible it may seem to us, a rather peculiar idea within the context of the world's cultures. (p. 59)

It is possible, of course, to study anything in more than one way. One can study the self in Western culture as a manifestation of the natural world, as Daniel Stern (1985), among many others, has done. Or one can study the self as one particularly significant creation of the culture we live in, as Erich Fromm (1941, 1947, 1955) and Philip Cushman (1990, 1991, 1995, Cushman & Gilford, 1999), among many others, have done. I believe that our field has benefited enormously from the work of all of these writers, although I believe that the benefit we have derived from Daniel Stern's work on the self is due less to his natural-science approach and more to his astute mother–infant observations and his incisive clinical and theoretical analyses of them. One does not need to accept Stern's observations as objectivistic or the theory as natural science to find both enormously useful.

In a hard-hitting critique of Stern's work on the self from a social constructionist perspective, Philip Cushman (1991), who calls for traditional, decontextualized psychology research on human universals to be replaced by research defining and studying phenomena in their social context, suggests (in one of his less critical conclusions about Stern's work) something similar to my own view:

Instead of universal laws, Stern articulated the shape of the cultural horizon at this historical moment. He did that by using methods that are valued by his professional colleagues, and in doing so collected information that is meaningful to us, in order to aid us in efficiently performing professional roles that are indispensable to our current Western way of life. (p. 209)

One can also study psychoanalysis and psychotherapy in different ways. One can define them as procedures composed of processes belonging to the natural world; or one can take the position that the processes that compose them, as well as the treatments themselves, are inventions of our culture that will change over time and may even disappear. In the former case, it ought to be possible to specify the underlying, universal processes that make up psychotherapy; this is what BCPSG attempts to do. In the latter case, it ought to be possible to describe in detail the processes that we see in psychotherapy, with an eye to identifying many different ways that the people of our time create and change meaning in their lives and many different ways that psychotherapists might therefore use in dealing with their patients (multiple solutions and contextual knowledge are hallmarks of this way of doing things, whether we call it hermeneutic or postmodern).

In the former (scientific) case, we agree to change the procedures of psychotherapy only when we believe the new procedures are closer to some kind of newly discovered truth about the subject matter. In the latter (hermeneutic) case, we agree to change the procedures because we sense that the world is a different place, and that we are therefore different from those who came before us; something different is demanded of us. In a similar vein, one can think of the people who practice psychotherapy and psychoanalysis and the people who come to them for the service they provide as human beings who are pretty much the same as human beings in any place or at any time; or one can think of patients and their therapists as human beings of a particular time and place, shaped according to the possibilities afforded them by the cultures into which they are born. It is a commonplace, for example, that since the 1960s there has been a broad shift in our culture regarding our relation to authority. We simply are not as willing to accept authority as people in our culture once were, when political leaders, teachers, doctors, and policemen could take respect and admiration for granted (which, of course, is hardly to say that the abuse of authority has ceased to be a problem). Because people are different today in this way, the kind of psychoanalysis that was practiced prior to the 1960s is simply no longer appropriate. People today are much less likely than they used to be to put up with analysts who feel that their patients must believe that the doctor knows the truth about them. And so in recent years Interpersonal psychoanalysis has emerged from its relative obscurity, and Relational psychoanalysis, with its emphasis on mutuality and its acceptance that the analyst's authority can be no more than ironic (Hoffman, 1998, pp. 69–95; Mitchell, 1997, pp. 203–230), has ascended. Actually, it seems to me very much to the point that until recently BCPSG would not have been able to publish their articles in the *International Journal of Psychoanalysis* (BCPSG, D. N. Stern, et al., 1998, 2002) or the *Journal of the American Psychoanalytic Association* (BCPSG, 2005), because in the past, what BCPSG does would not have been accepted within the boundaries of classical psychoanalysis. I do not think that these two mainstream journals accepted the BCPSG articles only because their editors believe that BCPSG has come closer to the truth than their intellectual predecessors; I think the editors of those publications were bending to changes in our culture's acceptance of a more democratic clinical practice. The readers of these two journals have also been affected in this way, of course, so that they are now interested in the papers of BCPSG—which, in circular fashion, is part of what makes the editors more likely to publish the work of BCPSG. Of course, the whole process works in both theoretical directions: The success of *Psychoanalytic Dialogues* can be partially pegged to the same factors.

BCPSG favors a natural science point of view. They are looking for the kind of regularities in psychotherapy that belong to the natural world; they write of "fundamental psychological processes" and "innate mental tendencies." My view is hermeneutic; I am looking at psychotherapy, including the transactions that take place in it and the experiences and cognitive processes in the minds of its participants, as a particular social practice in the here and now of our Western cultures.

The experience of presenting this point over and over again has taught me that I need to pause long enough to make it clear that my perspective is not relativistic. I do not take the position that one can say whatever one feels like saying. There exist constraints on our perceptions and thoughts; beyond them, our understandings are simply wrong, or crazy. There *is* a reality, then, and we sense it as a set of constraints that we must respect if we are to remain truthful and sane. But the possibilities that reality contains for our experience are manifold, which means that no single version of reality is possible to select as the correct one. There is always "wiggle room" in the next moment.[1] And if there is no single correct answer, and if we therefore choose our interpretations for some reason other than mere accuracy, every answer has a political aspect, visible or not.

I have just said that BCPSG favors a natural science approach to psychoanalysis, while I favor a hermeneutic one. But I have also made it clear earlier that BCPSG and I share some of the most important orientations about how to do psychotherapy and psychoanalysis. Given this similarity, why does it matter clinically whether we differ over something as abstract as the choice between natural science and social construction?

Philip Cushman (1990, 1991, 1995; Cushman & Fifford, 1999, 2005) would say that the difference matters because what he calls "decontextualized" psychology research, by which he means research that treats psychology as a natural science, takes an unintentional political position by treating current social conditions as a manifestation of the natural order, thereby reinforcing the status quo and the power relations that sustain it. Social constructionist research, on the other hand, is designed to formulate those same conditions as the expression of the values uppermost in our culture today, thereby exposing power and privilege and giving us a choice about whether to continue the status quo or change it.

Cushman's agenda is an important critique of the social sciences in general, but it really applies no more to Daniel Stern's research on the self or the work of BCPSG than it does to thousands of other research programs. However broad the reach of that kind of critique, though (Cushman is only one of many to mount it), it remains true that it does *also* apply to BCPSG. If we understand the transactions that make up clinical psychoanalysis as events of the natural world, in the same category as thunderstorms and the creation of diamonds, I believe that we give something up. I believe that viewing clinical practice that way makes us less likely to question whether what we are doing with our patients reflects unconsciously embraced values that we might prefer not to actualize—in a word, whether what we are doing with our patients is the manifestation of ideology. Very few, if any, of those who studied psychoanalysis in the 1950s, all of them employing a natural science perspective,

---

[1] Because of its multiple possibilities, reality is also never available in unmediated form. That is, since only one of the possibilities can become our experience, we cannot "know" reality without first giving it some kind of shape. We must somehow select which of the many possibilities facing us in every moment will become manifest for us, or formulated. Something must mediate reality to us. This "something" is culture and, on a smaller scale, the relational field and individual psychology. Culture, relationship, and character, that is, are the means by which we select and formulate that version of reality that comes to be our experience. For a more extended discussion of this view, which is rooted in Hans-Georg Gadamer (2004), see D. B. Stern (1997, 2002b).

noticed the influences of gender, sexual preference, race, class, and ethnicity on clinical practice; and if they did notice such things, there was nothing in a natural science view that encouraged them to view these problematic aspects of relatedness as anything other than phenomena of the natural world. Women just *are* passive and receptive; homosexuality just *is* psychopathological. It is the natural way. Psychoanalytic writers in those days seldom had reason to observe the authority relations between patients and analysts either, so much more rigid than they are today; this part of analytic relatedness was simply accepted as a part of the natural order, necessary to create therapeutic regression and the transference neurosis, which were in turn also considered aspects of the natural world that had been invisible until uncovered by psychoanalysis.[1] Today, in the same way, if we accept BCPSG's epistemology, we must accept (to cite just a few of BCPSG's most significant contributions) "moving along," "now moments," "sloppy process," and the "intention unfolding process" not just as useful ways of formulating our experience of doing analytic work, which they certainly are, but also as objective observations.

As a means of tying this argument down, let me cite and discuss how my argument applies to just one passage in the paper I am discussing. Near the end of their 2008 paper, in moving from the level of the individual to the level of communication between two people (after all, the two-person clinical situation, BCPSG agrees, is the point), BCPSG writes the following:

> The basic problem of the relation of the implicit and the reflective-verbal is paralleled in the two-person situation in terms of what is spoken and what is reflectively heard. We consider the spoken to constitute an implicit experience for the listener for the following reasons. The listener hears the spoken message, infers the underlying implicit experience that gave rise to the words, and feels the difference between the two. He receives a "gestalt." He must then, in an act of reflection, make a whole meaning of this gestalt. Again in this act, a disjunction/coherence is introduced between the implicit experience of hearing/seeing/experiencing the speaker's performance and the listener's reflected meaning. When the listener then becomes the speaker, the process continues, only in the opposite direction.
>
> The meanings (i.e., packages of implicit, reflective-verbal and their disjunctions) build on each other and reorient the direction as the dialogue advances, resulting in more global or summarizing intuitive grasps. In other words the meaning evolves in the course of the interaction. (p. 144)

---

[1] One of the few exceptions, maybe the only one written by a classical analyst, was Macalpine's (1950) observation that therapeutic regression is not a "natural" phenomenon at all, but a creation of the infantile relatedness set up and enforced in the analytic situation.

It is ironic that this precisely rendered passage is a fine description of the hermeneutic circle! This is exactly the process described by hermeneutic philosophers such as Gadamer (2004) as the source of meaning and the means by which meaning grows: One partner in the conversation offers a communication, and the other receives some kind of experience of that meaning, referred to as a "partial" meaning (BCPSG implies that the "gestalt" received by the listener is also an incomplete meaning); the receiver must then "complete" the meaning by making it into something recognizable, exactly as BCPSG says that the receiver must, "in an act of reflection, make a whole meaning of this gestalt." In the conception of the hermeneutic circle, the receiver makes the communication into a recognizable meaning by relating it to what is familiar—to expectations, or preconceptions. In felicitous circumstances, what is new in the communication is revealed by its contrast to what is familiar; in other circumstances, the new disappears into preconception. It seems to me that this hermeneutic process is pretty much identical to what BCPSG is describing when they say that the receiver, in making a meaning of the "gestalt," introduces a "disjunction/coherence ... between the implicit experience of hearing/seeing/experiencing the speaker's performance and the listener's reflected meaning." That is, some of what is conveyed in the communication is formulated into a meaning by the receiver and some of it is not. In either case, the one who has received the communication now goes on to respond to the first speaker, and as BCPSG says, "the process continues." In the hermeneutic literature, although the word "process" in this phrase would be more likely to be rendered as "conversation," the meaning would be the same. I see no meaningful difference between what BCPSG offers here and the idea of the hermeneutic circle.

And that raises the question of why we should bring science into the question of how treatment is conducted. Unless science adds something to our understanding that is not available otherwise, what is the advantage of bringing it to bear? Once again, if the science (NDST, in this case) is being used as metaphor by BCPSG, the question is moot, because then we are not talking about science in the literal sense. But I have the impression that BCPSG would say that they do intend their use of NDST to be literal.

My commentary on this passage has not yet addressed the reason that I presented it in the first place: science versus social construction in our investigation of the conduct of psychotherapy and psychoanalysis. Let me approach that problem by asking a question about the process of understanding being described in the passage I have just quoted from BCPSG's paper: How will it be decided what meanings are being communicated by the first speaker and whether (or to what degree) the second speaker has received them? To use NDST to answer that question in anything more specific than a theoretical sense, we need to be able to plot data points in an event space. And so we must know what the data *are*, in an objectively defined sense. Even if we only use NDST to create theory, a case can be made that we have to be able to believe that it is at least hypothetically possible to observe objectively defined data.

The developmental psychologists I mentioned earlier define actions by reference to points in space; and that seems straightforward enough. It is one thing to know objectively what a point in space is, though, and quite another thing to know objectively what a meaning is. Yet if we are to use NDST as BCPSG recommends, that is what we must know. We must be able to specify, in objective, consensually verifiable terms, the relevant meaning being communicated—or some data point, analogous to a point in space, according to which we can gauge meaning objectively. Only if it is possible to define a meaning in an objective way is an analysis of meaning that is rooted in an objectivist epistemology coherent.

BCPSG does make it clear that meaning is continuously changing, and so they might respond to what I have said by pointing out that meaning, because it is a relational event, cannot be pinned down, and is therefore beyond the reach of objective measurement. But flux is not inconsistent with objective existence. As long as they use NDST in a literal way, BCPSG is taking the implicit position that, in any particular moment of the clinical interchange, meaning exists in objectively verifiable form. That form may change over time, may even change very quickly—but it is fixed in any particular instant. I cannot see how the implication that meaning must be definable in objective terms can be escaped as long as one embraces an objectivist epistemology.

It is hard enough to believe that it is even theoretically possible to specify in an objective way either the meaning that the speaker in the quoted passage intended to convey or the meaning received by the listener. But that is just the beginning of the problems of objectivism in this context. We immediately reach another more difficult and significant conundrum: Even if we were to agree that an objectivist conception of meaning were possible, how would we decide what that objective meaning is in any particular case? How would we decide which, among a multitude of possibilities, is the "objective" meaning? There is no impersonal way to do that; there can be no "view from nowhere" (Nagel, 1986). A decision must be made. Who will decide which version of the meaning that the speaker conveyed to the listener is the objectively existing one, and who will select the objective version of what the listener received and then formulated? In other words, who will have the power to decide what meanings are the "correct" ones or the ones we study or interpret? Very quickly we come upon the necessity to acknowledge that the process of understanding is inevitably social and political.

From the hermeneutic perspective, on the other hand, the decision about what meanings are being communicated by the first speaker, and the question of whether (or to what degree) the second speaker has received them, is made by further hermeneutic inquiry. The questions about the events in the passage I have quoted, that is, are decided in just the same way that any other set of questions is decided: by the attempt to understand as best as one can, which requires frankly acknowledged intuition and interpretation, open to scrutiny and debate (at least when the event is public).1 The uncertainty does not go away. There is never a "bottom"; there are never objectively defined meanings that can make the process transparent and a final answer possible at last. Does that lead to endless questioning? Yes, that is exactly what it leads to.

I am prepared for BCPSG members to differ with my understanding of the implications of their objectivist epistemology. They may even disagree that their work should be characterized as objectivist. I am ready to listen to what they have to say and even to change my mind. I look forward to a dialogue about these issues. But at least at this point, I see their perspective in the way I have described. The position that clinical process can be given an objective significance leads to the conclusion that there is a correct way to view it, because that is the point of an objectivist epistemology: Truth inheres in the correspondence between what we say and what exists in the world, a correspondence that qualifies as objective because it exists prior to our observation of it. When we accept that truth exists apart from us, we inadvertently make the political and social influences on the construction of meaning invisible. I do not believe that anyone's psychoanalytic observations represent discoveries of preexisting truths about the world

---

1 BCPSG also uses the word "intuition" in the same context. But the implication, from within the NDST perspective, is that what one is trying to intuit is a meaning, however complex and affectively nuanced, that has an objective existence.

but are instead creations of new ways of thinking that will, in turn, be replaced by the next generation of thoughts. I believe that to take any other view is to take the chance of inadvertently defending invisible ideological aspects of the status quo and to risk making the revelation of these underlying influences more difficult and protracted.

BCPSG might respond to my argument by agreeing with me that psychotherapy and psychoanalysis are socially defined practices, but that they (BCPSG) are doing their best, within this socially defined set of procedures, to make objective observations. I can accept that characterization of their work, but it does not change the point I am trying to make.

I prefer less certainty than that. I trust that I have conveyed how fascinating and valuable BCPSG's work is to me. I teach it, and its lessons instruct me when I am with patients. But I see it as one of many formulations of psychoanalytic practice that could be made. I see the analytic process itself, including its perceptions, thoughts, and affects, its mutual unconscious enactments, mutual regulatory processes, and moments of intersubjectivity, as a social construction, valuable in so many ways, but no doubt serving more purposes than we know (or would be comfortable with, if we did know), just as the Western sense of self described by Geertz does. We all need to keep trying to articulate these hidden purposes, so that psychoanalysis maintains its primary value: its questioning stance toward everything. BCPSG and I share Fats Waller's sentiment about many things in psychoanalysis, but I would take it a step further to include our epistemology itself: "One never knows, do one?"

References

Alexander, F., & French, T. (1946). *Psychoanalytic therapy: Principles and application*. New York: Ronald Press.

American Heritage Dictionary of the English Language (3rd ed.). Boston and New York: Houghton Mifflin.

Aron, L. (1991). The patient's experience of the analyst's subjectivity. *Psychoanalytic Dialogues, 1,* 29–51.

Aron, L. (1996). *A meeting of minds: Mutuality in psychoanalysis.* Hillsdale, NJ: Analytic Press.

Aron, L. (2003a). Clinical outbursts and theoretical breakthroughs: A unifying theme in the work of Stephen A. Mitchell. *Psychoanalytic Dialogues, 13,* 273–287.

Aron, L. (2003b). The paradoxical place of enactment in psychoanalysis: Introduction. *Psychoanalytic Dialogues, 13,* 623–631.

Atwood, G. E. and Stolorow, R. D. (1984). *Structures of subjectivity: Explorations in psychoanalytic phenomenology.* Hillsdale, NJ: The Analytic Press.

Bach, S. (2006). *Getting from here to there: Analytic love, analytic process.* Hillsdale, NJ: Analytic Press.

Bartlett, F. C. (1932). *Remembering.* Cambridge: Cambridge University Press.

Bass, A. (2003). "E" enactments in psychoanalysis: Another medium, another message. *Psychoanalytic Dialogues, 13,* 657–675.

Beebe, B., & Lachmann, F. (1988). The contribution of mother-infant mutual influence to the origins of self and object representations. *Psychoanalytic Psychology, 5,* 305–337.

Beebe, B., & Lachmann, F. (1994). Representation and internalization in infancy: Three principles of salience. *Psychoanalytic Psychology, 11,* 127–165

Beebe, B., & Lachmann, F. (1998). Co-constructing inner and relational processes: Self- and mutual regulation in infant research and adult treatment. *Psychoanalytic Psychology, 15,* 480–516.

Beebe, B., & Lachmann, F. (2002). *Infant research and adult treatment: Co-constructing interactions.* Hillsdale, NJ: Analytic Press.

Benjamin, J. (1988). *The bonds of love.* New York: Pantheon.

Benjamin, J. (1990). Recognition and destruction: An outline of intersubjectivity. In S. Mitchell & L. Aron (Eds.), *Relational psychoanalysis: The emergence of a tradition* (pp. 183–200). Hillsdale, NJ: Analytic Press.

Benjamin, J. (1995). *Like subjects, love objects.* New Haven: Yale University Press.

Benjamin, J. (1998). *Shadow of the other*. London: Routledge.

Benjamin, J. (1999). Afterword to "Recognition and destruction: An outline of intersubjectivity." In S. Mitchell & L. Aron (Eds.), *Relational psychoanalysis: The emergence of a tradition* (pp. 201–210). Hillsdale, NJ: Analytic Press.

Benjamin, J. (2000). Intersubjective distinctions: Subjects and persons, recognitions, and breakdowns: Commentary on paper by Gerhardt, Sweetnam, and Borton. *Psychoanalytic Dialogues, 10*, 43–55.

Benjamin, J. (2002). The rhythm of recognition: Comments on the work of Louis Sander. *Psychoanalytic Dialogues, 12*, 43–53.

Benjamin, J. (2004). Beyond doer and done to: An intersubjective view of thirdness. *Psychoanalytic Quarterly, 73*, 5–46.

Bernstein, R. J. (1983) *Beyond objectivism and relativism*. Philadelphia: University of Pennsylvania Press.

Bion, W. R. (1962). *Learning from experience*. London: Heinemann.

Bion, W. R. (1963). *Elements of psycho-analysis*. London: Heinemann.

Bion, W. R. (1970). *Attention and interpretation*. London: Tavistock.

Bion, W. R. (1980). *Bion in New York and São Paulo*. Perth: Clunie Press.

Black, M. (2003). Enactment: Analytic musings on energy, language, and personal growth. *Psychoanalytic Dialogues, 13*, 633–655.

Blechner, M. (1992). Working in the countertransference. *Psychoanalytic Dialogues, 2*, 161–179.

Bollas, C. (1983). Expressive uses of the countertransference. *Contemporary Psychoanalysis, 19*, 1–34.

Bollas, C. (1987) *The Shadow of the object: Psychoanalysis of the unthought known*. New York: Columbia University Press.

Bollas, C. (1989). *Forces of destiny*. London: Free Association Books.

Bornstein, M. (Ed.) (2008). Is unconscious fantasy central to the theory and practice of psychoanalysis? *Psychoanalytic Inquiry, 28*(2).

Boston Change Process Study Group (BCPSG). (2002). Explicating the implicit: The local level and the microprocesses of change in the analytic situation. *International Journal of Psychoanalysis, 83*, 1051–1062.

Boston Change Process Study Group (BCPSG). (2005). The "something more" than interpretation revisited: Sloppiness and co-creativity in the psychoanalytic encounter. *Journal of the American Psychoanalytic Association, 53*, 693–729.

Boston Change Process Study Group (BCPSG). (2007). The foundational level of psychodynamic meaning: Implicit process in relation to conflict, defense, and the dynamic unconscious. *International Journal of Psychoanalysis, 88*, 843–860.

Boston Change Process Study Group (BCPSG). (2008). Forms of relational meaning: Issues in the relations between the implicit and reflective-verbal domains. *Psychoanalytic Dialogues, 18*, 125–148.

Botella, C. & Botella, S. (2005). *The work of psychic figurability*. Hove & New York: Brunner-Routledge.

Boulanger, G. (2007). *Wounded by reality: Understanding and treating adult onset trauma.* Mahwah, NJ: Analytic Press.

Brison, S. (2002). *Aftermath: Violence and the remaking of a self.* Princeton, NJ: Princeton University Press.

Bromberg, P. (1998). *Standing in the spaces: Essays on clinical process, trauma, and dissociation.* Hillsdale, NJ: Analytic Press.

Bromberg, P. (2000). Response to reviews by Cavell, Sorenson, and Smith. *Psychoanalytic Dialogues, 10,* 551–568.

Bromberg, P. (2006). *Awakening the dreamer: Clinical journeys.* Hillsdale, NJ: Analytic Press.

Bronfenbrenner, U. (1979). *The ecology of human development: Experiments by nature and design.* Cambridge: Harvard University Press.

Bruner, J. (1979). The conditions of creativity. In *On knowing: Essays for the left hand,* (expanded edition, pp. 17–30). Cambridge: Harvard University Press.

Bruner, J. (1986). *Actual minds, possible worlds.* Cambridge: Harvard University Press.

Bruner, J. (1990). *Acts of meaning.* Cambridge: Harvard University Press.

Bruner, J. (2002). *Making stories: Law, literature, life.* Cambridge: Harvard University Press.

Bucci, W. (1997). *Psychoanalysis and cognitive science: A multiple code theory.* New York: Guilford.

Bucci, W. (2007a). Dissociation from the perspective of multiple code theory, Part I: Psychological roots and implications for psychoanalytic treatment. *Contemporary Psychoanalysis, 43,* 165–184.

Bucci, W. (2007b). Dissociation from the perspective of multiple code theory, Part II: *Contemporary Psychoanalysis, 43.*

Chasseguet-Smirgel, J. (1990). On acting out. *International Journal of Psycho-analysis, 71,* 77–86.

Chefetz, R. A. (2003). Healing haunted hearts: Toward a model for integrating subjectivity: Commentary on papers by Gerald Stechler and Philip Bromberg. *Psychoanalytic Dialogues, 13,* 727–742.

Chefetz, R. A., & Bromberg, P. M. (2004). Talking with "me" and "not-me." *Contemporary Psychoanalysis, 40,* 409–464.

Corbett, K. (2001). More life: Centrality and marginality in human development. *Psychoanalytic Dialogues, 11,* 313–335.

Cushman, P. (1990). Why the self is empty: Toward a historically situated psychology. *American Psychologist, 45,* 599–611.

Cushman, P. (1991). Ideology obscured: Political uses of the self in Daniel Stern's infant. *American Psychologist, 46,* 206–219.

Cushman, P. (1995). *Constructing the self, constructing America: A cultural history of psychotherapy.* Reading, MA: Addison-Wesley.

Cushman, P. (2005a). Between arrogance and a dead-end: Gadamer and the Heidegger/Foucault dilemma. *Contemporary Psychoanalysis, 41,* 399–417.

Cushman, P. (2005b). Clinical applications: A response to Layton. *Contemporary Psychoanalysis, 41,* 431–445.

Cushman, P. (2007). A burning world, an absent god: Midrash, Hermeneutics, and relational psychoanalysis. *Contemporary Psychoanalysis, 43*, 47–88.

Cushman, P., & Gilford, P. (1999). From emptiness to multiplicity: The self at the year 2000. *Psychohistory Review, 27*, 15–31.

Damasio, A. (1994). *Descartes's error: Emotion, reason and the human brain.* New York: G. P. Putnam's Sons.

Davies, J. M. (1996). Linking the pre-analytic with the postclassical: Integration, dissociation, and the multiplicity of unconscious processes. *Contemporary Psychoanalysis, 32*, 553–576.

Davies, J. M. (1997). Dissociation, therapeutic enactment, and transference–countertransference processes: A discussion of papers on childhood sexual abuse by S. Grand and J. Sarnat. *Gender and Psychoanalysis, 2*, 241–257.

Davies, J. M. (1998). The multiple aspects of multiplicity: Symposium on clinical choices in psychoanalysis. *Psychoanalytic Dialogues, 8*, 195–206.

Davies, J. M. (1999). Getting cold feet defining "safe-enough" borders: Dissociation, multiplicity, and integration in the analyst's experience. *Psychoanalytic Quarterly, 78*, 184–208.

Davies, J. M. (2003). Falling in love with love: Oedipal and postoedipal manifestations of idealization, mourning, and erotic masochism. *Psychoanalytic Dialogues, 13*, 1–27.

Davies, J. M. (2004). Whose bad objects are we anyway? Repetition and our elusive love affair with evil. *Psychoanalytic Dialogues, 14*, 711–732.

Davies, J. M., & Frawley, M. G. (1991). Dissociative processes and transference-countertransference paradigms in the psychoanalytically oriented treatment of adult survivors of childhood sexual abuse. *Psychoanalytic Dialogues, 2*, 5–36.

Davies, J. M., & Frawley, M. G. (1994). *Treating the adult survivor of childhood sexual abuse.* New York: Basic Books.

Defoe, D. (1957). *Robinson Crusoe.* New York: Charles Scribner's Sons. (Originally published 1719).

Dell, P., & O'Neil, P. (2009). *Dissociation and the dissociative disorders: DSM-V and beyond.* New York: Routledge.

Dostal, R.J., (ed.) (2002). *The Cambridge companion to Gadamer.* Cambridge: Cambridge University Press.

Ehrenberg, D. (1992). *The intimate edge.* New York: Norton.

Eigen, M. (1981). The area of faith in Winnicott, Lacan and Bion. *International Journal of Psychoanalysis, 62*, 413–433.

Elkind, S. (1992). *Resolving impasses in therapeutic relationships.* New York: Guilford.

Ellenberger, H. F. (1970). *The discovery of the unconscious.* New York: Basic Books.

Elliott, A., & Spezzano, C. (1996). Psychoanalysis at its limits: Navigating the postmodern turn. In O. Renik (Ed.), *Knowledge and authority in the psychoanalytic relationship* (pp. 61–92). Northvale, NJ: Aronson.

Eshel, O. (2004). Let it be and become me: Notes on containing, identification, and the possibility of being. *Contemporary Psychoanalysis, 40*, 323–351.

Farber, L. (1956). Martin Buber and psychoanalysis. In *The ways of the will: Essays toward a psychology and psychopathology of will* (pp. 131–154). New York: Basic Books.

Fain, M., & David, C. (1963). Aspects fonctionnels de la vie onirique. *Revue Française de Psychanalyse, 27,* 241–343.

Fain, M., David, C., & Marty, P. (1964). Perspective psychosomatique sur la fonction des fantasmes. *Revue Française de Psychanalyse, 28,* 609–622.

Feiner, A. H. (1982). Comments on the difficult patient. *Contemporary Psychoanalysis, 18,* 397–411.

Felman, S., & Laub, D. (1992). *Testimony: Crises of witnessing in literature, psychoanalysis, and history.* New York: Routledge.

Ferro, A. (1999). *The bi-personal field: Experiences in child analysis.* London: Routledge.

Ferro, A. (2002). *In the analyst's consulting room.* London: Brunner-Routledge.

Ferro, A. (2005a). Bion: Theoretical and clinical observations. *Int. J. Psycho-Anal.,* 86:1535-1542.

Ferro, A. (2005b). *Seeds of illness, seeds of recovery: The genesis of suffering and the role of psychoanalysis.* London: Brunner-Routledge.

Ferro, A. (2006). *Psychoanalysis as therapy and storytelling.* London: Routledge.

Fingarette, H. (1963). *The self in transformation: Psychoanalysis, philosophy and the life of the spirit.* New York: Basic Books.

Fischer, K. W., & Rose, S. P. (1999). Rulers, clocks, and nonlinear dynamics: Measurement and method in developmental research. In G. Savelsbergh, H. van der Maas, & P. van Geert (Eds.), *Nonlinear developmental processes* (pp. 197–212). Amsterdam: Royal Netherlands Academy of Arts and Sciences.

Flax, J. (1996). Taking multiplicity seriously: Some implications for psychoanalytic theorizing and practice. *Contemporary Psychoanalysis, 32,* 577–593.

Fonagy, P., Gergely, G., Jurist, E., & Target, M. (2002). *Affect regulation, mentalization, and the development of the self.* New York: Other Press.

Foucault, M. (1980) Truth and power. In: The Foucault Reader, ed. P. Rabinow. New York: Pantheon, 1984, pp. 51-75.

Fourcher, L. (1992). Interpreting the relative unconscious. *Psychoanalytic Dialogues, 3,* 317–329.

Frie, R. (1997). *Subjectivity and intersubjectivity in modern philosophy and psychoanalysis.* Lanham, MD: Rowman & Littlefield.

Freud, S. (1895). Project for a scientific psychology. In J. Strachey (Ed. & Trans.), *The standard edition of the complete psychological works of Sigmund Freud* (Vol. 1, pp. 281–387). London: Hogarth Press, 1950.

Freud, S. (1918). From the history of an infantile neurosis. In J. Strachey (Ed. & Trans.), *The standard edition of the complete psychological works of Sigmund Freud* (Vol. 17, pp. 1–122). London: Hogarth Press, 1955.

Friedman, L. (2000). Are minds objects or dramas? In D. K. Silverman & D. L. Wolitzky (Eds.), *Changing conceptions of psychoanalysis: The legacy of Merton Gill* (pp. 146–170). Hillsdale, NJ: Analytic Press.

Fromm, E. (1941). *Escape from freedom.* New York: Rinehart and Company.

Fromm, E. (1947). *Man for himself.* New York: Rinehart and Company.

Fromm, E. (1955). *The sane society.* New York: Holt, Rinehart and Winston.

Gadamer, H.-G. (1976). *Philosophical hermeneutics.* Trans. & ed. D.E. Linge. Berkeley, CA: University of California Press.

Gadamer, H.-G. (1975). *Truth and method.* G. Barden and J. Cumming, Trans. New York: Seabury Press.

Gadamer, H.-G. (1965/2004). *Truth and method.* J. Weinsheimer & D. G. Marshall, Trans. London: Continuum. (Original work published 1965).

Galatzer-Levy, R. M. (1978). Qualitative change from quantitative change: Mathematical catastrophe theory in relation to psychoanalysis. *Journal of the American Psychoanalytic Association, 26,* 921–935.

Galatzer-Levy, R. M. (1996). Psychoanalysis and dynamical systems theory: Prediction and self similarity. *Journal of the American Psychoanalytic Association, 43,* 1085–1113.

Galatzer-Levy, R. M. (2004). Chaotic possibilities: Toward a new model of development. *International Journal of Psychoanalysis, 85,* 419–442.

Gartner, R. B. (1995). The relationship between interpersonal psychoanalysis and family therapy. In M. Lionells, J. Fiscalini, C. H. Mann, & D. B. Stern (Eds.), *The handbook of interpersonal psychoanalysis* (pp. 793–822). Hillsdale, NJ: Analytic Press.

Geertz, C. (1974). "From the native's point of view": On the nature of anthropological understanding. In *Local knowledge* (pp. 55–70). New York: Basic Books, 1983.

Gerber, L. (1990). Integrating political-societal concerns in psychotherapy. *American Journal of Psychotherapy, 44,* .

Ghent, E. (1989). Credo—The dialectics of one-person and two-person psychologies. *Contemporary Psychoanalysis, 25,* 169–211.

Ghent, E. (1990). Masochism, submission, surrender—Masochism as a perversion of surrender. *Contemporary Psychoanalysis, 26,* 108–136.

Ghent, E. (1995). Interaction in the psychoanalytic situation. *Psychoanalytic Dialogues, 5,* 479–491.

Ghent, E. (2002). Wish, need, drive: Motive in the light of dynamic systems theory and Edelman's selectionist theory. *Psychoanalytic Dialogues, 12,* 763–808.

Gianino, A., & Tronick, E. (1988). The mutual regulation model: The infant's self and interactive regulation. Coping and defense capacities. In T. Field et al. (Eds.), *Stress and coping* (pp. 47–68). Hillsdale, NJ: Erlbaum.

Gill, M. M. (1982). *The analysis of transference: Volume 1.* New York: International Universities Press.

Goldner, V. (2004). Review essay: Attachment and Eros: Opposed or synergistic? *Psychoanalytic Dialogues, 14,* 381–396.

Goldner, V. (2006). "Let's do it again": Further reflections on Eros and attachment. *Psychoanalytic Dialogues, 16*, 619–637.

Green, A. (1975). The analyst, symbolization, and absence in the analytic setting. *International Journal of Psychoanalysis, 56*, 1-22.

Green, A. (1976). The dead mother. In *On private madness* (pp. 142–173). London: Hogarth Press.

Green, A. (2000). The central phobic position: A new formulation of the free association method. *International Journal of Psycho-Analysis, 81*, 429–451.

Greenberg, J. (1991). *Oedipus and beyond: A clinical theory.* Cambridge: Harvard University Press.

Greenberg, J. (1999). Analytic authority and analytic restraint. *Contemporary Psychoanalysis, 35*, 25–41.

Greenberg, J., & Mitchell, S. A. (1983). *Object relations in psychoanalytic theory.* Boston: Harvard University Press.

Grondin, J. (1997). *Introduction to philosophical hermeneutics.* New Haven, CT: Yale University Press.

Grossmark, R. (2007). The edge of chaos: Enactment, disruption, and emergence in group psychotherapy. *Psychoanalytic Dialogues, 17*, 479–499.

Guignon, C. (2004). *On being authentic.* London: Routledge.

Habermas, J. (1971). *Knowledge and human interests.* Boston: Beacon Press.

Harris, A. (1996). The conceptual power of multiplicity. *Contemporary Psychoanalysis, 32*, 537–552.

Harris, A. (2005). *Gender as soft assembly.* Hillsdale, NJ: Analytic Press.

Hirsch, I. (1996). Observing-participation, mutual enactment, and the new classical models. *Contemporary Psychoanalysis, 32*, 359–383.

Hirsch, I. (2000). Interview with Benjamin Wolstein. *Contemporary Psychoanalysis, 36*, 187–232.

Hoffman, I. Z. (1998). *Ritual and spontaneity in the psychoanalytic process: A dialectical-constructivist view.* Hillsdale, NJ: Analytic Press.

Hoffman, I. Z. (2006, January). Doublethinking our way to "scientific" legitimacy: The desiccation of human experience. Plenary address at the American Psychoanalytic Association meeting. New York.

Howell, E. (2005). *The dissociative mind.* Hillsdale, NJ: Analytic Press.

International Association of Relational Psychoanalysis and Psychotherapy. (2005). *Online colloquium: What happens when love lasts? An exploration of intimacy and erotic life.* New York: Psychoanalytic Connection.

Jaffe, J., Beebe, B., Feldstein, S., & Crown, C. (2001). *Rhythms of dialogue in infancy: Monographs for the society for research and child development.* New York: Wiley.

Kavanagh, G. (1995). Processes of therapeutic action and change. In M. Lionells, J. Fiscalini, C. H. Mann, & D. B. Stern (Eds.), *The handbook of interpersonal psychoanalysis* (pp. 569–602). Hillsdale, NJ: Analytic Press.

Kieffer, C. C. (2007). Emergence and the analytic third: Working at the edge of chaos. *Psychoanalytic Dialogues, 17*, 683–703.

Knoblauch, S. H. (2000). *The musical edge of therapeutic relatedness.* Hillsdale, NJ: Analytic Press.

Kohut, H. (1984). *How does analysis cure?* Edited by A. Goldberg & P. Stepansky. Chicago and London: University of Chicago Press.

Lacan, J. *Ecrits: A selection.* New York: Norton.

Lachmann, F., & Beebe, B. (1996). Three principles of salience in the patient-analyst interaction. *Psychoanalytic Psychology, 13,* 1–22.

Lakoff, G., & Johnson, M. (1980). *Metaphors we live by.* Chicago and London: University of Chicago Press.

Lakoff, G., & Johnson, M. (1999). *Philosophy in the flesh: The embodied mind and its challenge to western thought.* New York: Basic Books.

Lashley, K. S. (1950). In search of the engram. *Society of Experimental Biology Symposium, 4,* 454–482.

Laub, D. (1992a). Bearing witness or the vicissitudes of witnessing. In S. Felman & D. Laub (Eds.), *Testimony: Crises of witnessing in literature, psychoanalysis, and history* (pp. 57–74). New York and London: Routledge.

Laub, D. (1992b). An event without a witness: Truth, testimony, and survival. In S. Felman & D. Laub (Eds.), *Testimony: Crises of witnessing in literature, psychoanalysis, and history* (pp. 75–92). New York and London: Routledge.

Laub, D. (1995). Truth and testimony. In C. Caruth (Ed.), *Trauma: Explorations in memory* (pp. 61–75). Baltimore: Johns Hopkins University Press.

Laub, D. (2005). Traumatic shutdown of symbolization and narrative: A death instinct derivative? *Contemporary Psychoanalysis, 41,* 307–326.

Laub, D., & Auerhahn, N. (1989). Failed empathy: A central theme in the survivor's Holocaust experience. *Psychoanalytic Psychology, 6,* 377–400.

Layton, L. (1998), *Who's that girl? Who's that boy? Clinical practice meets postmodern gender theory.* Hillsdale, NJ: Analytic Press.

Layton, L. (2002). Psychoanalysis and the "free" individual. *Journal of Psycho-Social Studies, 1.*

Layton, L. (2004a). Dreams of America, American dreams. *Psychoanalytic Dialogues, 14,* 233–254.

Layton, L. (2004b). A fork in the royal road: On "defining" the unconscious and its stakes for social theory. *Psychoanalysis, Culture, and Society, 9,* 33–51.

Layton, L. (2005). Notes toward a nonconformist clinical practice: Response to Philip Cushman. *Contemporary Psychoanalysis, 41,* 419–429.

Lecours, S., & Bouchard, M. (1997). Dimensions of mentalisation: Outlining levels of psychic transformation. *International Journal of Psycho-Analysis, 78,* 855–875.

Levenkron, H. (2006). Love (and hate) with the proper stranger: Affective honesty and enactment. *Psychoanalytic Inquiry, 26,* 157–181.

Levenson, E. A. (1972). *The fallacy of understanding.* New York: Basic Books.

Levenson, E. A. (1983). *The ambiguity of change.* New York: Basic Books.

Levenson, E. A. (1984). Follow the fox: An inquiry into the vicissitudes of psycho-analytic supervision. In A. H. Feiner (Ed.), *The purloined self: Interpersonal perspectives in psychoanalysis* (pp. 111–125). New York: Contemporary Psychoanalysis Books.

Levenson, E. A. (1988). The pursuit of the particular. *Contemporary Psychoanalysis, 24,* 1–16.

Levenson, E. A. (1991). *The purloined self: Interpersonal perspectives in psychoanalysis.* A. H. Feiner (Ed.). New York: Contemporary Psychoanalysis Books.

Levenson, E. A. (1994). The uses of disorder: Chaos theory and psychoanalysis. *Contemporary Psychoanalysis, 30,* 5–24.

Lionells, M., Fiscalini, J., Mann, C. M., & Stern, D. B. (Eds.). (1995). *The handbook of interpersonal psychoanalysis.* Hillsdale, NJ: Analytic Press.

Loewald, H. W. (1960). On the therapeutic action of psycho-analysis. *International Journal of Psychoanalysis, 41,* 16–33.

Luquet, P. (1987). Penser-parler: un apport psychanalytique la thorie du langage. In R. Christie et al. (Eds.), *La parole trouble* (pp. 161–300). Paris: Presses Universitaires France.

Lyons-Ruth, K. (1991). Rapprochement or approchement: Mahler's theory reconsidered from the vantage point of recent research on early attachment relationships. *Psychoanalytic Psychology, 8,* 1–23.

Lyons-Ruth, K. (2003). Dissociation and the parent-infant dialogue. *Journal of the American Psychoanalytic Association, 51*(3), 883–911.

Lyons-Ruth, K., Bruschweiler-Stern, N., Harrison, A. M., Nahum, J. P., Sander, L., Stern, D. N., et al. (1998). Implicit relational knowing: Its role in development and psychoanalytic treatment. *Infant Mental Health Journal, 19,* 282–289.

Lyons-Ruth, K., Connell. D., Zoll, D., & Stahl, J. (1987). Infants at social risk: Relationships among infant maltreatment, maternal behavior, and infant attachment behavior. *Developmental Psychology, 23,* 223–232.

Lyons-Ruth, K., Connell. D., Zoll, D., & Stahl, J. (1950). The development of the transference. *Psychoanalytic Quarterly, 19,* 501–539.

Macalpine, I. (1950). The development of the transference. *The Psychoanalytic Quarterly, 19:* 501–539.

Mandel, A. J., & Selz, K. A. (1996). Nonlinear dynamical patterns as personality theory for neurobiology and psychoanalysis. *Psychiatry, 58,* 371–390.

Marty, P. (1990). *La psychosomatique de l'adulte.* Paris: Presses Universitaires France.

Marty, P. (1991). *Mentalisation et psychosomatique.* Paris: Laboratoire Delagrange.

McDougall, J. (1985). *Theaters of the mind.* New York: Basic Books.

McLaughlin, J. T. (1996). Power, authority, and influence in the analytic dyad. In O. Renik (Ed.), *Knowledge and authority in the psychoanalytic relationship* (pp. 189–223). Northvale, NJ: Aronson.

Merleau-Ponty, M. (1964a). Introduction. In *Signs* (pp. 3–35). Evanston, IL: Northwestern University Press.

Merleau-Ponty, M. (1964b). Indirect language and the voices of silence. In *Signs* (pp. 339–383). Evanston, IL: Northwestern University Press.

Merleau-Ponty, M. (1973). *The prose of the world*. Evanston, IL: Northwestern University Press.

Messer, S.B., Sass, L.A. & Woolfolk, R.L. (eds.) (1988). *Hermeneutics and psychological theory*. New Brunswick, NJ: Rutgers University Press.

Miller, M. (1999). Chaos, complexity, and psychoanalysis. *Psychoanalytic Psychology, 16*, 335–379.

Mitchell, S. A. (1988). *Relational concepts in psychoanalysis*. Cambridge: Harvard University Press.

Mitchell, S. A. (1991). Contemporary perspectives on self: Toward an integration. *Psychoanalytic Dialogues, 1*, 121–147.

Mitchell, S. A. (1993). *Hope and dread in psychoanalysis*. New York: Basic Books.

Mitchell, S. A. (1997). *Influence and autonomy in psychoanalysis*. Hillsdale, NJ: Analytic Press.

Mitchell, S. A. (2000). *Relationality*. Hillsdale, NJ: Analytic Press.

Mitchell, S. A. (2002). *Can love last? The fate of romance over time*. New York: Norton.

Mitrani, J.L. (1995). Toward an understanding of unmentalized experience. *Psychoanal Q., 64*:68-112.

Modell, A. (1984). *Psychoanalysis in a new context*. New York: International Universities Press.

Modell, A. (1990). *Other times, other realities*. Cambridge: Harvard University Press.

Modell, A. (1991). The therapeutic relationship as a paradoxical experience. *Psychoanalytic Dialogues, 1*, 13–28.

Modell, A. (2003). *Imagination and the meaningful brain*. Cambridge: MIT Press.

Moran, M. (1991). Chaos theory and psychoanalysis: The fluidic nature of the mind. *International Journal of Psychoanalysis, 18*, 211–221.

Nagel, T. (1986). *The view from nowhere*. New York: Oxford University Press.

Nahum, J. (1994). New theoretical vistas in psychoanalysis: Louis Sander's theory of early development. *Psychoanalytic Psychology, 11*, 1–19.

Nahum, J. (2000). An overview of Louis Sander's contribution to the field of mental health. *Infant Mental Health Journal, 21*(1–2), 29–41.

Nelson, K. (Ed.). (1989). *Narratives from the crib*. Cambridge: Harvard University Press.

Ogden, T. H. (1994). *Subjects of analysis*. Northvale, NJ: Jason Aronson.

Ogden, T. H. (2004). The analytic third: Implications for psychoanalytic theory and technique. *Psychoanalytic Quarterly, 73*, 167–195.

Onishi, N. (2007, October 12). Death reveals harsh side of a "model" in Japan. *New York Times*.

Orange, D. M. (1995). *Emotional understanding: Studies in psychoanalytic epistemology*. New York: Guilford.

Palmer, R.E. (1969). *Hermeneutics*. Evanston, IL: Northwestern University Press.

Palombo, S. R. (1999). *The emergent ego: Complexity and coevolution in the psychoanalytic process*. Madison, CT: International Universities Press.

Piers, C. (2000). Character as self-organizing complexity. *Psychoanalysis and Contemporary Thought, 23*, 3–34.

Piers, C. (2005). The mind's multiplicity and continuity. *Psychoanalytic Dialogues, 15,* 229–254.

Pizer, B. (2003). When the crunch is a (k)not: A crimp in relational dialogue. *Psychoanalytic Dialogues, 13,* 171–192.

Pizer, S. (1998). *Building bridges: The negotiation of paradox in psychoanalysis.* Hillsdale, NJ: Analytic Press.

Pizer, S. (2004). Impasse recollected in tranquility: Love, dissociation, and discipline in the analytic process. *Psychoanalytic Dialogues, 14,* 289–311.

Plato. (1956). *Protagoras and Meno.* W. K. C. Guthrie, Trans. London: Penguin Books.

Poland, W. S. (2000). The analyst's witnessing and otherness. *Journal of the American. Psychoanalytic Association, 48,* 17–34.

Polkinghorne, D. E. (1988). *Narrative knowing in the human sciences.* Albany, NY: State University of New York Press.

Quinodoz, J.-M. (1997). Transition in psychic structures in light of deterministic chaos theory. *International Journal of Psychoanalysis, 78,* 699–718.

Racker, H. (1957). The meanings and uses of countertransference. In *Transference and Countertransference* (pp. 127–173). New York: International Universities Press, 1968.

Racker, H. (1968). *Transference and countertransference.* New York: International Universities Press.

Renik, O. (1993a). Analytic interaction: Conceptualizing technique in light of the analyst's irreducible subjectivity. *Psychoanalytic Quarterly, 62,* 553–571.

Renik, O. (1993b). Countertransference enactments and the psychoanalytic process. In M. Horowitz, O. Kernberg, & E. Weinshel (Eds.), *Psychic structure and psychic change* (pp. 135–158). New York: International Universities Press.

Richardson, F., & Zeddies, T. (2001). Individualism and modern psychotherapy. In B. Slife, R. Williams, & S. Barlow (Eds.), *Critical issues in psychotherapy: Translating new ideas into practice* (pp. 147–167). Thousand Oaks, CA: Sage.

Richardson, F., & Zeddies, T. (2004). Psychoanalysis and the good life. *Contemporary Psychoanalysis, 40,* 617–657.

Richman, S. (2002). *A wolf in the attic: The legacy of a hidden child of the Holocaust.* New York: Haworth Press.

Richman, S. (2006). Finding one's voice: Transforming trauma into autobiographical narrative. *Contemporary Psychoanalysis, 42,* 639–650.

Ricoeur, P. (1970). *Freud and philosophy: An essay on interpretation.* New Haven, CT: Yale University Press.

Ricoeur, P. (1977). The question of proof in Freud's psychoanalytic writings. *Journal of the American Psychoanalytic Association, 25,* 835–871.

Ricoeur, P. (1981). *Hermeneutics and the human sciences.* Cambridge: Cambridge University Press.

Ringstrom, P. (1998). Therapeutic impasses in contemporary psychoanalytic treatment: Revisiting the double bind hypothesis. *Psychoanalytic Dialogues, 8,* 297–315.

Ringstrom, P. (2001). Cultivating the improvisational in psychoanalytic treatment. *Psychoanalytic Dialogues, 11,* 727–754.

Ringstrom, P. (2007). Scenes that write themselves: Improvisational moments in relational psychoanalysis. *Psychoanalytic Dialogues, 17,* 69–100.

Russell, P. (1991). Trauma, repetition, and affect. Presented at the First Symposium, Massachusetts Institute for Psychoanalysis. *Contemporary Psychoanalysis, 42,* 601–620.

Russell, P. (2006a). The theory of the crunch: The collected papers of Paul Libbey Russell, MDH. *Smith College Studies in Social Work, 76*(1–2), 9–21.

Russell, P. (2006b). The collected papers of Paul Libbey Russell, MDH. *Smith College Studies in Social Work, 76*(1–2).

Sander, L. W. (1962). Issues in early mother-child interaction. *Journal of the American Academy of Child Psychiatry, 1,* 141–166.

Sander, L. W. (1988). The event-structure of regulation in the neonate-caregiver system as a biological background for early organization of psychic structure. *Progress in Self Psychology, 3,* 64–77.

Sandler, J. (1976). Countertransference and role-responsiveness. *International Review of Psycho-Analysis, 3,* 43–47.

Sarbin, T. (1986). *Narrative psychology: The storied nature of human conduct.* New York: Praeger.

Sass, L.A. (1988). Humanism, hermeneutics, and humanistic psychoanalysis: Differing conceptions of subjectivity. *Psychoanal. Contemp. Thought, 12:* 433-504.

Schafer, R. (1983). *The analytic attitude.* New York: Basic Books.

Schafer, R. (1992). *Retelling a life: Narration and dialogue in psychoanalysis.* New York: Basic Books.

Searles, H. F. (1975). The patient as therapist to his analyst. In *Countertransference and related subjects* (pp. 380–459). New York: International Universities Press.

Searles, H. F. (1976). Psychoanalytic therapy with schizophrenic patients in a private practice context. *Contemporary Psychoanalysis, 12,* 387–406.

Segal, H. (1957). Notes on symbol formation. *International Journal of Psychoanalysis, 38,* 391–397.

Seligman, S. (2005). Dynamic systems theories as a metaframework for psychoanalysis. *Psychoanalytic Dialogues, 15,* 285–319.

Sennett, R. (2008). *The craftsman.* New Haven: Yale University Press.

Shane, E., & Coburn, W. J. (Eds.). (2002). Contemporary dynamic systems theories: Innovative contributions to psychoanalysis. *Psychoanalytic Inquiry, 22.*

Singer, E. (1971). The patient aids the analyst: Some clinical and theoretical observations. In B. Landis & E. Tauber (Eds.), *In the name of life: Essays in honor of Erich Fromm* (pp. 56–68). New York: Holt, Rinehart and Winston.

Slavin, M. O. (1996). Is one self enough? Multiplicity in self organization and the capacity to negotiate relational conflict. *Contemporary Psychoanalysis, 32,* 615–625.

Slavin, M. O., & Kriegman, D. (1992). *The adaptive design of the human psyche.* New York: Guilford.

Slavin, M. O., & Kriegman, D. (1998). Why the analyst needs to change: Toward a theory of conflict, negotiation, and mutual influence in the therapeutic process. *Psychoanalytic Dialogues, 8,* 247–284.

Smith, L. B., & Thelen, E. (1993). *A dynamic systems approach to development: Applications.* Cambridge, MA: MIT Press.

Spence, D. P. (1982). *Narrative truth and historical truth: Meaning and interpretation in psychoanalysis.* New York: Norton.

Spence, D. P. (1987). *The Freudian metaphor: Toward paradigm change in psychoanalysis.* New York: Norton.

Spruiell, V. (1993). Deterministic chaos and the sciences of complexity: Psychoanalysis in the midst of a general scientific revolution. *Journal of the American Psychoanalytic Association, 41,* 3–44.

Stein, A. (2003). Dreaming while awake: The use of trance to bypass threat. *Contemporary Psychoanalysis,* 39: 179–197.

Stein, A. (2004). Fantasy, fusion, and sexual homicide. *Contemporary Psychoanalysis, 40,* 495–517.

Stein, A. (2006). *Prologue to violence: Child abuse, dissociation, and crime.* Hillsdale, NJ: Analytic Press.

Stern, D. B. (1983). Unformulated experience. *Contemporary Psychoanalysis, 19,* 71–99.

Stern, D. B. (1989). The analyst's unformulated experience of the patient. *Contemporary Psychoanalysis, 25,* 1–33.

Stern, D. B. (1990). Courting surprise: Unbidden experience in clinical practice. *Contemporary Psychoanalysis, 26,* 452–478.

Stern, D. B. (1991). A philosophy for the embedded analyst: Gadamer's hermeneutics and the social paradigm of psychoanalysis. *Contemporary Psychoanalysis, 27,* 51–58.

Stern, D. B. (1994). Empathy is interpretation (and who ever said it wasn't?). *Psychoanalytic Dialogues, 4,* 441–471.

Stern, D. B. (1996). The social construction of therapeutic action. *Psychoanalytic Inquiry, 16,* 265–293.

Stern, D. B. (1997). *Unformulated experience: From dissociation to imagination in psychoanalysis.* Hillsdale, NJ: Analytic Press.

Stern, D. B. (2000). The limits of social construction: Discussion of Dyess and Dean. *Psychoanalytic Dialogues, 10,* 757–769.

Stern, D. B. (2001). Comments on the clinical material presented by Jill Scharff. *Psychoanalytic Inquiry, 21,* 499–512.

Stern, D. B. (2002a). Words and wordlessness in the psychoanalytic situation. *Journal of the American Psychoanalytic Association, 50,* 221–247.

Stern, D. B. (2002b). What you know first: Construction and deconstruction in relational psychoanalysis. In S. Fairfield, L. Layont, & C. Stack (Eds.), *Bringing the plague: Toward a postmodern psychoanalysis* (pp. 167–194). New York: Other Press.

Stern, D. B. (2002c). Language and the nonverbal as a unity: Discussion of Neil Altman's "Where is the action in the 'talking cure'?" *Contemporary Psychoanalysis, 38*, 515–525.

Stern, D. B. (2003). The fusion of horizons: Dissociation, enactment, and understanding. *Psychoanalytic Dialogues, 13*, 843–873.

Stern, D. B. (2004). The eye sees itself: Dissociation, enactment, and the achievement of conflict. *Contemporary Psychoanalysis, 40*, 197–237.

Stern, D. B. (2005). Introduction. In E. A. Levenson, *The fallacy of understanding and the ambiguity of change* (pp. v–xvi). Hillsdale, NJ: Analytic Press.

Stern, D. B. (2006). Opening what has been closed, relaxing what has been clenched: Dissociation and enactment over time in committed relationships. *Psychoanalytic Dialogues, 16*, 747–761.

Stern, D. B. (2008). On having to find what you don't know how to look for. In A. Slade, S. Bergner, & E. L. Jurist (Eds.), *Mind to mind: Infant research, neuroscience, and psychoanalysis* (pp. 398–413). New York: Other Press.

Stern, D. B. (2009). Dissociation and unformulated experience: A psychoanalytic model of mind. In P. F. Dell, J. O'Neil, & E. Somer (Eds.), *Dissociation and the dissociative disorders: DSM-V and beyond* (pp. 653–663). New York: Routledge.

Stern, D. N. (1971). A micro-analysis of mother-infant interaction: Behaviors regulating social contact between a mother and her three-and-a-half month-old twins. *Journal of the American Academy of Child Psychiatry, 10*, 501–517.

Stern, D. N. (1977). *The first relationship*. Cambridge: Harvard University Press.

Stern, D. N. (1985). *The interpersonal world of the infant: A view from psychoanalysis and developmental psychology*. New York: Basic Books.

Stern, D. N. (1995). *The motherhood constellation*. New York: Basic Books.

Stern, D. N. (2004). *The present moment in psychotherapy and everyday life*. New York: Norton.

Stern, D. N., Sander, L. W., Nahum, J. P., Harrison, A. M., Lyons-Ruth, K., Morgan, A. C., et al. (1998). Non-interpretive mechanisms in psychoanalytic therapy: The "something more" than interpretation. *International Journal of Psychoanalysis, 79*, 903–921.

Stolorow, R. D. (1988). Intersubjectivity, psychoanalytic knowing, and reality. *Contemp. Psychoanal., 24*: 331-338.

Stolorow, R. D., Brandchaft, B. and Atwood, G. E. (1987). *Psychoanalytic treatment: An intersubjective approach*. Hillsdale, NJ: The Analytic Press.

Sugarman, A. (2008). Fantasizing as process, not fantasy as content. *Psychoanalytic Inquiry, 28*, 169–189.

Sullivan, H. S. (1953). *Conceptions of modern psychiatry.* New York: Norton, 1950.

Sullivan, H. S. (1950). The illusion of personal individuality. In *The fusion of psychiatry and social science* (pp. 198–226). New York: Norton, 1971.

Sullivan, H. S. (1954). *The interpersonal theory of psychiatry.* Edited by H. S. Perry & M. L. Gawel. New York: Norton.

Sullivan, H. S. (1956). Selective inattention. In H. S. Perry, M. I. Gawel, & M Gibbon (Eds.), *Clinical studies in psychiatry* (pp. 38–76). New York: Norton.

Symington, N. (1983). The analyst's act of freedom as agent of therapeutic change. *International Review of Psycho-Analysis, 10,* 283–292.

Tauber, E. S. & Green, M. R. (1959). *Prelogical experience.* New York: Basic Books. Republished by Routledge (New York), 2008.

Tauber, E. S. (1954). Exploring the therapeutic use of counter-transference data. *Psychiatry, 13,* 332–336.

Tauber, E. S. (1979). Countertransference reexamined. In L. Epstein & A. H. Feiner (Eds.), *Countertransference* (pp. 59–69). New York: Aronson.

Thelen, E., & Smith, L. (1994). *A dynamic systems approach to the development of cognition and action.* Cambridge, MA: MIT Press.

Tronick, E. Z. (1989). Emotions and emotional communication in infants. *American Psychologist, 44,* 112–119.

Tronick, E. Z. (Ed.). (1998). Interactions that effect change in psychotherapy: A model based on infant research. *Infant Mental Health Journal, 19*(3).

Tronick, E. Z., & Weinberg, K. (1997). Depressed mothers and infants: The failure to form dyadic states of consciousness. In L. Murray & P. Cooper (Eds.), *Postpartum depression and child development* (pp. 54–85). Hillsdale, NJ: Guilford.

Tulving, E., & Craik, F. (Eds.). (2000). *The Oxford handbook of memory.* Oxford: Oxford University Press.

von Bertalanffy, L. (1968). *General systems theory.* New York: Braziller.

Warnke, G. (1987) *Gadamer: Hermeutics, tradition and reason.* Stanford, CA: Stanford University Press.

Winnicott, D. W. (1945). Primitive emotional development. In *Through paediatrics to psycho-analysis* (pp. 145–156). New York: Basic Books.

Winnicott, D. W. (1949). Hate in the countertransference. In *Through paediatrics to psycho-analysis* (pp. 194–203). New York: Basic Books.

Winnicott, D. W. (1960). Ego distortion in terms of true and false self. In *The maturational processes and the facilitating environment: Studies in the theory of emotional development* (pp. 140–152). New York: International Universities Press.

Winnicott, D. W. (1971). *Playing and reality.* London: Tavistock.

Wolstein, B. (1954). *Transference.* New York: Grune & Stratton.

Wolstein, B. (1959). *Countertransference.* New York: Grune & Stratton.

Wolstein, B. (1971a). *Human psyche in psychoanalysis.* Springfield, IL: Thomas.

Wolstein, B. (1971b). Interpersonal relations without individuality. *Contemporary Psychoanalysis, 7*, 75–80.

Wolstein, B. (1972). Interpersonal relations without individuality again. *Contemporary Psychoanalysis, 8*, 284–285.

Wolstein, B. (1974a). Individuality and identity. *Contemporary Psychoanalysis, 10*, 1–14.

Wolstein, B. (1974b). "I" processes and "me" patterns. *Contemporary Psychoanalysis, 10*, 347–357.

Wolstein, B. (1975). Toward a conception of unique individuality. *Contemporary Psychoanalysis, 11*, 146–160.

Wolstein, B. (1983). The pluralism of perspectives on countertransference. In *Essential papers on countertransference* (pp. 339–353). New York: New York University Press.

Zeddies, T. J. (2002). More than just words: A hermeneutic view of language in psychoanalysis. *Psychoanalytic Psychology, 19*, 3–23.

Zeddies, T. J., & Richardson, F. C. (1999). Analytic authority in historical and critical perspective: Beyond objectivism and relativism. *Contemporary Psychoanalysis, 35*, 581–601.

Index